THE SCOTT AND LAURIE OKI SERIES

IN ASIAN AMERICAN STUDIES

THE SCOTT AND LAURIE OKI SERIES
IN ASIAN AMERICAN STUDIES

From a Three-Cornered World: New and Selected Poems
by James Masao Mitsui

Imprisoned Apart: The World War II Correspondence of an Issei Couple
by Louis Fiset

Storied Lives: Japanese American Students and World War II
by Gary Y. Okihiro

Phoenix Eyes and Other Stories
by Russell Charles Leong

Paper Bullets: A Fictional Autobiography
by Kip Fulbeck

Born in Seattle: The Campaign for Japanese American Redress
by Robert Sadamu Shimabukuro

*Confinement and Ethnicity: An Overview
of World War II Japanese American Relocation Sites*
by Jeffery F. Burton et al.

*Judgment without Trial:
Japanese American Imprisonment during World War II*
by Tetsuden Kashima

*Shopping at Giant Foods: Chinese American Supermarkets
in Northern California*
by Alfred Yee

*Altered Lives, Enduring Community: Japanese Americans
Remember Their World War II Incarceration*
by Stephen S. Fugita and Marilyn Fernandez

Eat Everything Before You Die: A Chinaman in the Counterculture
by Jeffery Paul Chan

Eat Everything
Before You Die

A Chinaman in the Counterculture

JEFFERY PAUL CHAN

UNIVERSITY OF WASHINGTON PRESS

SEATTLE AND LONDON

This book is published with the assistance of a grant from the Scott and Laurie Oki Endowed Fund for the publication of Asian American Studies, established through the generosity of Scott and Laurie Oki.

University of Washington Press
P.O. Box 50096, Seattle, WA 98145, U.S.A.
www.washington.edu/uwpress

Library of Congress Cataloging-in-Publication Data

Chan, Jeffery Paul.
Eat everything before you die : a Chinaman in the counterculture / Jeffery Paul Chan.—1st ed.
p. cm.—(The Scott and Laurie Oki series in Asian American studies)
ISBN 0-295-98436-8 (pbk. : alk. paper)
1. Chinese Americans—Fiction.   2. Asian American gays—Fiction.
3. Counterculture—Fiction.   4. Brothers—Fiction.   5. Orphans—Fiction.
6. Gay men—Fiction.   7. Cooks—Fiction.   I. Title.   II. Series.
PS3603.H3558E23   2004
813'.6—dc22   2004012534

The paper used in this publication is acid-free and recycled from 10 percent post-consumer and at least 50 percent pre-consumer waste. It meets the minimum requirements of American National Standard for Information Sciences—Permanence of Paper for Printed Library Materials, ANSI Z39.48-1984.

Excerpts from *Eat Everything Before You Die* first appeared in *Asian Pacific American Journal* 3, no.1 (1994).

Acknowledgments

I would like to acknowledge the help, support, and encouragement of friends, patient and dear, who lent themselves with no other expectations than to see this work done—most especially Alfred Wong, Leslie Friedman, and Scilla Finetti. I also want to express my gratitude to my editor, Kerrie Maynes, for her scrupulous attention and her witty, insightful remarks.

I wish to thank the California Arts Council and the Marin Arts Council for their timely and generous awards in support of this work.

And, finally, to my wife, Janis, loyal companion, helpmate, thank you.

For Alice, for Esther

Eat Everything
Before You Die

1

The fourteenth of June, 18:56 PDT, mid-Pacific. Seven hours down and seven more miserable hours to go for Hong Kong International. In the economy class of a United Airlines 747, we are packed like galley slaves momentarily freed by a fretful wind filling the sails with illusory choices. I shop the in-flight magazine, watch the movie, numb myself with the music channel loop, one eye following the unraveling seam that fastens the antimacassar to the seat in front of me.

I admit to no one seriously my gratitude for, my addiction to manufactured foods. I love airplane chicken, that unthreatening loaf of breast meat in a non-lactose cream sauce with four karats of peas and a diadem of mushrooms. I mash the separate grains of salty pilaf into the *jus blanc,* then prize strands of chicken into soft knots. I sweeten the potage with the cobbler's fructose as time passes like magic. Very tasty. I follow with a Pepcid and a Zocor, a daily act of contrition, these small but necessary prophylactics acknowledging my mortality that, in turn, inspires such sweet nostalgia for events in the past as well a confidence in the future that this hour, this minute, this flight will end. Such minutiae serve me when I fly—or, rather, when I'm flown. Despite the physical inconveniences, these cramping constraints, I feel oddly joined in this environment. We are fellow passengers hurtling through space, sharing the same physical needs, the same end; we invent a social order, an etiquette that varies only fractionally, by class, by seat order. And food—food we manipulate to suit whatever illusory appetite we fancy—sustains us. What more can I ask?

I should have ordered the vegetarian alternative. It's big brother's recipe, Peter's pan-Asia surprise, his *WokTalk* curry wrap or our corporate facsimile. But I didn't; sibling spite, of course. We're family. Everybody's imitating us now that we've learned to imitate everyone else. Our made-up family of facsimiles, of uncles and aunts, of orphans and secrets, of inventions, of disguise, is rock solid. We're incorporated. So much hard work

3

and sacrifice, such diligence, so that all our generations could learn to climb the golden staircase. Each in our turn has reached the summit. There's nothing left to do but jump.

Oh my Lord,
Thank You for these Thine gifts,
the fruit and body.
Free at last, Jesus,
I fly. I plummet.

I know my history matters not a whit to those who came before; I'm speaking to the anonymous generations who left us orphans in a Chinatown diaspora, to invent ourselves as we might. The dead are dead. But there is that gnawing desire, always, to link ourselves to some past, to figures more immediate if less substantial than, say, the Great Wall of China, forever disconnected, a defense against nothing, but incorporated, certainly. There was Lincoln, Uncle Lincoln, who remains a strong presence in my memory, substantial, independent, many years gone. And there was Mary, Auntie, who tended all of her orphans together, who made all of us family. She died; there's no one left to tell, no one left to listen. She shaped me, watched me, so carefully, so successfully. Or so I like to remember.

Mary, my Auntie Mary, had observed the bridges that spanned her family's generations with the same wary attention our Chinese American upbringing requires, to conceal as much as to reveal, inventing the strategies of imitation that assimilation makes necessary, to span the gaps, the chasms, the identities we all construct to link our immediate past to our presence as aliens, new citizens, the American-born, hoisted just this side of the Golden Gate in a city surrounded by all varieties of cantilevered, drawn, and pontooned contraptions. "Admire the view, but consider both ends," she counseled. She would remind me of the arched footbridge in the Japanese Tea Garden in Golden Gate Park, designed by a Chinese immigrant in a time when we were all Orientals because of Exclusion, because of the War. To stand at either end of the bridge meant choosing to be the despised enemy alien or martyred refugee. Instead, we stepped gingerly to its middle.

Mary—the fifth child, fifth daughter and last surviving female of three boys and five girls, born in America and raised in San Francisco's Chinatown—imagined herself as a bridge of sorts, the product of two cultures, moral opposites, indelibly stamped by blood, by genes, somehow straddling the Pacific Ocean, awkwardly balanced, her skirts delicately raised to avoid the surf lapping the two shores, the muddy alluvial waters of the Pearl River Delta and the foggy shores of San Francisco Bay. It was, after all, a familiar formula that the American-born children of pre–World War II Chinese immigrants were taught by the China-born children of the Christian missionaries to memorize in their mutual catechisms, to recite, to rationalize to each other while growing up during the Exclusion in Chinatown's missionary ghetto: Baptist assemblies, Protestant settlement houses, kirks in cobbled alleys, a cathedral, parochial schools, a Paulist friary, convents, nunneries, all manner of ecclesiastic services, from a Catholic daycare to a Jesuit university on a hill. Sundays, the bells of St. Mary's at the center of Chinatown drew pilgrims disguised as tourists to worship before the facade of a gas station built to resemble a pagoda. In this sundry, crowded tidal pool, Mary had few opportunities to swim. More often, she simply observed the rise and fall of the tide, her arms outstretched, her hands reaching for opposite shores. Of course, Uncle Lincoln thought we'd all climbed Wick's belfry, and, observing the tumult from on high, we'd jumped.

In her dotage, without Uncle Lincoln to shout and curse, she mildly complained and conspired, but if there is any toll left unpaid for our crossing, any accumulation of injustice, of debts left unsatisfied, of persons left waiting or abandoned, no one who could remember is left to pay. Fifty years, a hundred years later, the shadow the Exclusion casts over the new Chinatown malls teeming with pregnant families is quite pale, nearly transparent. The old migrant bachelor society is dead. Young mothers squat at tanks of tilapia, carp, catfish, frogs, turtles, a bounty of live edibles. Life is rich; the markets, abundant. All the prayers we were taught to pray have been prayerfully answered. We are all of us forgiven. Mary's family, forgiven. Uncle Lincoln, Auntie Mary, forgiven. Peter, Winnie, Melba, my wife forever, even me—all forgiven by those who have trespassed against us. Even Wick, Theodore Candlewick, our ex-divine, forgiven by merciful amnesia, by the mercy of time passing unremarked, corrupted by human frailties, the blessings of senility and dementia.

I remember twenty years ago sharing a pew with Mary hiding her tears at her family's griefless funeral for our paper kin, my paper father, every-body's Uncle Lincoln. Lincoln Wong, aloof, bluff, preemptory, a bachelor who began his relationship to Mary's family while operating a short-order takeout in the desert near the Mexican border right after World War II, earning our family's bad reputation by providing marriage and his citizenship to women slipping past the bamboo curtain, the beaded curtain of Macanese gambling palaces, the lace curtains of a Taipei barbershop—perhaps my own mother included—all of whom he called Daisy.

Whether Lincoln's Daisies were plucked from Toisan or American-born baby girls recalled to China to be repackaged as emigrating paper sons, to satisfy the legal exigencies of the Chinese Exclusion Act, Lincoln joined in fraternity with Wick, with Mary loyally conspiring to satisfy the need for Confucian family order before the War. Lincoln had become an especially sharp thorn in the side of Mary's brothers, railing against the male heirs who had sent Mary and the rest of her orphans packing, all according to the Chinese patrilineal code of inheritance whose Confucian mien masked their own Jesus enough to disguise their greed. All that might have been contested, but Mary, with Lincoln and Wick's help, had her own investments in various immigration schemes—that is, our travel agency, some gambling, and other properties—to tide us over; we were all of us Mary's orphans, Wick would joke, with Lincoln to lead us out of exile. Legal proceedings against Mary's brothers would have exposed everyone unnecessarily, so it was only Lincoln who pecked and worried at old wounds. Besides which, such family scabs are more or less traditional, Mary would remind us, looking over her shoulder at what might have been just another idea of China exacerbated by the illusions peculiar to exile.

"Jesus taught us to forgive, but Chinese people never forget," eulogizes big brother Peter, who was chosen—who is always chosen—to speak a few words despite his orphan past because he is so impeccably Peter Pan in his soft gray Italian jacket, charcoal dress shirt, and black and white paisley tie. That he is present, that he attends is so much face for our family gatherings—our own Peter Pan, the eponymous global gourmand, the pan-Pacific chef—the brothers can ignore the gibes lightly disguised in his pagan sermonette. Lincoln's obituary becomes our shared orphan history, just paper, as Lincoln was the only surviving son of an only surviving son of a paper father, and Peter and I, his grateful wards, at last, legitimate orphans.

The truth was that if Mary's younger brothers had not survived their childhood and World War II, or had had no sons, no male heirs, our provenance might have been quite different. When three legitimate boy cousins were finally born, Peter and I were disposable, although we were ever present evidence at reunions, Mary's reward. If truth be known, Peter and I were immigration stratagems, finally unnecessary, like most of our generations born under the shadow of the Exclusion, raised under the direction of various mission welfare agencies that ministered to our assimilation: the Catholic Church; the YMCA with its pool and warm showers, the orphan's Chung Mei Home for the disposables and the dispossessed, and Wick's settlement house, Shepherd's Haven.

Wick is here at Lincoln's funeral, still here, defrocked, deranged, still dressed in his familiar mufti, black sweatshirt, white turtleneck, khaki bush jacket: the Reverend Candlewick, whom Lincoln's funeral has rescued for the occasion. He is on furlough from his happy house, some glebe the missionary board keeps in the country where their fallen can consider the misuse and abuse of their misconduct, the erosion of their spiritual discipline and direction. Words, words, the whisper of dried pages in a corrupted text, pederast words, sodomite words so long forgotten, so long forgiven.

And here is Winnie, our wife.

Auntie raises her chin proudly towards the mourning nave at Winnie, whose veil has slipped elegantly about her slim shoulders—our Winnie, Uncle's publicly acknowledged widow, Auntie's carefully groomed protégée whom she saved from a poorly conceived green-card scam with hapless me. From a village in Hunan south over the mountains to Guandong Province—or was it Saigon, Macao, Hong Kong, Honolulu—then on to Berkeley via Vancouver, Seattle, she sits in repose, listening to the subdued but not unseemly laughter curling like smoke over the pews cluttered with families surnamed Wong, the sounds of reunion, the aroma of incense, a hint of garlic and ginger drifting in from the street.

I remember that for the interment, the public-safety-minded family association provided two limousines and a bus to carry the mourners to

Colma's Chinese cemetery, not wishing to risk the usual parade of family sedans in mid-morning cross-city traffic, the endless detour through the park. We stood assembled at the grave site, uncomfortably warm in the unshaded near-noon sunshine, the sweet loamy aroma of the dead's perfume mixed with the smell of sweat and dark worsted-wool suits. There was a delay. After reading the gravestones, the association secretary, Dr. Wong, waved to a clutch of old men mopping the perspiration from their gray heads, fanning themselves with their hats. They conferred. They agreed. The gravediggers had exhumed the wrong Wong family plot, distant cousins still, but the wrong branch of the Wong family. It was an easy mistake to make. Uncle Lincoln had ensured a place farther up the hill in a group plot, a purchase he'd transacted when there had been a minor flurry of émigrés returning to China in November of '49. Mao Tsetung declared that a new kingdom had arisen. Party loyalists, who had maintained a Chinatown soviet of folk culture and propaganda to the embarrassment of the republican Kuomintang, left a step ahead of the Confession Program, the congressional hearings investigating the presence of Communists disguised as Chinese in America. Just so the record would be clear, a king-sized double grave site sandwiched between two bachelors named Wong had been recorded in the burial association books. Imagine—such ruses and strategies, plots to hold out hope against the threat of extinction during the Exclusion. And both Lincoln and Mary— really, their entire generation—always had a good eye for real estate.

We waited an hour while they dug a fresh hole, everyone visiting over the graves of people they knew or wandering about looking for shade. It was Winnie who calmed the young folks who thought it all a little grisly. Passing easily through the crowds of family and friends, the loose ends of her scarf the color of ash fluttering like transparent wings, she said she didn't think Uncle would mind the extra hour in the sun. How well suited she was, soft-spoken, forgiven and forgiving as she claimed her place at the right hand of Auntie Mary.

Mary's brothers had gathered in craven knots, renewing their faith at their favorite touch points in the church. Grown prosperous on the family's money, divided in traditional fashion among the boys (daughters are only other men's wives), each of them was well invested in real estate holdings whose price successive waves of new Chinese immigrants have mandated toward heaven since the end of the Exclusion. They fingered their rosaries in the memory palace that is Old St. Mary's, its plaster epiphanies nudging the Confiteor or the Apostle's Creed to come mumbling, spilling out in fearful awe of their mortality, assuaging their guilty lives, avoiding Mary's sharp eye, their sister, their father's daughter. Peter saved an especially accusing, baleful gaze for the cemetery as they approached to offer a quick condolence. Then his television smile, "You're still with us, Uncle."

Uncle Pius, Uncle Paul, and Uncle Joseph, the youngest, in their mortal terror—or so I like to imagine—genuflect before the stained glass transoms of their namesakes, their rosaries hanging from their lips, each Hail Mary a bead they catch with the tips of their tongues. St. Mary's Catholic Chinese congregation displays a crèche, regardless of the season, with Oriental features, the baby Jesus looking not unlike the fairytale Peach Blossom boy, white porcelain cheeks, rouged lips, mounted on a peach the color of raspberries, Kwan Yin, the multi-armed androgynous goddess of mercy, his mother. Uncle Lincoln lying in his casket threatens to rise up and curse the proceedings, to make them choke on their beads. "You cheap bastards," he exclaims at their division of the family money. "Goddamn missionaries," he says, even though we've all drunk from the same well. "No divorce, no money. Thieves." He rips the mourning scarves from his collar and stalks the stone statue of St. Paul, rendered as a white-eyed balding Confucian scholar, wispy gray beard trembling in terror. Carefully knotting the pale yellow silk scarf, he slips it around Uncle Joe's neck and locks an elbow behind his ear. Lincoln stares hard at me, his lips drawn tight against his teeth, and I hear the radio, organ music on a familiar theme, emanating from his throat; he seems to speak, to remind me of old radio themes I once heard in my infant's sleep.

At the cemetery, the uncles cannot avoid his shadow. Winnie takes their hands in hers, offers a light touch on their sleeves. The widow (too young, too pretty) reminds them (her pale kiss, her chaste embrace) of Lincoln's revenge, the mortality they share.

It was a few years after the War—or was it during another war?—when I was sent toddling away to live with him. He reluctantly kept me for an entire summer as I recovered from a suspicious shadow on a Community Chest X ray, or so the story goes. I remember him wrapped in a fullbibbed apron and stained T-shirt, skinny arms and elbows leaning on the aluminum-frame back door of the trailer kitchen takeout, a wet cigarette glued to his lower lip, glowering across the interstate, irritable, squinting at the malevolent desert sunset chasing the faint glow of taillights trailing from Barstow. I heard the radio as if it were Uncle's voice, Gabriel Heatter complaining with more bad news.

At the post-interment buffet, the traditional half-banquet—four side dishes with take-out boxes conveniently adjacent to the plastic settings—was laid at the Neon Moon Cafe, once the best Cantonese banquet palace in Chinatown, but now specializing in quick steam table lunches and at night becoming a jazz venue for locals addicted to the copy artists that ply the Pacific Rim from Honolulu to Kuala Lumpur. Peter's friend Twig and his band, the Tree of Heaven, once had two big weekends there, to attract a Nikkei reunion of World War II veterans from Honolulu who were conventioning at the South Pacific Inn at the bottom of Grant Avenue.

At these family gatherings, Mary was always surrounded by a crisp garland of grandnieces, a new Daphne, a baby Rose, even a Daisy, who's four but says she's five, and Kristi who sits closest to Auntie because she doesn't like to eat just anything, who whispers to her favorite auntie in English with a slight lisp that Auntie in her dotage finds irresistible.

"What's that stuff, Auntie?"

"That's duck, Kristi girl. You like that." Mary pulls the dark meat away from the bone and plops a square of sweet duck skin on top. "Remember? You told me you like duck. Donald Duck, Daffy Duck. This is a cousin, roast duck, hah?"

"Auntie, do I have to eat it?"

"Just put some in your mouth and if you don't like it, put it back on the plate, okay? Chew the skin, it's very sweet."

"I don't want it," she pouts.

Auntie pretends to cover Kristi's eyes, plucking the offending piece from her bowl and concealing it under her napkin. "All gone!" Her precious garland giggles around her, a wreath of tittering cute. "We'll let the boys eat it."

Here is the final reward, the steam table display of terminal abundance, the greasy stuff that will kill us all in the end, as it certainly did Uncle, lying there with funereal makeup frosting his sharp, expressionless face sunk beneath fat cheeks and chins, in a starched black suit, shirt cuffs shot a fashionable three quarters of an inch, arms crossed over his chest. Winnie hands Peter a stack of telegrams. Her mourning dress, a tight black chemise, turns heads as Peter directs a recitation of condolences in Cantonese to the head table where Winnie confers with family association representatives. A low murmur sweeps across the room, the company pointedly ignoring unlucky remarks, their eyes on Winnie's provocative bottom. The mention of the dead is always bad luck.

The mortician has forgotten to powder Lincoln's hands. The dark mahogany fingers poke from under the mourning scarves, hands and nails the color of barbecue, of the deep fryer's peanut oil, of the roast duck skin Kristi won't eat. I remember Uncle Lincoln's hard hands sowing the landscape with the greasy crackling of old rice and yesterday's noodles the texture of a potato chip. A carton of that and a formula of catsup, pineapple juice, inky soy—hell, he could give that away in little white boxes, condiments for the gravied morsels, all-you-can-eat, two ninety-five. Uncle's largesse: Some of it even found us at his final buffet.

At all wakes and family celebrations, cousins by the dozens arrive from their suburban retreats. A new generation of children—cassette players, ear cuffs, cameo T-shirts splashed with color, linen jackets, a rainbow of sneakers—stare at one another with mutual contempt, milling beyond the baleful stares of their parents, mute, embarrassed by the Chinatown look of Cathay Mortuary wakes and buffet banquets. The immediate family of the dead are sober in black and white and gray. Mary spies the first grandnephew, her brother's daughter's son, iron-cross earrings, a thin twist of packing cord around his wrist, cropped skull, burnt orange hair, a witty tattoo of a barcode on the back of his neck. Auntie Mary nods, staring at her nephew. "Very nice. Looks just like death," she murmurs in Cantonese.

Had Melba been there for Lincoln's funeral? But no. Her postcard had her leading tourists along the Inca Trail from Cuzco to Machu Picchu disguised, she said, as a Quechua guide, providing a postcolonial analysis for the New Age ecotourist.

All the boys-become-men look funny to Auntie's Chinatown generation. They smell foreign, too much milk and meat, too often caught nibbling at the crisped noodles, the kind Uncle stored in lard cans for the take-out customers, sour breath, a mask of fresh pimples, allergic, asthmatic, swollen and clumsy. They smell American, smell like white people, poisoned by prosperity, the final solution.

From the podium, Peter sweeps the assembled, his eyes and teeth glittering, recalling Lincoln's words as an entreaty to negotiate a fragile benediction. It was only yesterday, he says, a year, maybe five, right here at the Neon Moon, that Lincoln repeated that the only practice the Chinese observe religiously is eating. If I turned around, would I see Wick smiling? Surely that was his. By eating, we inspire the living. We can even evoke the dead.

It's been twenty years and some time more. I can hear Peter conducting lunch at the Ming Garden Grill in the fog-shrouded Sunset District: "Eat everything before you die. It's a couplet you repeat to yourself. You write it on walls. Then it's yours forever. Uncle Lincoln?"

"Keep talking, boy," Uncle says with his mouth full. Lincoln preferred to eat among the new immigrants in the suburban avenues, leaving Chinatown to the tourists. Uncle Lincoln could only be caught dead eating in Chinatown at the Neon Moon.

It was after Winnie had accompanied Lincoln to China to rescue another orphan for Mary, after the curtain had fallen on the Cultural Revolution. A Ming Garden lunch in the Sunset District meant bean-cake stuffed with fish paste, steamed bacon and preserved mustard greens, salty black bean clams, a steeped chicken breast with iced scallions and seasoned salt, oyster sauce hearts of chard, rice, the house soup, a California Chardonnay for his orphans, Chinese beer, tea, and Lincoln's Hennessey, a bottle the kitchen always left for our table. Potted cut flowers wrapped in congratulatory red ribbons were stacked against the engine housing of the holding tanks, commemorating the restaurant's new ownership, a quarterly occurrence to accommodate new investors, a killing at the paigow tables in Reno, or a funeral.

Eat to live, eat, kill, die so that we may eat. Here are the pioneers who blazed the omnivorous path Chinese immigrants followed, picking the spicy bits from shimmering pools of tepid sauces, catsups of brown bean, fermented red bean, fat fingers of bean cheese, the land a banquet of legumes. We pluck bits of fish from the gravy, a cheek, the eyeball accompanied by the appropriate allusion to erotic foreplay. We hold our chop-sticks as if we're were about to chisel a poem, mark lunch's epitaph on the plate. The new Chinese paint the walls verdant green, the front door red, bright red, Chinese red. Red is for luck. For the old immigrant, it must stand for the blood spilled in the diaspora by the first generation as they murderously attacked and were attacked by their children, who ate what was demanded of them.

Peter works the Ming Garden crowd as Peter Pan, the Oriental epicure, but Lincoln senses the crowd, his audience. At the window table a crew of house painters in splattered coveralls, a study in the gray daylight stab-bing through the smoke, sprawl with their backs to the holding tanks, drinking tea, nodding with cigarettes dangling from their lips, no livelier than the lobsters that peek over their shoulders, the catfish, the bottom feeders keeping company in the post-lunch haze.

Peter reaches across the table to offer food, pour wine, asking, "How was the village, Uncle?"

"Primitive, really old-time stuff, poor. Mary's cousin, her niece's old-est son, brought *bak jum gai* over to her house for lunch. Boiled chicken, right? But at the end of lunch, he took the half we didn't eat back home. They're still hungry. Blanched chicken is a big deal. Everybody wants money. Everything you need is free, but everything you want needs American do re mi."

A diner with spackle in his hair sitting at another table agrees. *"Gum hai law."* That's the way it is.

Uncle loved the story as much as the telling. He drank his Hennessey, sucked clams, talked with his chin constantly pointing for attention. "'Course, the niece can't come over. No papers left. And she already had two girls, right? Well, she refused to have her tubes tied. So the Red Guard guys punish the family by taking the family door. Just took it off the frame, right? Not your ordinary door, now. I could call it antique, thick as a wall. Probably been in their family for centuries. Bandits come. Japanese army. War. Now what? Cultural revolution. Anything and everything bad. When all hell breaks loose, they just close the door, right? Worked forever until the damn Communists made the kids Red Guards. Then the kids just opened the door. Anyway I had to write a letter to show she had overseas relatives, the *wahque* connection, and say we would support the family, so any extra babies would not be a burden on the government. In the meantime, I paid the neighbors to steal the door back. I even got a thank-you note from the authorities after we already got the door re-hung. I donated a color TV and money for the new school. Everybody in the village knew where the door was. No place to hide anything anywhere in that place. Door must be eight by eight with iron straps. Big as a car. They just dumped it behind the town hall. Lucky we stole it first."

The guys at the window table nod. *"Gum hai law,"* familiar ironies, stories from home; that's just the way it is, they agree.

The funeral buffet once laid—white food for those who are required to mourn, sweet and sour glazes and noodles from the steam table—leads to a tower of take-out cartons and a deck of paper bags for Uncle's gravesite, spirit food to sustain our memory of him. The clan gathered celebrates the end of Uncle's exile. Now Uncle is buried in a spot where he can be safely recalled at graveside picnics in the spring, at Ching Ming when we climb the mountain to honor the departed, the safely contained.

At Ming's, Peter describes the banquet scene embroidered on a tablecloth that opens his cooking show. "Notice how these figures do not relate to one another. There's contempt, irritation, arrogance among them when anyone, any adult with a memory, refuses food. Blood enemies sit across steaming tables and eat as an act of defiance, of challenge. The epics of China, the rise and fall of kingdoms, begin and end with a disturbance in the food chain. The entrails preparatory to a feast are probed for the future. Even the dead are fed."

He seduces his audience with the challenges that confront the Chinese gourmand. "Remember, the best noodles are fried in lard on the street. You understand what the flavor of the frying pan is, the breath of the wok, the taste of cooked oil, cooked explosively in the marketplace, clouds of incinerating oil crusting live shrimp, the crusty patina ladled on fresh fish flesh, beancake. There's a taste of mud in the sablefish, catfish, carp, the iron taste of alcohol-fermented soybean, and scallion, washed down with the heady perfume of fresh steamed rice and smoked tea."

"Well, my dear Christopher, now we really feel like family. Let's remember what we want to remember." Auntie nods her head as our Peter recites our names on this day, becoming the voice of our mute divine, Ted Candlewick, sitting conspicuously alive but silent and undone several pews behind a clutch of ancient Catholic clergy seated front and center with the uncles.

My memory is never timely, never chronological, of a piece. It rises and falls like pressure in my ears. I remember Lincoln's last birthday, his eightieth or so we agreed, replete with an Eastern Onion Singing Telegram and a delivery from Balloon Delights. The food was the usual Styrofoam potluck that can be eaten in your lap on a bus, on a train, a hydrofoil dividing the Pearl River Delta, a ferryboat to Kowloon, a junk plying aimlessly across the South China Sea. In the chitchat, the babble of dialects, the straining sensibilities concealing the cracks in the communion of diaspora, there was the accountant from Taipei, some friends of Winnie's from Hong Kong, the Wong family from Saigon by way of Heinan who ran the local takeout in Mira Vista Square and catered the affair. That evening was devoted to vacation videos. Winnie and Lincoln provided a tour of the backrooms of kung fu studios where the esoteric mysteries of the Chinese physic are practiced like massage, dentistry, and barbering in the ancient marketplace. Winnie's new role as Lincoln's wife, no longer his nursemaid, no fictitious adoption, made her uncomfortable, a little too saucy, for a wife of substance.

But Uncle loved Winnie. We all loved Winnie better as Lincoln's helpmate than as my green-card mistake.

"I always liked Winnie," Auntie says. "So Hong Kong gay."

After Uncle had gone to the village to save Mary's cousin's family door, he and Winnie had spent the rest of their time in Hong Kong, shopping and making home videos of their honeymoon to show the rest of the family. And out comes the tape they shot of a qi gong master demonstration of the ironshirt exercise that encourages the flow of chi and develops the peroneal muscles, seen as the foundation muscles of the horse stance. For the ladies, Winnie passes around various weights of metal eggs to be inserted in the vagina and held there to encourage the muscles and to stimulate the autonomic channels that run from the perineum up the spine and over the crown to the nose, then from the nose straight down to grandmother's house. The video crackles in a mix of Cantonese and Mandarin as the master and assistants are introduced on tape. I attempt to encourage some explanation in English of what we're observing. I ask as disingenuously as possible where they put the weights on the man. Then the video answers the question. We see Winnie standing next to a skinny guy in a sarong. She tries to lift 165 pounds of iron weight plates tethered to a steel bar. The verity of the weights established, the camera swings to the guy's genitals, which he exposes. His scrotal sac and penis are cinched by a scarf. Their color looks vaguely necrotic, not even blue—as if the videotape has never recorded such a color before—and is in sharp contrast to the garish tints the video captures of, for example, the red door, Winnie's cosmetic pallor, the Hong Kong Bank calendar on the wall, and the color of the wall itself, a bright jade green.

The subject proceeds to tie one end of the scarf to the weights as he squats over them in classic horse position. Then he lifts the weights by standing upright and begins to swing them back and forth between his legs, his genital flesh stretching nearly to his knees as he swings the weights to and fro.

Uncle Lincoln, in his hospital bed, listening, growls, "I could do that."

Winnie provides a running voice-over translation in English. "He does this forty to sixty times each session for best results. He cannot have ice cold or hot and must not ejaculate before beginning these exercises." She smiles at Peter, who smiles back. Then she holds up the smallest weighted egg in a set from a silk-lined teak box and asks, "Would any of the ladies like to try this one?"

I recall that when we first started sleeping together, Winnie offered only parts of herself for me to examine, to fondle. She hid beneath the sheets, offering a foot, her knee, an elbow, each with a plaintive warning: "Don't hurt me, please." And after I had sworn a thousand times, she would always say, "I knew you would."

"No takers." Uncle wheezes and coughs. The graph duly records his spasms.

Further demonstrations of the exercise include beating with a very heavy steel brush, which is very stimulating as long as you focus on your trunk or major muscle groups (I hit myself with it to see how it felt). Uncle

Paul's wife drops a large iron egg onto her Styrofoam tray, which splits and deposits mu shu pork in her lap.

At Uncle's funeral, Auntie crosses herself elaborately, slowly, so her garland can follow, left shoulder, right shoulder, forehead, lips, palms together.

"Where's your wife now?" everybody always asks. The question follows immediately after asking if I have eaten. On his deathbed, Lincoln asked.

"I came by myself, Uncle." He'd forgotten. Melba was already halfway to Cuzco, to Amsterdam, to Rome.

"I see. That's all right. Winnie's here right now." He opens his eyes wide and glares at me so there's no misunderstanding. "You got a cheap ticket?"

"Of course." An Air Avianca destined for Rio de Janeiro. I was upgraded to the empty business class by a sympathetic sales agent when I told him I was visiting my dying uncle. I always kill someone near and dear if I have to make a plane reservation. My flying requires a blood sacrifice.

"You stay at my house tonight. I told Winnie it's okay."

He dozes. I duck into the toilet, stick my finger down my throat, and purge the Tequila Sunrise I had for breakfast on the plane. From the window, a clear view of Vista Del Mar, a retirement community west of the Long Beach sprawl, across the freeway overpass and guarded by a shopping mall whose retail prices keep the newly arrived and the perennially poor from crossing over, surrounded by golf courses and long boulevards with timed traffic signals that prevent loitering at intersections and keep the curbside retailers, the rose peddlers, the garlic gangs, and the orange sellers from molesting the traffic.

An errant staph infection in ICU requires that I mask and glove. A pretty dark-haired nurse, tan and ripe with youth, warns against hospital-borne infections that are nearly immune to antibiotics. We have to scrub before going in and after we leave the unit. The room is covered with greeting cards and messages, a poster made by the children of fictitious relatives, Uncle's adopted brood, exhorting him to eat and breathe, to live, in broad Pentels and vivid rainbow washes. He has tubes running from his neck metering Dobutamine, a tube running into his penis to drain his bladder. His arms and legs are scarred the color of coffee stains. A large scar runs the length of his chest and another down the inside of his right thigh. The room pulses with the wheezy sound of his breathing passing through the respirator, the heart monitor emitting squeaks and whistles as the computer acknowledges his heart rate, from 52 up through 100 when he needed to hoist himself on the bedpan. Every five to ten minutes he indicates that he needs to be suctioned and Winnie sends a vacuum tube into his throat while he holds his breath. All the nurses are young, pretty, and speak with various accents. There's a Southerner, slightly older than the rest, who calls Winnie "Boss." A young Filipina nurse recites for me the invocation of hope—eat, breathe, sit up—as I stare deeply into her soft dark eyes. To imitate life, visualize recovery. Smile. Be happy.

I take a break and have lunch at a Vietnamese noodle palace in the evolving Long Beach ghetto.

Winnie chirps, *"Hai leng, hai peng,"* a couplet that means pretty and cheap. "Two dollah-fifty cent" still buys you more than you can eat in ultra thin noodles with four varieties of beef and sessile organs, four unsweetened deep-fried doughnuts, a condiment plate of raw bean sprouts, serrano chilis, lime quarters, and a beer served with a glass of chipped ice, a tropical habit that has adapted well in Southern California. You would love the place, Uncle, a menu and a venue after your own heart. It is his heart we worry over. We've all adopted the same malady.

Winnie worries, pacing, and natters on about how thin he is—the good wife. "Tell him what you had for lunch. He likes that." She peppers our meal with advice and warnings. "He weighs as much as I do, but shoot, I'm five-one and he's five-ten. It's all right when I'm one hundred pounds, but not for him." She sips a plastic tumbler of hot tea. She's always been slight but athletic. She complains about some fictive cousin's son who is an athlete but on a constant diet that encourages bulimia. "Have you ever heard of such a thing? Throwing up all his food?" Winnie avoids elevators, bounding up the stairwell, hips forward. "I'm small, compact, petite, but I'm strong and well and healthy," she says, cursing illness, embracing the inevitable. She's very competent at what she does, paying social calls on everyone's children, stepchildren, grandchildren, and even estranged nephews. Even though she's only been in Long Beach less than a month and is living in a corporate suite, she's adapted to the SoCal lifestyle. She shops. She points out the best malls. She's trained herself to drive on the freeways and broad boulevards of Los Angeles, and she drives quickly, efficiently. "I like to make all the lights so I don't have to stop." She's stopped drinking and smoking for his sake.

"She's smarter than you are." Uncle's respirator squawks in strangled agreement.

At his evening meal, she scolds him petulantly. "You have to eat, Lincoln. If you don't, you know what that means." She threatens, cajoles.

He holds up his hand. "I die, right?"

They are fearless together. "You want to die before I spend all your money?" she asks as directly as she knows how to do. She never shrinks from the words, a mix of English and dialect, childish humors, the no-nonsense scolding as she maneuvers his bedpan, suctions the steady flow of saffron ichor clotting his throat as the uneasy beeps from the over-cautious monitor, the steady flow of numbers marking his vitals, set a rhythm of slow expiration, of slow dying. "Don't die, Lincoln." She stamps her foot, "Don't you die. You've left food on your tray. Eat a little more."

Before I leave the next day, I feed him his lunch. Spaghetti, vanilla pudding, apple yogurt, 7-Up, coffee, beef bouillon, and a container of a thoughtful cousin's bitter melon and beef over noodles that his Manila-brown nurse offers to microwave. I am waiting to leave, but she takes some time to do it.

"Sorry, honey, I got caught behind a burrito," she laughs through her damp mask.

We try to choose his menu for the next day. Spaghetti again, beef stew, coffee, soups, salads. He points at carrots. The thought of tomorrow's menu furrows his brow. He mouths words carefully. He draws words in the air that only Winnie can follow. He writes, he raises his eyebrows, looks around the room for what he wants. He has everything he ever wanted from me. When we all used to eat together, it was Peter who knew how to give him respect, stimulate the appetites. And he has Winnie. He needs them, Peter and Winnie, not me. I never say good-bye. Not those words, anyway.

I smell the smell of crushed ailanthus, the aroma of popcorn in the tea Winnie brews. I will forever wash it from my clothes, rinse my hair in the incense of his food. It exudes from me like living itself.

He dies, all labored breath, grape smells and orange stains discoloring the stiff white pillowslips, sheets artfully folded to hide blood spots, a water glass stamped with his fingerprints, a box of hospital tissue, a pale rose across Mary's rosary, a white missal, and a picture of Jesus, his right arm cradling the sacred heart, his left palm raised to reveal a festering wound.

The mounds of flowers tremble gently as the coffin sinks past the freshly turned sod.

With his chopsticks Peter slides the cheek from the head of the sea bass carcass into Uncle's rice bowl and tops it with the eyeball. Uncle drums his fingers on the table as we pour another round of Hennessey into the teacups.

Uncle loves the company of men. "I guess you can tie weights on your balls for the show. But the real test is to swing a hot one between your legs, no hands, right?" He'd say that.

All of us at the table raise our arms over our heads and cheer loudly enough that the kitchen empties, chef Wong in the lead, to drink a cup for the meal he cooked for us.

Peter stands and toasts the cook. "Thank you, kitchen master. Uncle here was inspired by the food and was telling us about his exploits in the kitchen."

"Yeah, well, you know that's real." The chef carefully dries his hands on his apron, helps himself to a cigarette from the packs left open on the table, and blows smoke across his brandy, tipping the cup in Lincoln's direction before he drains it and leans forward for a refill: "Everything I know he taught me." Bottle in hand, he pours a round while the dishwasher, a woman recently arrived from Hong Kong—wrapped in a thick blue denim apron, a headband of the same material knotted around her head, the lank strands of hair stuck to her forehead, wearing oversized knee-high rubber boots—cradles two jugs of high octane fruit brandy to the table. Her boots glisten with fish scale and bits of vegetable. The crowd divides, parted by the sharp smell of detergent and oil smoke that follows in her wake. She pours for herself and shuffles back towards the wall, leaning against an empty chair, sipping, smacking her lips, murmuring her thanks to no one in particular. Her rubber gloves are jammed down the front of her apron and she leans against the wall, a generous haunch bouncing easily against the loose veneer paneling on the side of a holding tank as she takes quick sips of her drink.

"You don't have to say that, chef," Uncle says grandly. "Just because it's true."

"And don't say anything more because a lady's listening," Peter adds.

"You men never learn, do you? I'm nobody's lady, assholes," she chirps. "I'm the kitchen cleaner. You can say what you want. I'm not tying apron strings to your balls. Go fuck chickens. You guys are all turtleheads anyway."

In Cantonese, the language of Chinatown diasporas around the world, the image of the turtle's head is particularly obscene, from the lips of a woman always hilarious, and in the dishwasher's bright Hong Kong dialect, ribald but rather fetching. "I already know that. You all would have me swinging a pig head between my legs."

Uncle found himself blotting drool from his lap, he laughed so hard when Winnie held up the iron eggs of the Chinese sexual physic. "Start with the small ones for practice. When you are stronger, the big one won't be any problem."

"*Jun hai,*" Mary responds automatically. Auntie says "*Jun hai,*" which means "that's right" or "that's reality," or "*Jun hai law,*" an encouragement to continue, "tell it the way it is. That's not a lie."

"*Gum hai law,*" says Peter to close the loop.

"Well, Lincoln's dead now. Everybody's free. We are all family now. We'll just remember what we want to remember. That's America."

Confession. How much to tell? Can I tell everything? How can I tell everything? I can't remember, I don't know how much he wants to hear or when to stop; it becomes a habit of mind, for a lifetime, to recall, to recite, to confess, to repent, to find absolution, forgiveness, to seek perfect contrition in Rome.

Aunt Mary says, "You only confess what you think you've done wrong. And if you are truly contrite, you will be forgiven, even the ones too little to remember, Christopher. I'm sure that's what Sister meant."

Uncle Lincoln mutters, repeating "Stupid," or words to that effect: unread, knowing nothing, useless, the litany one generation employs to distance themselves from the next.

Big brother Peter says to tell them how I make pictures of the sisters with beards eating hot dogs on Fridays. Auntie turns as if to brush her sleeve, examining the fabric of her cuff, testing a button. A child, I would fumble my way to her lap to catch the look on her face, exploring the enigma of her smile, patience, perhaps resignation. She's soft, the folds of her dress are silk, cool; I feel her body yielding to me, unlike the nuns, whose habits are starchy and stiff.

Am I really so stupid? I ask her wordlessly. And is that why I am sent away each day, why I must leave her company, why I am so wrong that I must confess? I was a misery, allergic, clinging, with a shadow on my lungs, prone to infection, the last orphan, much to everyone's relief.

Auntie gives me a nickel to buy candy. I favor Necco wafers, pastel discs that taste of peppermint, chocolate, citrus chalk, setting them one by one on my tongue in preparation for my first communion. When the moment finally comes, the Host is a disappointment, the texture of paper that dissolves into a paste I've been instructed not to chew. It has no flavor, but the aroma of sacramental wine on the priest's warm breath lingers like perfume as I finish my recitation. There would be no miracle, no introduction of the sacred body of Christ into me, nor would there ever be the salvation of Jesus Christ resurrecting me from my purgatory, because I could never offer a complete confession. There never would be, how could there be, so much to confess, all of my life.

Peter pouring old scorn in my ear asks, "How contrite can you be?" I can never escape. After China, I've come to Italy, to Rome to arrange a divorce from my second wife, Melba. "Columbus in pursuit of Marco Polo?"

"Polo's paramour. She has me staying in Rome's Chinatown." Esquilino, an old, evolving Roman neighborhood, February, the end of Festiva, the beginning of Lent. Cold, bright sun. Melba has stuck me in one of her rentals for the dozens of Chinese restaurants in the neighborhood. Huddling in my dark first-floor apartment, I'm trying to recover from the jet lag that envelops me entirely. Yesterday there was a *sciopero,* a labor strike that shut down the transportation system, the bus, the tram, and the subway until lunch. I was headed for the laundry near the Colosseum and noticed there was no traffic on Labicana. The working-class quiet and tranquility in this ancient Roman neighborhood became the high flutter of circling helicopters, the occasional claxon, the speeches over bullhorns. I hear "We Shall Overcome" in English, reminding me of school, when I first met Winnie. I like Rome; it welcomes all travelers and reminds them of where their memories have been shaped, especially my own, among a Chinese diaspora in a Catholic North Beach neighborhood; the coincidence is always delicious. And here in Rome, especially in Esquilino, an ancient neighborhood overrun by new immigrants, I can have pizza and Chinese takeout on the same block. *Paradiso.*

Peter's friend, Umberto, comes for dinner, arriving alone, no Melba. He's a pleasant enough fellow, allowing for pauses, a word here or there in Italian, and cultural silences, little gaps. He makes cautious enquiries about Peter in Amsterdam. They were together six months ago in this same flat, he tells me. They have equal shares in a small *enoteca* in Centro. They'd walked through the August heat to the bottom of the hill and spent a few hours luxuriating in San Giovanni di Laterano's cool enormity.

Berto, an Italian communist, shares Peter's satiric anxieties over the megaliths of mother church and holy Roman stone that surround the ancient city. He recalls Peter's observation that the huge interior spaces of cathedrals require filling by the obelisks erected in the piazzas adjacent. I've heard it all before, Peter impious, Peter profane: "From big erections to huge space, to each according to his capacity. Look with envy, Ozymandias. Never big enough, hard enough, long enough," Peter whispers sharply enough to send his words rebounding across the dim, cavernous space, Peter's act of contrition, Peter contrite, the apostate, home at last in exile he commutes, today Amsterdam, yesterday, Rome.

I serve up olives and cheese with my own anecdotes about my recent trip to China that I had practiced with Winnie. "Peter makes me the bag man. I carry contraband ingredients all around the world to inspire his culinary repertoire. I sabotaged every scent hound from Schiphol to SFO, my duffel filled with gift bags of Sunwei County dried orange peels. My luggage stinks of citrus."

Berto finds me mildly amusing, distracting enough, worth any word, any tidbits about Peter that might fall. Melba keeps him in a posse of Peter's Roman familiars. Berto's recently divorced, out of the closet, addicted to homeopathy and Peter. He's brought a loaf of warm bread, a five-seed studded with whole almonds, as macrobiotically dense as Peter's Chi Bars. He ignores my veal stir-fry and basmati rice plate.

So many of Peter's friends require restrictive diets. A dose of soy and chiseled ginger in the olive oil, stir, it's all good. Berto's vegan, so he just nibbles the bread he baked and sips the bottle of red he's brought. He describes being sick and alone this winter with the flu; here is a man who has been married for two decades, now separated and living alone, realizing what alone means. His son visited once; his ex, once. He keeps cats, so I avoid his apartment, even though he lives nearby and we could meet quite often, as we do anyway, with Melba and friends for a bite of something small and dense.

During dinner, even though I have not opened the old wooden shutters in the dining room, I can hear the rain falling hard, a sudden downpour splattering in the garden. The drain pipes rattle for a few minutes, then stop. Berto's bread is offered as the Host as we made bread so long ago to seek and celebrate such communion, if not with God, then with the God in our communion. Oh, stop it, Peter. You're not even here. Enough irony. My jaw aches. He just smiles. Forgive us, oh Lord, for these our sins we are about to commit again, amen. Mares eat oats, and does eat oats. Berto walks home. The next morning, the rain reappears, a steady drizzle. I eat the rest of Berto's five-seed loaf for breakfast. I take a walk up the hill to the marvelous spectacle of mosaics at Santa Maria di Maggiore, looking for the self-service laundry Berto said was next to the international marketplace, the sweet smell of curry, raw fish, the rank poultry stand, a cook's tour Peter might lead.

It's always Peter: Peter's friends, Peter's absence; I'm always Peter's "little brother." His friends are loyal, gay, witty, informed like Berto—even the women I fuck on those occasions when they are left without partners after feasts that stretch into the dawn, always a crowd for breakfast. Peter and Melba, my soon-to-be ex-wife, are always better as friends than as family, but here we are again.

Our Winnie stands apart as head of the family now, straddling our east and west, sending me swinging like a pendulum across the oceans to Asia, to Europe. She needs to be careful for all of us. Peter spends too wildly and Melba knows too much of the family's history and remains still married to me. And there's me, especially, whom Winnie trusts will fall into foolish circumstances, even though everything we have, everything Auntie left us, is under her direct stewardship. So, finally, a last bit of business for me. It's time to divorce, do the paperwork please, take Melba's signature off the records. Ironic because it's Winnie who worried about her own legitimacy until the old man married her as compensation for staying with him till he died. It was fair. Auntie thought it was fair. It looked odd only if you were an old-timer and remembered the rumors that Winnie had married the youngest one, the "little brother," for a green card. Our family was known for its connections to the immigration trade and their use of the missionary house to hide their business. It might have all been exposed except for the scandal that so dramatically distracted from the traditional disguises and strategies illegal entries require. Poor Wick, reduced to the funny guy who liked little kids.

Elusive sleep. After Berto left, I napped, but woke at three and read till dawn, unable to still the voices of the past, of the present: Melba's familiar, compliant murmuring, too close again, always affecting me; Hanif, the notary, a long-lost cousin of the real-estate agent who brokered the travel agency; Lazio, Melba's latest paramour, a retired football player who practices yoga; Ramdas Steinman, the vegan chef from San Francisco she persuaded Peter to hire for their *enoteca; et tu*, Berto?

Winnie and Melba still conspire. Melba left me her cell phone so I could call the States. Winnie already has the number and calls to remind me to sign the divorce papers before the end of the month, please. Several items have been on the selling block for months since Auntie Mary's death, including the travel agency, which still has Melba's name attached. "Please. Bring some dried citrus peels—orange, tangerine, pomelo." And divorce. "Please, Chris. It has to be soon or we wait until the next tax quarter. Say hello from me. If you speak to Peter, tell him to call or e-mail or something just to show he is alive, please. Tell him I made his pan-Asian gravlax recipe that *Cooks* published and it was very good, the tamarind pulp, especially."

Finally, it's Melba's voice on Melba's cell, although the window identifies the caller as Lazio.

"I thought you were coming to dinner with Umberto last night. He says there's a new Chinese place around the corner on Vicolo Dante. The veal is excellent." I'm whining.

"Sorry, but something came up at the last minute. An old friend."

Not so old. Yes, not so old, I leave unspoken. "Can you be ready at four? Hanif thinks he'll be back. He's driving down from Orvieto right after lunch. We can all have a drink and emancipate ourselves or whatever Winnie tells us needs doing. Don't you think it's sad when we let the words just fall, just to hear them, Chris? We've been married fifteen years, come July third. Is it possible? But Winnie says we must finally divide in order to multiply. We have to trust her and poor Mary's judgment in these matters. Did you get any sleep?"

"A little. I'm napping."

"Go for a walk, get some sunlight. You're five blocks from St. Peter's finger and fragments of the cross. Santa Croce di Gerusalemme. There's a Chinese-Japanese place right on the corner. Peter said it was good. Did I tell you that before her stroke Mary wrote me and told me what I should do? I'm sure she had premonitions. I cherish, that after all these years, she kept me in mind."

Mary probably included terms for a substantial payoff. I could hear another voice. "You're breaking up. I'll be here or I can call a cab."

"All right. I'll ring."

"Ciao?" I offer uselessly. She never disconnects, always waiting for the other party to resign. I listen for a moment more and hear the old friend whispering before I surrender the connection. I will improvise on this theme forever, whetting that appetite, measuring my physical need for her still, all this artifice, the dance in mind, my pursuit of her never over. I want illusion. I don't want release. When we first met, she offered to tell me everything I wanted to know about her, anything. I needed simply to ask.

She rattles on through my groggy blur. "I teach a yoga class on Thursday nights. Does that appeal to you?" In my dreams she whispers about how, in a Roman bathhouse, young boys serve the languid and supine. "In these times of plague, I keep their backs to me. I surround them with my flesh, the sight of which I disguise these days. They feel my nipples harden against their lumbar muscles and my hands reaching for their genitals."

It's evening, again, after six. It's dark outside. I must have slept. I walk myself through the city, across the Campo to Trastevere. I thought I saw a pretty Mei ducking through Piazza San Cosimato. In Rome, every Chinese rose peddler with a pretty smile reminds me of Toisan Town, of Mei and the month I'd just spent in Guandong Province hustling real estate for Winnie, smothered by the gingko harvest for Peter, and handling the purchase of the Hoipeng Close development Winnie wants to market to the overseas Chinese, all over the world. She sees a market for vacation condos for men in a village their wives and children could discretely avoid, for those homesick immigrant daddies suffering their independent wives and foreign children.

I see Mei wherever I travel, even here in Rome; I hear her voice still, thick with tears, on the expiring cell phone: "Perhaps we will meet in another lifetime, perhaps in heaven." When we last spoke, she was on a train, halfway home. But she knew it was me without looking at the display on the tuneful cell phone she always wore around her neck. No one else had the number. Perhaps it was because we had repeatedly said goodbye, how impossible we were together, soap opera, but in my mind I could imagine Lincoln's Daisies. So she knew it was me. She held her voice in check. I could imagine the crowded train compartment. Everyone, behind their newspapers, the noisy chatter, and the video on the TV monitor, would be listening intently. Who would waste money on a call to a girl traveling single hard seat to Fut Ow Town and beyond? A husband could wait. A lover would not.

I smell camphor chasing the mildew in the closets of my Roman apartment and see my provincial China. Camphor, to drive out the cockroaches, to staunch and stay the cut earlobes sent to the parents as motivation for quick ransom. In the deep ruts left by weighted freight, by the dusty sandal tracks of village bandits stalking the returning sojourners to their Toisan roots laden with the weight of a gold mountain on their backs, I smell their goods, their despair. What would Peter think, what would Lincoln have said about the return, and Melba and Winnie and Auntie? Camphor—the smell of it fills the salon of the ferryboat moving up the Pearl River as the salesgirls load an infomercial into the video machine and the TV monitors fill with Dr. Ho and his kung fu medicinal ointment, as the boat carries me back to Toisan Town. The girls work the aisles with open samples that reek of camphor.

Where was that new development? The locals called it Commune 49, a pun in dialect that means "dead dog." It was advertised as Hoipeng Close in the British press and American ads. Winnie knew the family of the jailed developer whose wife was from Hoipeng. He named it nostalgically for her and her family's connections before the bottom dropped out of the investment market as he was trying to leverage their monies. Several units had been completed, a brick-lined lane in the middle of the city with village homes newly renovated and recently rediscovered by Winnie. When the Commies threatened to confiscate farmland again, there was a building boom of new housing construction to homestead private holdings. Then there'd been a disastrous economy. Money for the construction market leeched into the fields as fertilizer. So we were in there pitching for bargains.

Beijing, Shanghai, yes, but I'd never been to the district the ancestors came from, and, truly, we could buy almost without looking further than the prices, but the locals like to see a warm body—a male, preferably—spreading gifts, who they can wine and dine. "Chris. So you go. It's quite near where Mary's family came from. Lincoln made the trip once, you remember. For Mary. Visit the graves, you know; we want to show them we can market them all over again. No place like home," Winnie laughs pleasantly.

I know. They know. That's why you all left.

"We can buy three-plus bedroom units for less than twenty thousand. Go. They will treat you well. You'll see. Learn something new. Your Chinese will improve, just by listening."

So I went, Guandong Province, Canton City, Toisan Town, by ferry, no less, and a quick look at the remains of Bok Tsek village from the back of a motorcycle, just to needle Mary's brothers who have never been. Then I met a girl, a baby, really, who spoke in the dialect of my Chinatown childhood, all those familiar sounds.

Mei caught me when I thought I was just looking, when I thought I'd forgotten how to hear, to look without listening. A stocky farm girl with strong legs, a blunt haircut, her shoulders and arms made a tight fit in her white polo turtleneck, looking sixteen, her face still ivory under the protection of those wide-brim hats they wear to preserve their pale, transparent complexions until they marry or wither. She arrived at our table late one afternoon and was invited to sit and pour while my new partners tested my American point of view and my memory of the local *sze yup* dialect. Most had been sojourners abroad, in Europe, the Hispanic Americas, Miami, New York, Los Angeles, San Francisco, but because of language or culture, they preferred life in Toisan Town to spending their afternoons at a Doughnut World in a Chinatown diaspora. But the talk was the same. I was reminded of Lincoln bantering with the same languor.

Mei let the foam spill as she poured the new beer the owner's niece brought to the table. Mild cursing at the farm girl, "That's clumsy. But we have to let her learn. She's just arrived." Mei kept her head up as she mopped up. Then she dropped the wet napkins under the table and the niece erupted: "Stupid and clumsy! This is not the village! You're in a house with wooden floors. You can't throw garbage everywhere!"

Retrieving the sodden papers, Mei held them by her side, not knowing what to do. The niece held out the tray with the empties and nodded. Mei gratefully let the napkins fall and sat again, pouring more beer into glasses that she carefully tilted to avoid the spill.

"What kind of girls do you prefer, Mr. Christopher? Do you like Chinese girls?"

"I like women I can talk to, who talk back, who can be friends. My Cantonese is so poor, it's difficult to develop a friendship without English."

Ah Mei in Toisan spins a careful couplet, letting it curl around the table. "If she speaks English, she'll be home before you will." Her riposte wins the table, a murmur of approval. She has heart. I choose her. She claims to be nineteen, but she tells me later that she's actually twenty-four. I would guess a few years older, but they have to lie if they want to be considered. Of course, she's strong, with the stamina that comes from a life on the farm, and has been carefully coached in the methodical use of condoms: check for leaks, dispose of them promptly, shower quickly. We watch the soap operas on the TV and she explains who she would like to be, how her own life resembles the heroine, how our days together might be like those on the screen.

We take a taxi to spend a few days by the sea. The city ripples from the center with new enterprise, the demands of pending free-trade opportunities carved into the translucent valleys shimmering with the coursing river, small streams, the flooded rice paddy, the gleaming ponds. In anticipation of China's entry into the WTO, a broad new highway carves past several kilometers of nurseries all specializing in a single variety of plant product. Here, Bonsai trees—a thousand clones, all black pine, all sweeping, all in blue glazed ten-liter pots—snap by like icons on a computer screen. We arrive in a village with two resort hotels, almost empty, very discreet, where the authorities do not demand a woman's identity card, where she can reside as a woman with no name.

At the shore, the owner's wife, a cousin of my host in Toisan, entertains us with stories as she serves exotic morsels the locals traditionally invent for visiting sojourners, invaders, the homesick, the hapless enemy, the swaggering conqueror, their overseas brethren, all of whom are welcomed and fleeced. Fried duck tongue on the beak is as poised and mannered, as exotic, as native as dried ear lobes off kidnapped children as inducements for ransom. Sea turtle soup, a fiery dance of hot peppers to stir the extremities, a fish gut pudding: I eat everything.

My first evening in Rome passed quietly. Umberto was good company. He described spending a late afternoon closing the St. Peter's post office, Peter sending multiple postcards telling how to prepare the rabbit for Easter, then wandering the center of Catholicism's most sacred space.

Berto worked his fingers through the winter tangerines from Sicily. "As we shuffled out of St. Peter's when the buzzer sounded the close, perhaps two hundred people filtered through the exits to watch the twilight swirling of swallows that create the shadowy mobiles, black Calder-like sculptures twisting, shifting in vast flocks in the sky above Rome. Peter was surprised. He thought we'd been alone in that enormous space, so vast, so isolating."

The rain had stopped. "It was like that for me in China, Shanghai, Beijing. I thought I was alone, free to do, to be anything. Ancient cities. No one conquers a courtesan. By the way, I hear Peter's coming to Rome— by train, no less. He's just out of the hospital so he's traveling with our uncle Wick." With Mary gone, who else is left to watch over us but our senile divine? Wick had recited Mary's eulogy spontaneously, extemporizing as if he were swinging from the Tree of Heaven—or smoking its leaves, I heard a nephew remark. Not a pretty picture. Nor Peter, the breathless courtesan turned wheezy, a bit blue at the ends of his fingers from poor circulation, aging, in decline. Nor I, Chris. Waiting for life to begin, I'm suddenly sure that as life begins, it begins again. What was I waiting for all these years, something more momentous than what, that I would understand my place in a family, in a religion, in a community of idealism, in service to my people, to mine own self? None of it and all of it. A half-century spent with hopes of a goal, a reward, a clear recognition, of compensation for time spent living. And I discover that it's only living that is its own reward. I forgive everyone and I forgive myself. I thought everyone was watching over me, watching my every move; I lived to fulfill the expectations of others. All illusion. I live, I eat, I devour the days and the past, garlic skins evaporating in a flash.

In Rome, it's Chinatown again, an international district certainly, where the immigrants have begun their relentless search for new roots that sprout an array of foodstuffs and ingredients, the emporia of the world, a district lit at night by the paper lantern glow that signals a Chinese restaurant. Waiting for Melba's call, I'm napping through time warps. Daylight crashes against my eyes. I've opened the window and a nun peeks out from between the fall of lace curtains that shades the windows of the convent across the alley. She looks familiar yet foreign, Sri Lankan, Tamil, Indian. It must be morning. We both watch as a fat little Chinese girl, ten, eleven years old, dressed in a turquoise warm-up suit her parents might peddle on the sidewalk, trudges up the cobblestoned *vicolo* all by herself, school pack on her back, past the nunnery where the nun, her dark Dravidian features framed in her white wimple, peers expectantly. Does she know by my face that I'm apostate? I'm still dreaming that the cell phone rings, Winnie in San Francisco trying to close a deal, Mei in Toisan Town asking if she can join me, Melba in Trastevere showing flats to an American couple, reminding me that our divorce papers await my signature. I'm in Rome, and I'm a kid again, ten years old, growing up in San Francisco's North Beach, still in the Chinatown diocese, attending catechism. I've lived for more than half a century. The dark-eyed sister in the lacy window-length wimple meets my eyes but withdraws without any acknowledgement that she's seen me or the little girl walking to school alone. I'm at the center of a triangle of three Catholic churches, and I am weeping, tears streaming down my face for the child in me that remains, at heart, alone.

2

I see now that what I have embarked on is a narrative of my life that is essentially an invention, cobbling snatches of sensory impressions, all of appetite, very little of intellectual or intuitive insight I may have realized or been taught, nothing from stumbling past a door of perception left ajar by some New Age pharmaceutical. This narrative is, however, a reassuring justification, a wall that I might fix against the tide, to chart the shoal, that forms the backwater where Auntie Mary wades still. So I recall these moments as significant milestones that not only marked the beginning and end of my two attempts at marriage, but also the progress of life itself. At the time, I was still young enough, naive enough, to ignore the intimations. I could only imagine myself beginning and beginning again while those around me were preparing their farewells, all in the guise of food.

Uncle Lincoln had his first coronary incident not long after he took Winnie with him to Hong Kong on a business junket for Mary. Peter would joke that it was the honeymoon that took him down that road, that finally killed him. Before Winnie moved him down to Long Beach, he'd spent a few days two floors above the emergency ward at County General (where I would later find myself). Hospitals and graveyards manufacture such coincidence.

Auntie called from Uncle's Embarcadero penthouse to tell me that she had persuaded him to see a distant cousin, who was a heart specialist in Monterey Park, for further evaluation. Winnie would go with him. Then, almost as an afterthought, she invited me to have dinner with her. It was the first of the many meals she would prepare for me alone, that we would share together whenever we were home, until she died last year.

"I'm staying at their place while they're gone. I'm helping them because there was no time for them to unpack. Why don't you leave your car in the garage and walk over after work? I want to tell you what Ah Lung Gong said in the hospital." Using the name I called Uncle when I was a child, she made her invitation a command from the old man himself. Auntie's invitation was audacious and revealing, almost code between us. There was no mention of brother Peter gone to Waikiki or Wick in hiding. "I'll make something. Nothing special. Just us."

I imagined an invitation to a conspiracy. There was always a rivalry in the preparation of a meal, a declaration of family loyalties.

Peter and Lincoln were always fused together, some sticky concoction left too long in the glaze. When we were young, I knew Peter was always much closer, knew Uncle much better, than I ever could. They fought in a Chinese I identified as belonging to the older generation, a different vocabulary, bereft of concerns for my physical well-being, the state of my hair, my clothes. Peter was an adult in a language where I would forever be the adolescent. He would always be my senior, with all the affection and rivalry, jealousies, and the mutual contempt that attends. But he respected Lincoln, where I was merely afraid. Peter still fondly recounts that when Uncle was in the kitchen, he took no prisoners at the range. The heat and combustion of his cooking required quick hands and the temper of a sapper taking out the bridge over the River Kwai. Peter says Uncle infused the breath of the wok into everything he made: the Cantonese stir-fry, hot and salty, dancing in the high fire-blast furnace that turns salt-and-pepper prawns into a pink tangle of lace leaves, sweet peppers and onions al dente. On TV, Peter did imitations of Uncle, growling at Twig, who played the native pantry boy, "It's all in the wrists, bra'." Peter would remind me how Lincoln used to sing along with the radio as we listened to "The Hit Parade" or croon with Bing Crosby as he slipped wontons one by one into the deep fat fryer or pitched a smoking mound of onion and tomato into the air, catching it in his pan like some live thing he needed to drown for the sauce. It was like a wrestling match on black-and-white TV. He would warn me off with a sweep of his arm as the wok threw flames that scorched the ceiling of the trailer and bubbled the plastic molding. Preening like Gorgeous George, he'd warn, "Watch it now, hot stuff. Don't come near."

Peter and I shared such zany links, a common language of old radio and black-and-white TV, all of us children in a loony paradise. That we were company for a middle-aged Chinese bachelor lonely for friends, for family, occurs to me only now as I recall the discrete moments of time we actually spent together. The explosions, the smoking grease fires that filled the kitchen trailer with thick black clouds, were an invitation to join him. Peter would leap for the door, pushing it open to let the smoke out, while Lincoln dragged a can of flour from the pantry, and we would throw handfuls at the burning pan to smother the flames. As the smoke billowed, we pitched drifts of flour to extinguish the blaze, dusting the three of us until we finally fell outside, Lincoln wiping the flour from my face with a corner of his apron while I whipped them both around the back parking lot with a dish towel, singing along with Spike Jones to that classic recording of "Chinese Mule Train." He had a genuine six-shooter, a single-action revolver he would fire off just to hear the echo bounced off a distant canyon wall. Made the dogs howl.

Peter smirks. There are so few of my generation that I can confide in, and only Peter shares life with Uncle as I did. My little recollections res-onate in him. "I remember I hated the dogs. Lucky One, Two, and Three. All that affection in a smelly pile of fur."

"'Chinese Mule Train.' I still remember all the words. How can we have memories that we love and still hate to recall?"

"That is what makes sense of us." Peter always has an answer. "It's con-tempt, self-contempt. It's the legacy of victims passed down over gener-ations. You have to be born to it. Makes you a Chinaman, boy."

"We were always together."

"We were in hiding." Peter laughs at me. "We were Siamese, if you please."

I could name that tune in six notes; Peter, in four.

On the phone, Auntie fell easily into the chatter of food that we all share as a strategy to ease the undigested bits we don't acknowledge, the inti-macies we obliquely include. Is Ah Lung Gung well? Will he live through the day, the week, the month? Winnie was hiding out with Uncle, till death do them part.

"Nothing special tonight. Look for something good when you walk down the hill. I'll cook it. We're just the two of us tonight, right? I feel like *dah bin low,* a little hot pot. Anything fresh is good. But don't buy too much. There's lots of stuff in the refrigerator already."

So I left the office a little early, before the markets closed. Shoppers crowded the fishmongers' aquariums, pushing for a glimpse of catfish, crab, or eel that could link the flavor of bean sauce, sesame oil, something salty or sweet, something rank and stinky, the molecular logic of pheromones, the whiff of the familiar, to stimulate the appetite's imagination.

"You're just like Ah Lung Gong. You like the stinky stuff. Buy some for yourself. If it's not too much of a bother, buy some fish paste too. You know how to say it? Ask for *yu jeung*."

Auntie knows I follow my eyes, my nose, and point.

A battered delivery van, its side doors blocked open with folding chairs, has claimed a parking space across the street. A line of chipped enamel pans in the shadow of the bakery's awning lines the sidewalk. Fresh crustacea, snails nesting in coils of watercress, tiny shrimp, turtles, all manner of live stuff freshly gathered, collected from the lakes and streams in Golden Gate Park or the mudflats of the Bay where the gleaners have illegally planted Asia's culinary fauna, are on display. A golden carp rests in a bucket beneath a card table stacked with Styrofoam ice boxes. The public health department does a monthly sweep to record for the state's Department of Fish and Game what new species have immigrated to America. The city requires a sign, often ignored, warning of shellfish contamination. The red tides that contaminate the oyster and clam beds are more lethal to the immigrants than the INS. A woman sits resplendent on a stack of old newspapers, surrounded by a small forest of herbs and grass in plastic planters wrapped in crinkled foil, selling freshwater snails in chipped enamel dishpans.

I point, and as I point, the gesture itself—the poking toothpick to extract the meat—brings the taste of the snails to my tongue. The word falls easily from my lips: *"Tin law."*

"Gai daw, ah?" she asks, dismissing the familiar, the extravagant rote of particulars that describe their freshness, details for preparation. She knows.

I am immediately reduced to a hand signal. I know my numbers, but I'm helpless without the words for measures: a pound, a catty, a handful, a bushel and a peck. She silently includes a boa of watercress without another glance at me.

Uncle's words come to me in Cantonese, in English, without any bidding on my part, and leave as abruptly. It's no coincidence that I have kept the nouns for foodstuffs. Eat everything before you die. Eat everything before somebody else eats it. Eat everything before it goes bad. Eat all you can eat.

I catch myself humming something that sounds vaguely liturgical, vaguely pentatonic. It's Twig, Peter's ex-lover. Twig's composition for his band, the Trees, loops, mindlessly seductive, a flashback that occurs with no warning, my toe tapping at Lincoln's funeral when I sat with Auntie Mary as she lipped her rosary beads like the Anna Magnani she had loved with Burt Lancaster at the Orpheum, and I feel suddenly blinded by the light flooding out of the projection booth into Peter's kitchen, always the exploding glare that catches me looking for words whenever we try to describe ourselves.

Peter prompts me. "There you have it, a key."

"I don't get it."

"We're talking about successive generations of victims. Lincoln didn't want to play 'pass it on/no pass back.'"

"Baby talk," Peter cautions. Lincoln's sacrifice, to disguise, to obscure, to hide the past. Peter prompts me again. "That's the only talk we all have in common. Baby babble. What is it you wanted from Lincoln? Be realistic. What could he give you? What could he say that you could repeat, that wouldn't give us back to the Indians?"

"The Indians?" I don't want to understand.

"Why would he want us to be what he had to be?" Peter snaps impatiently. "He hadn't anything to pass on. There's nothing to tell. Don't you get it?"

Wick said once, "Orphans don't have answers for themselves or for others, much less for the sons of orphans." I dream that I can finally turn to look at him, stare defiantly past his solicitous pardon, only to realize my eyes are tightly shut. I won't cry. He accepts my blinking, my embarrassment, with an expression brimming with compassion, inviting tears, a communion of absolution.

Exit the confessional. Father Peter, Dr. Wick, the patient divine standing in the kitchen, both of them always looking for more, helping me to re-examine the leftovers. But then how successful were they or any of us at realizing who we were and what we might become?

So this is what we were. We grew up in Chinatown with Auntie Mary in the decade after World War II. Peter, whom I called *dai gaw*, and I lived on the corner of Washington and Brenham, right above Portsmouth Square, with a view of police headquarters down the hill to the east. We had the second balcony facing north, looking directly into the double-windowed doors to the second-floor banquet hall of the Sun Hong Heung restaurant back when Washington Street hill was still paved with cobblestones. When I was very young, the steep incline of Washington Street on a rainy April morning, with the sun peeking past clouds over the East Bay hills, resembled the back of a prehistoric monster, a dragon, some dinosaur's backside reticulated with gray and blue plating, its scales glistening as it rose from the black Bay waters. The dried, the preserved, the raw miasma of the markets when they hosed the stalls in the early morning lingered until the deep fryers in the restaurants started rendering pork skin, covering the smell of the live poultry in wooden crates, the ducks, the geese, the chickens murmuring singsong in the cool shade of the alleys.

When the sun broke through the clouds, I would watch old men wipe the park benches dry with newspaper and sit with them as they nibbled dried fruit and cracked seed, chewed slices of fresh sugar cane and spit sweet fiber on newspapers spread at their feet. In the evenings, when I was sent to dump the household garbage in the trash barrels in the park, I could smell the scum of vegetable matter and cardboard, slip from the produce market, the cold exhaust of fog and sewer gas.

My first organized education in English came from the nuns at St. Cecilia's, Irish and Italian women who in their lifetimes had seen the neighborhood shift from immigrant Italian to Chinese and Mexican, from World War II to the Korean police action. On the Broadway littoral that separates Chinatown from North Beach, where Italian, Mexican, Chinese, Basque, and Navajo boxcar children were catechized, I was taught a funereal vocabulary I even now recall with every visit to a mortuary. We napped in solariums, held vigils in the columbarium for the stations of the cross. I learned the rosary, sang "Ave Maria" in Latin, went costumed in the motley of the Swiss Guard, learned the love of legumes (particularly yellow peas, strung like those sacred beads) while listening to a Brahms lullaby and closely observing the pendant Christ whose discreet loin wrap but wanton knee akimbo tickled my earliest pubescent fantasies. Startling collisions of a Renaissance heaven, buff and ripped martyrs, the milky blue breasts of the fallen and the ascendant played against the ceramic Taoist and Buddhist iconography of Chinatown, the abdominal and the bald against the hirsute and fleshly, wimpled martyrs and cloisonné figurines, Christ and Kwan Kung, the naked and the enraged, the sublimity of Christian surrender and martyrdom challenging the rule of revenge for disloyalty and inevitable, erosive amalgamation. These icons figured on the ceiling of the solarium where we lay with Christ while Sister Stanley manned the record player, the silibant hiss, the introductory static crackling, that sweet lullaby engraved in the spinning black vortex, repeated over and over.

Offenbach's dreams, Brahms's lullaby became "Baubles, Bangles and Beads," "The Dickie Bird" and "The Old Master Painter" when a new record invited us to juice and fruit. My right hand was engulfed by the pale, chaste grip of Sister Joseph. In my other hand I held a chum's sticky fingers. A chain of corduroy cherubim, we were led through the halls, through the streets of Chinatown, marked by the old men as the victims of their immigrant ambitions. There we were, guarded by wimpled white women, untouchables now, destined to become the martyrs for acceptance in America. They called to us in Chinese, in the *sze yup* dialect of common households, and we pretended not to hear, not to understand. Linked hand in hand to Sister's firm grip and her admonition to hold tightly to one another, we paraded past the old uncles of Chinatown, who in their turn kept their silent greetings to themselves with perhaps a prayerful admonition to family, to children across the oceans to remember those who had not forgotten them.

When I was older, I began to follow Peter to the Protestant settlement house, Shepherd's Haven. He was old enough to be a counselor and was quickly promoted, becoming one of Wick's assistants in the Saturday school where we were taught American manners, the etiquette of the toilet, and the history of the Haven. He loyally handed down to me the sacred relics of a childhood spent awash in the surplus of WWII souvenirs, models he had already built and painted, authentic holster webbing, box carts with skates for the hill slides, all his precious treasures, trading cards, comic books, records. Just as I wore his corduroys and maroon wool sweaters to parochial school, I kept his fish tanks, painted turtle shells, and ping-pong paddle covers, the smell of glue, of ink, of camphor and mothballs, and our love for Wick. The Haven was originally established to rescue Chinese women from the clutches of

Chinese men like Uncle. Unfortunately, even as we made our escape from the ghetto enclaves of Chinatown bachelor societies, there was Wick and his unfortunate addiction for embracing young boys too closely— no haven for some of our generation of cultural orphans, but he saved me, saved Peter, even Auntie Mary, although I didn't know how or why at the time.

I only knew then, as now, as it will be on earth as it is in heaven, fresh watercress floating in plastic buckets on the sidewalk, muddied coriander, scallions bunched with fuzzy twine, their tips gleaming albino spiders on a plank, onion grass that's grown without sun to capture a pale sweetness for the soup stock, stalks of chard, baby chard, mature chard, flowering chard, leafed, unleafed, dried chard, then spinach, the roots, the fruit from the tropical diaspora, all at home in Chinatown America. Soybeans, fresh or frozen, boiled in salted water for an appetizer, become tofu—soft, medium, hard, fresh, dried, boiled in soy sauce, and dried for soup. The Chinatown emporia teems with such bounty that only a necromancer like Auntie can encompass, manipulate, and control it.

I spy some fresh asparagus that Auntie and I won't get to this evening. It's too much already. But I'm always intoxicated by Auntie's invitations, the sumptuous repasts, so I buy a bottle of wine and two bean sauces in jars with labels I haven't seen before. Peter's right, always, always. My earliest memories are locked in Chinese I can't translate, more sensations than words, just single sounds, phrases that can make me itch and sneeze or feel feverish, crave a taste for food I eat only when I have a cold or when I'm blue. When that happens, I have this irresistible urge to prove I can count to ten in Chinese. Auntie taught me my numbers, taught me to count to ten, to disguise my foreignness, that I might make familiar sounds in a way that she could find some comfort from me, an act that requires I start with one and end at ten, the only two numbers I can immediately recall and pronounce out of order. Counting to ten in Chinese strips away the years, a mantric baby talk that evokes a forgiving continuity, a tender succession of sensations, the sigh of the wind in the trees, the sun-stiffened cotton nubs of a bed sheet, the hot grass smell of a summer pasture, and food, of course, thick rice gruel with stew beef that separates from its rind of fat and tendon in strings.

The number one is me, the baby, the youngest on the first day, the day, daily, every day. It's a hot, sultry evening at the back door of my Lung Gung's kitchen. I'm trying to scramble my way down the wooden stairs past the garbage cans, scratching my knees, scuttling across a field singing ten times ten, trying to cross a hundred steps beyond the neon circle that glares through the night, so I can lie down beneath trees that smell like toasted rice. During the day, the dogs prostrate themselves in their dirt enclosure, snap at flies swarming their leftovers. A hot wind fills the curtain of two thick scrubs of ailanthus some pioneer herbalist scattered at the edge of a knoll, upwind forever, where the grass lies thick and green, brilliant under vast sunfalls of light against the surrounding valley, sere yellow, scrub and brittle hiding the Sierra granite beneath a shock of thin grass and sand. Further downwind, the trees' progeny hug deep pockets of topsoil, stunted brush where the table water disappears. Mortarless field-stone walls like old bones divide pasture from orchards. Stone weirs across the riverbed streaming long coils of moss and water-cress mark the fish traps.

These are the landscapes I imagine. For me, this is where I began, where Uncle Lincoln began, here, with one of Auntie's mysterious cousins, always Daisy, my mother, my auntie, my very own. I was told that I was born in a cycle of bad business years, at a rest stop called Columbia. So the first stories have us criss-crossing the interior of the state. Uncle worked as a short-order cook, then a pantryman in a hotel resort southeast of the Sierra Buttes on the northwest edge of the Sacramento Valley, where he had the kitchen concession for a season. Lincoln would migrate down through the central valley, all the way to the Anza-Borrego Desert where a Daisy I can never recall would wither and die in a converted Sunstream trailer, a roadside takeout with a few picnic tables and benches in front of the delivery window.

Or was it when Lincoln, Daisy, Peter, and I lived as a family in Paradise, in the shadow of the thinning Sierra forest, where dead summer leaves hang brittle, beaten copper, and the bad air rising from the valley smells like fever, like mud behind the restaurant, where a dog lay chained to the wheelrim of a semi. The dog was always old, a dusty misery that rose only to follow the sun's shadow like a sundial, guarding its food under a cloud of black flies. The first dog I could call was named Nine. In Cantonese, "dog" sounds like "nine" or "old." I thought I had submerged myself in

Chinese habits by naming the dog "Old Nine." But everything Chinese already has a name, and every word a hundred homophones. Uncle would play the nines with me until it became, "Enough!" *Gow law!*

Uncle called the dog Lucky in English, in Chinese, Dog. Every dog he ever owned was named Lucky. A dog at the door foreshadows riches. "Come, Lucky; here, Lucky. Here, Dog." He recited the numbers so I could keep my place. When I rhymed nonsense with Chinese syllables or recited for his country cronies, performed for them, I'm sure I was a dire warning, a Chinese son who could not speak Chinese except to fetch numbers in a strangled singsong voice, his first wife's nephew or second wife's cousin or some relative by marriage. Then, a white missionary with the fanciful name Candlewick, passing through Columbia, named me eponymously the same. They'd all shake their heads and sigh and recount similar circumstances that produced such odd coincidences, adding up to a sum that was neither three, nor four, not this or that. Here was Columbus, and here, America. What a thing, what a place.

Lincoln hid us among the last brotherhood of bachelor exiles fending for themselves away from the family responsibilities and public humiliations an urban persona requires. A part of him was escaping from the marriage Auntie Mary's family had arranged between Lincoln and one of the Daisies who might or might not have been my mother. Peter told me being a single Chinaman running the local takeout gave Uncle freedom from any family fealties Auntie Mary's inventions and conspiracies would target. Wick said it was to escape from the hostility white people automatically exhibit when they encounter more than one of a different kind. I know now that Mary did choose Wick. But together, all of them were saving us, hiding us, feeding us, layering us with enough history to be able to explain ourselves when we were old enough to speak.

Auntie Mary told me I was sent to live with her family in San Francisco after I was diagnosed with valley fever. Daisy had died from it and Lincoln couldn't care for an infant. But when I was older, maybe eight or nine, I was suddenly sent back to Lincoln. They said I had tested positive for TB. My good uncles thought I was infected and wanted to send me to some sanitarium, but Auntie Mary told me she had persuaded bad Uncle Lincoln to take me, a lonely reunion in exile. I remember thinking only that I was being sent away to my father. Of course, he wasn't. He never said that. Neither did Mary. (There were times when I wished Wick could be, of course.)

All the old men of Lincoln's generation were "Uncle"—I'd always called him Uncle. Never telling me that he was my father or that I ever had one, Lincoln let me inherit the legend of orphans, told me stories about his own orphan past. He told me that it was during the War, when he left San Francisco to run a restaurant outside of Sacramento, in a town the Chinese called Second City before there ever was a Sacramento, that he met a man who had known his father, the man Uncle called "Uncle." Lincoln carried a photograph of his uncle, the one who taught him how to cook, standing on the veranda of a two-story clapboard building, the front porch of a sweet shop in Lovelock, Nevada, circa 1910. The black-and-white snapshot catches this man improvising a smile, mouth open, standing among but not with a group of dark-skinned men dressed in quilted black jackets and cuffless pants, two with queues coiled roguishly under flat pancake hats with unrolled brims, gandy dancers, boxcar cleaners for the Tahoe Truckee Sierra spurs. Their faces, mouths agape, eyes wide with surprise, that expression of dull worn shock, of a lingering sickness all pioneers exhibit, suggest mental retardation, some blow to their mental faculties, something of the immigration experience that they hadn't quite recovered from, all of them refugees from a collapsing dynasty, seeking refuge or oblivion in the scrabble and granite of the Sierras.

Uncle would finger the face of each man in the group, asking me, was this one Chinese or Indian? There were ten faces in the photograph, and only two of these sun-darkened figures from his obscure origins were *tong gen,* yellow people. Number One, the oldest looking one in the picture, Uncle's uncle, had scars on his legs from his childhood when he dove for pearls in the village. In America, he had worked for the Southern Pacific in Lovelock and Sparks, where the freight trains made scheduled transitions from the mallet engines that drove the freight cars backwards across the Sierras to the drivers that would complete the route to the Oakland Mole. He had worked variously as a cook, a dealer, a procurer. Uncle recalled a bordello on the Truckee River near Reno where this man, his father, had cooked for the women, hung the laundry, brewed the medicinal teas that made a lone Chinaman valuable to any community. The old man had been addicted to opium. Uncle would watch him smoke, then fall asleep on pallets in a room with no windows, a boarding house for Chinaman railroad workers up Six-Mile Canyon.

Lincoln said his uncle did laundry and track surveys, swept boxcars, and cooked. He lived with an Indian woman. Taught her to count money, make change in Chinese, the numbers, how to stoke a fire and feed its heat up a chimney to fire a wok. I suppose Uncle thought that was the least he could do for me, too, a legacy of numbers that count for something.

While he was still at Shepherd's Haven, Wick lined his study with old photos of immigrants of Lincoln's "uncle's" period. At fellowship gatherings, he would project slides of the old photos of the gold country above the site of the church camp on the windows facing Chinatown, mingling the images of the old and new. "These are the refugees from a collapsing dynasty, surrounded by Americans on the move, fading Indians on the frontier, decades of anti-Chinese venom from the American laboring classes and the pursuit of the immigration authorities, driven from the cities by a conspiracy of natural earthquakes and the inevitable insurance arson teams that followed. They seek oblivion in the scrabble and granite of the Sierras, hide amongst the memories of cannibals at Donner Pass and the dreadful drifting fields of snow, finding refuge among the exiles." At about that time, Peter and Wick shared a discovery at church camp, a lightning strike exploded in a glory hole some Chinaman had filled for a fishpond. Blackened sugar pines and the screen of Chinese willow stood twisted and bare, skeletal reinforcing rods of a foundation of a building that no longer existed. After a Sierra deluge had extinguished the smoldering shrub and dry summer grass, the Chinaman had sown herbal plants from China in a garden that the wind had stretched for miles down the canyon. The sun glinted over the quartz debris he used to form the weirs. The channel to the stream that fed the pond was still intact and the hole some fifteen feet deep at bottom was nearly filled, threatening to erode a new channel to meet the stream. My first time in camp, we spent a summer clearing the drains and repairing the garden wall.

Lincoln drinks and smokes black cigars at the sink after lunch. Mopping his hands on his denim apron, he wipes the kitchen's oily sweat from his face with the red bandanna he keeps around his neck. The gamblers, unemployed bachelors wearing second-hand suits, sit with him in the kitchen or stand at the back door, blowing smoke, sipping Hennessey from teacups in the hour or two before the dinner crowd, soft tweed caps rolled in their pockets. They'd get drunk, then mean, the easier to butcher memory.

"I've done it many times, now. I know. Find a near-sighted woman, you can't go wrong. They don't pick at everything, not so fussy. Grateful and ugly with small feet is best. They stay close, learn to appreciate food every day, kids. Village girls. They never worry the small stuff, just whatever they can hold in both hands. So you get stuck with an ugly runt that trips over her big feet," he explodes, a wet, rich tearing in his chest, coughing up, tears flooding his eyes, streaming down his wrinkled cheeks. "Marry a midget." He pauses. An abacus snaps from the gloom of the front counter through the split door held ajar by the cardboard runner that catches spills, where an auntie with no number counts money, biding hours, pretending not to hear. "I can do that. Easy."

I see again the dishwasher at Ming's, a Daisy in her apron watering the flowers lined up against the holding tanks, a woman from Hong Kong, wrapped in a thick blue denim apron, a headband of the same material knotted around her head, the lank strands of hair stuck to her forehead, wearing oversized knee-high rubber boots.

When I first realized that Lincoln was talking to me, that he was drunk, I cried. But I taught myself not to shed tears in front of him. (Now that he's dead, I can't.) My tears caught him by surprise. He'd not been talking to me, not directly. But he was revealing a side of himself, his utter loneliness, his confession that he wasn't all that he should be. I think he forgot I was in the kitchen with all the rest of them, listening. I began to blubber, no other word for it. I couldn't stop. I don't remember if there were actually others in the kitchen, although it would have been unusual for there not to be. I know he was embarrassed, not for my sake, but for himself. And he shushed me, and when I couldn't stop, he gave me his apron and told me to go outside and wash up. Told me I could feed Lucky the slops. But I couldn't move. I wept never knowing why, how to stop, nothing. That was the last time I ever did. He never gave me another opportunity.

The McCarthy era forced everyone to hide their origins. Men like Lincoln held their secrets. Each auntie held her own secrets. The Catholic Church, settlement houses like Shepherd's Haven, helped disguise us.

Auntie had a cousin whose children had not only survived the Japanese invasion but were living as the hope of the Communist future. Her sister-in-law managed to smuggle them from an agrarian commune where they'd been revealed as the spawn of a revisionist entrepreneur, a baker with family land leased to his neighbors before the Revolution. One let it be known that a boy older than I had been declared an orphan and claimed by a group of Maryknoll missionaries in the New Territories. Politically neutral and religiously correct, an exchange was made. He was shipped to Paradise, named Peter, then sent to San Francisco. I was returned to San Francisco to live with my childless Auntie Mary left at home. The family sent us to parochial schools and the Presbyterian Church camp to reassure everyone of our perfect faith in the miracles of Jesus Christ, our loyalty and gratitude to the Christians who helped smuggle and shape us for acceptance in America.

Uncle's uncle had a different story. To Lincoln, he liked to say, "I don't think your daddy was all Chinese anyway. You know that, don't you? Your father didn't come on a boat. He's the unhealthy spill that dropped from a squaw lady from Denver who looked Chinese enough to make his father hard one time. That's all we all are. One time, right? Hell, if my daddy had sneezed in the wrong direction, I wouldn't be here. If your daddy had coughed at the wrong time, you'd be a girl, right? Same thing for your mama, only I think her daddy was aiming, of course, not for a girl, because they stay Chinese, but in the general direction of China, in a Chinese bed, you know?"

Uncle Lincoln poked a greasy finger at the photograph. "You see these guys? How can you tell anymore?"

He tipped the teapot lid for more hot water.

"Your aunties, they all hate me because I wouldn't keep them. Your grandpa and I talked. One for your daddy, one for me. Your ma, Daisy, she wanted me. But she was American. Me, too, of course. But she died."

At Ming Garden, around the table nearest the kitchen, we eat and drink and repeat the lies that console us in the waning years, the drift of our lives.

"The one thing your aunties knew how to do was to lift their dresses. I had all of them first to make sure they knew how to do it. It was my duty. I was like a father to them. Just like the whores. The whores call out that daddy has just been visiting. You know that. International settlement and all that. The Barbary Coast. Well, I sniffed them all up and I knew how to and they all wanted more, like let's get married, apply for welfare, you can work for my daddy. Like shit. Be daddy's servant and protect his sons until they're grown enough to inherit all the money? Son-in-law means pussy-whipped." Uncle coughs. "Uncle was a mean guy, but he told the truth."

The table is wreathed in cigarette smoke drifting over the carnage that was lunch.

"Anyway, everybody knows. All the men with daughters in America were church people, Catholic holy soldiers to protect them from me. They protect them by washing them in holy water. Not me. I piss on them, splash my yellow water all over them, makes them Chinese that way."

Peter's old enough to laugh when Uncle's drunk. Of course, he always had Wick to explain everything. Wick's antiquarian ways, his fascination with our Chinaman past. We were the most important people in Mary's life, the men of her family, but for no other reason than she willed it so.

More tea.

"I had them all at one time or another, every chance when they came to visit, bring you kids to the country for the summer time. You remember that one?"

I have his attention now. "Who was that one? The one who took care of me?"

"Daisy. She was always so beautiful. Something about her made me like her best. Maybe because she liked me best. Real short, kind of fat, but looked me straight in the eye, and I knew. She'd sit on my lap, under the trees. She would not let go until it was all finished. Hell," he begins coughing and spits wetly into a napkin, "I liked all your mamas. Tell your daddies, ah?"

Lunch over. "Rub a little sesame oil on it, garlic, a little parsley, soy, you can eat anything." He pauses, rubs a thumb over the face of Number One in the photograph. "Ten Indians, ah? But two, the first one and the last guy, they were Chinese." But Lincoln would often confuse the father he imagined for himself and the father he wanted to be.

In another story, Uncle Lincoln said that he was born in America. In Lovelock, Nevada.

"My father, he was Chin Lew Leong or Liu Lien or they called him

"Lo Chin" or Charlie, right? And he was from Bok Tsek, Toisan. And my mother was a woman named Yee Ah Yuk, of Denver, Colorado. Surprised? She was half Chinese and half Indian, a Ute *gen*. Her father had a laundry."

It is his memory of his father that becomes my memory of my father. He remembers living in Virginia City. He was young. He stayed week-days in town, slept at a soda fountain on chairs or in the back room near a stove when it was cold. "On school days, I remember falling asleep on two ice cream chairs, wire-backed stools, staring up at four propeller fans on the ceiling. But on Friday afternoon after school, I was supposed to leave town and head for home up Six-Mile Canyon. I remember I was always scared that I wouldn't make it home before dark. I used to run the last half mile or so, wouldn't stop, and when I saw the lights in the window, I would slow down, so I could walk in. And I remember my ma, she'd be ironing, using a very big iron and a big bowl of water she'd sprinkle on the shirts. The scorched shirt laundry smell means home to me. That uncle and the Indian woman, they had a boarding house."

Peter could repeat the same story word for word as if it were the truth of us.

Lincoln said, "They made me stay in Virginia City because I was always making a mess in the laundry. I remember drawing pictures with the ink and brush over the calligraphy that kept the laundry's records. I could understand their *sze yup* even though I could barely speak it then. I heard them argue in *sze yup*. Something about how my father bought tennis shoes that were too big and Ma stuffed newspaper to make them fit, but I never grew into them. First long pants, first leather shoes I remember in the fourth grade. Maybe I was ten."

It's time to cut my losses and move on. Alone, clapping dust from the cuff end of my cuffless denims, I step off into an interior of my own making, protected, insulated by a deep silence. Ghosts hardly ever talk; almost a first rule. And I remind myself that "one" in Chinese numerology is "corpse," not "god."

"So what did you want to know? Ask me anything. My bah was a real tough guy. I remember he and my ma sometimes voted. So he had citizenship, right? So that was the truth. Or at least they let him vote. Maybe

47

he was lying. Everybody knew who he was, that he was my father, that much I remember. Then they sent me away from that place. He went to jail; Ma died. And they told me to go to San Francisco with *ah bak,* then to Honolulu, then to Hong Kong, then back. I knew then that was the best way to live. Be free, open to opportunities, never look back. Memories drag you down. That's what I keep in mind, always. Not the people, not even my ma and bah. I mean, what were they? Nothing, real nothings.

"When I was a kid, I was just what they were. People knew me because they knew them. Bad reputation, living on the edge of town, washing clothes, smoking opium, gambling all the time. And she was a prostitute. So I had nothing important to remember except to try and forget everything that I came from. Your Auntie likes to say forgive and remember. I say forget it and you have nothing to forgive. They couldn't be anything else. They only had poor times, bad for Chinese people, bad for everybody in a country of orphans. Nobody stayed that had a home to go to. Even me, running down the road, chased by nightfall, welcomed by the aroma of toasted starch, medicinal herbs stinking in a glass pot, pine pitch, and creosote. I worried that I would be alone with them. I worried if they had company and if they were all drinking and smoking when they came for a bath or a haircut.

"When they came for haircuts, Ma cutting hair for company would be reminded to cut my hair too. She didn't need a bowl to make a pattern. She combed the water from the big bowl on the ironing table into my hair, making it hang flat. The front and back she cut straight across like a curtain. She sheared the sides as short as her thick iron scissors could manage, and I would cover my ears so she wouldn't cut them. Then she would start with the rest of them. Pa would laugh and make jokes, pour drinks, while Ma hacked away, sweeping hair off the side porch, shaking the flannel sheet she used to cover our clothes. Then she shaved the back of their necks with a straight razor and rubbed bay rum into their freshly shaved skin, and called for the next in line. I'd stand by when they opened their coin purses.

"'Gimme a nickel,' I would beg. *Ng ga chin.* I could say that in Chinese, in English, in Spanish. Most times, it was a Lincoln, you know. A penny. Two bits for a shave, a haircut, and a Lincoln for the kid. I guess I would be called Buffalo if I ever got more. If they gave me more than that, I would have to call them Uncle.

"One old guy I remember gave me a silver dollar. He was a butcher. He brought meat, chickens usually, but sometimes a part of a hog. I watched him make headcheese and sausage and he sang me a song I memorized: *Mares eat oats/ And does eat oats/ And little lambs eat ivy/ A kid'll eat ivy too/ Wouldn't you?*"

His squavering voice was so sweet to me in that offal stink of memory.

"One day I went to the back to the cold-storage box where he hung the meat. There was a barrel of white stuff I thought was ice cream, and I asked if I could have some. He gave me a bowl and a big wooden spoon and told me I could have as much as I wanted. I filled the bowl with as much as I could, then took it behind the store to eat so he wouldn't see how much I'd taken. Turned out it was cottage cheese. That was the first time I'd ever eaten that stuff. One bite and I just dumped it on the ground. Dogs liked it. I never did. He taught me to thumb my nose and hum 'Sweet Leilani.'"

Lincoln coughs deep in his chest. "It was a mean place, but I made my way."

Over a bad connection from Honolulu, I hear the same raspy sound as Peter jokes, "I remember him doing that, like a human kazoo."

Maybe I could raise the dead humming "Little Egypt." Lincoln loved best the songs his ears reinvented: . . . *ghost writers in the sky. . .* for the man who wrote letters for the dead.

I look down at Lincoln's corpse, anticipating a macabre movement, a twitching, a raised eyebrow, a smile that lets a silver coin slip from his painted lips. Revulsion in the form of heartburn, the uneasy breakfast of green bananas, soy milk, and rice gruel, the rising bile makes me shiver with dread. The stilled form preserves the appearance of intended movement, as if the world has stopped for a single instant while we convene to relive all that remained to be said.

First long pants, first leather shoes, the first taste of cottage cheese, the smell of burning starch, medicinal herbs, I heard him say. Or he never said it. He never spoke of himself, ever.

"There was always jobs being a short-order cook for Chinese businesses in the sticks. In fact, that's how I slipped under the Social Security Act. No pension, you know. But then I found a job paying benefits with a summer resort at Lake Tahoe, cooking for the crew. I cooked breakfast, lunch, dinner; lived in a one-room studio, an old motel the company kept to house the Chinese workers. I cooked the best, had the best ingredients, the restaurant's cold box was opened to me. Boy, everybody ate well. Pay was minimum, but housing and food were good. And it only took me two seasons to qualify for Social Security benefits, so it was worth it. Lucky, right?"

Auntie Mary remembers sending me to him with Chinese ingredients from the herb shops as an excuse for my visit. And it was there that he told me or at least made me understand in words we could not share, words that required Wick's translation. He told me that he was in all likelihood not my father, though in matters of that sort, no one could be absolutely sure. He taught me how to view paternity in his world, the way he had been taught by the man who had claimed him. But I understood that for him being a father wasn't a matter of the heart, but of loyalties, of oaths sworn and broken, of experiences that had taught him to be responsible to himself alone since in this mean country he had very little opportunity to care for more than himself. He might say, because he liked to brag, that he could never remember the number of opportunities he'd had to father children. He liked life to hold little surprises that could be wrapped and delivered whole and eaten on special occasions. So a kid here or there who presented himself might very well be a part of him. In America he left bastards all over the place. His own uncle had railed against this habit of dispossession but practiced it himself in a community of orphans and half-breeds, Chinamen too poor, too sick, too old to go home, like Indians who had no home left to them. In my imaginings, he hectored me like a teacher. But in truth, he kept silent, waiting for Wick or Peter to translate, or until no one was left to listen.

He had advice, however: achievement. Imitate those who are successful; eschew the lame and the halt. Look for balance. Eat liver to test balances. If you only eat gruel, you remain gruel. You must always test and challenge your appetites to achieve balance. Equanimity disguises the tension between opposites. The more radical the zig or zag, the broader the path of compromise and balance one can achieve. It's obvious. Holding very still is stupid. It's like sitting on a nail, on a pin; you are eventually impaled.

Uncle Lincoln's uncle was not a stupid man; neither was Lincoln. "Why return to China?" the exiled generations would argue. "America is the great Asiatic power China must confront. Fewer people to feed, a capitalist class who will risk themselves in great adventures, and McKinley, the great seer who built a winding path to China, from Hawaii to Manila, and floated the grand American fleet in the Pacific. Do you know this? Do you read? Better McKinley than the Japanese puppet emperor of China. Or do you think you're going home? Dumb shit."

Of course, I knew nothing of all that. I didn't know the questions to ask.

"Ask me anything you want, anything you want to know. I will tell you. Even things you really don't want to know I will tell you." Maybe he never really said that.

"Daisy didn't die in the desert."

"My mother?"

"Yeah. That was your real mother."

"And she didn't die?"

"Of course she died. Everybody dies."

"But not in Barstow?"

"Naah. Near Reno."

"And Auntie Mary?"

"Just an arrangement between her daddy and me. I thought he tricked me because she was so crazy when she was young, but Chinese people, you know, they trick everybody."

The Truckee River runs through the heart of downtown Reno. On any given day, the park the city built to contain the river is filled with the newly wedded and the freshly divorced. They eye one another and take each other's measure by the company they keep. Here in the shadow of the casinos, the sanctity of nonsectarianism in the psalms to matrimony and life are sacred. And while I have never heard of a funeral in a casino chapel, I know that if Lincoln had had his way, this is where he would have liked to be buried, in the company of blue-collar cowboys, casino dealers, the two waitresses smoking in the park, one black, one white. Here are Filipinos on holiday, warily eyeing the Chinese from the casino kitchens. We find ourselves among them, sharing the path and benches that line the concrete banks that funnel the river past our all-American parade of the dispossessed idling in the park at dawn.

Here, our ancestors straddle a concrete balustrade, warming themselves in the morning sunlight. I spy them as they spied on all of us, storytellers reciting Comstock tales for this good-natured, egalitarian march of matrimony and divorce. I hear their conversations in passing, ribald stories of the bedroom, lucky coins for the casinos, the thirty-nine-cent midnight breakfast. Their anecdotes float past quickly and are submerged in the sound of the river. We all pretend not to hear, but we snatch every single word, every inflection, every breath.

So early one morning Winnie and I found ourselves in a wedding chapel in Reno, where no one would find us except the ghost of Lincoln's uncle. Winnie was about to become my first wife; she would later be my uncle's last. I see the ghost of Uncle's uncle standing on a pedestrian bridge straddling the Truckee River. A busker sings folksongs for coins, a storyteller, a letter writer, a gambler, a thief, a dead demon, wandering far away from his homeland. *My country, 'tis of thee / Ching Chong Chinaman / Sittin' on a Fence / This land is your land / This land is my land.*

When we sang songs in the schoolyard, the lyrics changed. *My mother lies over the ocean / My father lies over the sea / My daddy lies over my mommy / and that's how they got little me.*

Even that, the act of conception, these imaginary confessions like acts of contrition, I'm not so sure I want to know.

Lincoln was a lucky man. Lincoln was lucky to have a dog, his own room in a trailer, a truck, a gun and a place where he could shoot it whenever he wanted, friends who thought he was the boss and who liked him a lot, able to cook everything for himself so he could eat anything he wanted to, whenever he wanted to. In a boy's universe, there's nothing better. He washed or didn't, left the radio on all day and all night, his TV lighting the dark corner next to his bed.

Auntie pours spring water into a portable butane-fired cooking pot in the center of a small dining table laid with wire handbaskets, small plates of thinly sliced meats, the flesh of beef, pork, and chicken, peeled prawns spiraling their tail fans, ringlets of squid, tofu cubed or in strips, and the fish paste I've brought scooped in a celadon bowl in the shape of a carp with its own silver hook. The hook is a small touch to capture the accumulation of pudding that sticks to any heated surface. She's heaped cabbage, watercress, cilantro, sticks of green onion, garlic tops, and two bundles of cellophane noodles in front of her table setting to order the development of the dish—tonight, a soup. The condiments of hot oil, mustard, sesame oil, soy, and bean sauces—yellow, brown, and red—sweet hoisin, mild curry, and a fermented shrimp paste that Lung Gung enjoys, remain capped but available in their own tray at the end of the table, an empty setting in front of the enormous bay window that captures the darkening eastern hills across the water illumined now by the lights of the Bay Bridge. Their sweet aromas blossom like yeast in the rise of steam.

I'm pouring one of Peter's suggestions, an Australian white, when Auntie appears with a ramekin of the water snails she's stir-fried with salt and garlic. "I didn't make rice. I didn't think we'd need it. There's just the two of us." She defies all convention. A meal without rice: the phrase resonates in my memory, some ancient stricture cursing privation that recalls crows winging across a shattered field of broken dikes, stagnant pools, broken stones, and a door hanging by a single hinge to a half wall. Is there a guardian against famine to whom such an appeal is addressed? Have I skipped lightly over the graves of all my dead aunties who turn suddenly, a light temblor under my feet? I feel safe in Auntie's hands.

She turns the fire up and piles a load of watercress, cabbage, onion, and a few peeled garlic cloves into the pot.

"Wine?"

"Just a little, please. I'll lose track of what's in here." She stokes the steaming kettle with her chopsticks, folding the recalcitrant cabbage as it softens, splitting each garlic clove as it softens.

I eye the resolving stock and admit, "I pour a can of chicken broth."

"Yes, sometimes I do that." She studies the chard, then peels a long fiber from an older stalk. "When I want to make chicken soup and I don't have a chicken. This one, I want the vegetables to make the stock. It's very quick, and that way, you can taste everything separately. I don't want to make a stew. Drink some more wine. Eat your *tin law*. They look good. This should be ready to cook in a minute."

I choose a toothpick from its caddy and pick a snail free. It looks all the world like a shriveled homunculus, an evolutionary fetus for which

I feel kinship, each morsel some sacramental host, exquisitely oiled, succulent. "They're perfect, Auntie." Prizing the tender knots from their uniform coils, I imagine that each little twist suggests a different agony, imparting subtle differences in taste and texture. Auntie catches me stacking their little sarcophagi in a pyramid on my plate. She watches as I fill her glass.

Lately, I am as forgetful as she, starting a task and forgetting to end. There are the ragged edges of Peter's sojourn in Europe. Wick has disappeared again. There are discount fares, one-way tours to Machu Picchu. In the office, we've dubbed tours I've mangled "the shining path."

"Men are little boys when they eat with their fingers." She heaps a handbasket of squid and prawn into the stock. "You and Peter have Lincoln's eating habits. I loved the way you boys would vacuum the meat from the poached fish. Everything goes, even the shine on the bones."

When Peter was a little boy, he loved to suck the lips, sharing the eyeballs with Lincoln. "What do fish see, I wonder." Lincoln is on her mind. She adds a touch of rank lemongrass to mellow the sweet garden aromas becoming the field and beyond, the encroaching jungle.

"I love that acrid stink, the lemongrass," she says. "It makes the marriage, doesn't it? We never used it before, when Lincoln cooked."

"Vietnamese. New immigrants."

"It should be fresh, of course. But the arrangement is important, to please the eye, not just your nose and tummy. What does Peter say all the time? It's always a contradiction, a paradox. It's all so many leaves and grass, and a little meat." She extends her grip on her chopsticks to keep her fingers from the hot steam.

What are we talking about, Auntie? Food? Marriage? Romance?

"That's when a man is cooking, always a new romance. Women have to cook every day. They like experienced lovers. Used lovers? Abused lovers?" She laughs, her smile flashing across me, hot steam from the boiling pot. She nods, a half bow to the assembled ingredients. "Now you're making me forget. The prawns are ready in an instant. Don't let them drown or they overcook."

She's set an uncracked egg in each of our rice bowls and now raps hers sharply against the porcelain edge, filling her bowl with raw egg, then whipping it with her chopsticks. She pours a little chili oil, a little soy into the mixture. "You know I like mine spicy."

I follow suit, then net a prawn which I bathe in the cool, raw egg I've mixed with ginger strips, soy, and sesame oil. "Wick says eating is a religious experience that marries the sacred and the profane, like church."

"Please, no Candlewick talk right now. He's left the city. *Kai dai yeh* doesn't know how to eat anymore." She retrieves a stick of scallion from the roiling broth and cooling it first in egg, snaps it between her teeth. "Very good." She lowers the flame. "Everything's going to cook too fast. Beef? Chicken?"

I never mean to mention Wick. But he is everywhere and absent at the same time. I wonder how the two of them managed for so many years.

"Amen." I feed the body, I am the body, I consume myself. Where should I start, what shall I do with my clothes, my toes, my woes?

And so the pacing of the meal. Thin shreds of beef bleed for an instant, then, cauterized by the broth, are quickly eaten. Chicken breast settles to the bottom to swim with lost prawns, slices of mushroom, and pillows of tofu. The pork sugars the broth, its trim of fat melding the flavors together. Fish paste, white fish whipped with egg white to form a glutinous pudding, cooks into irregular balls the texture of cheese, so mild they absorb all the flavors of the stock, billows of tender succulence rising to the surface as the paste congeals. Auntie adds strips of semidried abalone and fresh watercress to freshen the stock, and another round of cooking and eating begins.

During our meal together, she confides, "We're worried about Ah Lung Gung. He's not well, Christopher. He even admits it to me, that he's feeling weaker. He said he misses the dry heat in the desert where he used to have a restaurant."

"I remember a take-out joint in a trailer."

"He likes to exaggerate. Really, he hated it every second. But it kept him alone and safe. Free from temptation. He's a very good man, you know." She carries her bowl down the table to sit closer to me. "When he was young, he took care of you and Peter."

"And Daisy?"

"They all helped each other. They were very brave. And Wick helped too."

I make rude noises sucking the juice from a snail shell. "There were lots of Daisies?"

Auntie smiles indulgently. "He held the lamp outside the door while they slept."

If there never had been a Lincoln or a Candlewick, if it were always a mild summer evening, Auntie and I might camp outside on the balcony. How mild an imitation of the windswept desert plains of North China, no horses raising dusty clouds, no dogs howling beyond the concrete terrace. She would light charcoal in a brazier in the fireplace, then load the hot coals into a Mongolian cooker, a smokestack with a metal ring around its middle, resembling a chimney rising from a moat. The meats would be laid on the side of the rounded hot flue where they would grill and drip their juice into the surrounding catch-basin filled with stock and vegetables. But more often than not, the oil and smoke from the grilled meats overpower the stock. Only the root vegetables deserve a bite or two. Tonight, with only the two of us grazing across the vast bounty of the marketplace, carefully sifting each ingredient and snatching it from the pot before its essence is transmuted, allowing only those components that mellow the brewing to remain, we arrive at the final detail.

"I told Winnie to stay with Lincoln now. He's sick. He needs someone to take care of him."

"Why does she have to live with Lincoln?"

"Because Lincoln asked her." Auntie reaches out, brushing my cheek with fingers. "Don't be so mad at him all the time. You and Peter are always angry with him. He's old now. You don't need to fight anymore. And it's best for Winnie. She needs to stay here."

"What about me? What will people think?"

"We thought we could adopt her, but the law says she has to be married. Christopher, you don't have to stay in the same place all the time. Do what you want now. Live with Melba, that's what you want. We have a house you can live in across the Bridge, big yard for a garden. Melba can grow her tomatoes. She won't refuse."

"I can't speak for her. She hasn't really made up her mind yet. Whether she wants to be with me."

"I know some of the reasons." Auntie looks straight at me, smiling. "You know I like her. We talk together.

"I have a proposition for you. We have this big house in Santa Lucca, a big piece of property. We have people working there, Wick and I. There is also Peter's friend, Twig. When he first came to America, he was part of the Huynh family Uncle helped to immigrate from the camp in Hong Kong. Wick has them working on the properties we have there. There's even a small house nearby for you." She turns the flame up for the final time and heaps the brittle nest of bean threads into the pot. "We have all these investments in Santa Lucca. But we have no one to watch over the family business things."

"Why doesn't Uncle ask Peter?"

"He's not asking you." She takes my hand in hers. "I am."

And Wick. Was it Wick after all?

After resigning from the Haven, Wick had begun sponsoring small groups of Yuon he helped move from their entry point in Atlanta to the public housing tracts of Oakland. Wick had organized them into their own labor exchange. They were a desperate but disciplined group of men, women, and children who had organized themselves into a family grouping in the Shekou refugee camp in Hong Kong to facilitate their escape, taking advantage of the INS preferences for families. Mary and Lincoln financed their several enterprises, a silent partner to these cousins who saw business opportunities everywhere, from scrap paper to the verdant untrimmed suburban landscapes. They commuted from the East Bay by bus at first, and then the flatbed transporting the women and kids suddenly began appearing on the narrow hillside road in the wooded suburban canyon community, then converted stake trucks hauling great weights of cardboard and newspaper, plastics, and new pickup trucks filled with garden and construction equipment as their enterprises prospered.

The brittle wire bundle of cellophane noodles Auntie drops into the broth collapses instantly as the tendrils touch the boiling stock, then sink to the bottom from their own rehydrated weight. In their soft tangle, the detritus of this rich stock has been netted.

"There is no one to watch the children. It draws the neighbor's attention when they run around in the streets. And Wick wouldn't be appropriate."

"I don't know. I have to talk it over with Melba."

"Well, now. This is what Melba and I have already discussed."

"What did she say? She hasn't mentioned any of this to me. It may be something she wants to keep between you and her. Or she would have said something to me."

"Well, she hasn't given her answer yet. She's probably waiting to speak with you."

She retrieves our bowls of egg sauces, whipping them together with her chopticks as she pours them into the broth. My tongue is numb with chili sauce and hot onion.

Auntie ladles the hot stock into my bowl, poaching the egg's emulsion into soft strings of a colloid that traps the essence of all that has bathed at the bottom of my rice bowl. We sip wine. I capture soft shapes of egg and draw up the net of noodles with its collection lying at the bottom of the pot. The dish is complete. The soup is done.

3

A mordant Toisan couplet describes the road home as a dusty track with deep furrows dug by the weight of the sojourner's luggage, followed closely by the sandal prints of thieves. I am seen to encourage such misbehavior in my hapless pursuit of family, ignoring every obstacle Uncle Lincoln or Aunt Mary might have invented, Wick's unholy crucifixions, and Peter, ten steps ahead. Searching for relief, I am bound to follow that same dusty path I imagine all my familiars have taken before me, leashed to a grotesque, multi-limbed chimera bearing more than a faint family resemblance, bound for home.

I was eighteen, and, save for the summer or two I had spent with Uncle in his trailer in the desert, I'd always had a room of my own from which I was always imagining escape. Now I had the choice of living in Peter and Wick's empty flat or staying with Auntie. There was, God forbid, always a bed with one of Auntie Mary's brothers, and their endless relief whenever they saw me in the neighborhood in the company of girls they recognized as classmates forever, from public kindergarten through high school. In groups, we appeared normal, destined to mingle, to produce the next generation. In fact, the thought of romance among us was mutually repellant, suggesting a kind of social avoidance anthropologists of the day suggested arose naturally from the enforced intimacy racial segregation brews from childhood memories, the aromas, visual and auditory cues, of incest. This phenomena was felt especially strongly in me, at least. It would have been like dating a sister. But in all other respects, I appeared utterly normal, save for the odd collection of aloha shirts among the broadcloth button-downs, khaki chinos, penny loafers in black and oxblood, and the variety of pornography at the bottom of Peter's closet. I'd even been seen by a family spy climbing out of a taxi in downtown Reno. It was assumed I had been visiting the bordellos pitching camp down County Road 49. Those floodlit aluminum house trailers clustered in an enclosure, even fenced by armed electrical wire, must have recalled my early years with Uncle in his aluminum caravan.

The circumstances of my sexual development were the uncles' greatest concern because tales of Wick's early indiscretions had begun appearing in print. The victims had been ten or eleven years old. They were at least beginning to get it right. Wick didn't bugger babies. And Peter had reached the age of consent.

When I finished high school, I was assimilated into the final wave of nondescripts that institutions of higher learning would absorb before their decades-long collapse as the Vietnam War ended and the state withdrew its tax support of public education entirely. Peter's success—thus local notoriety—as the gay host of *WokTalk* isolated me further. It was assumed that I spent my free time flying back and forth to the Islands when I wasn't working at the travel agency. I wore flowered shirts and cultivated a tan. I incorporated a few pidgin phrases Peter repeated, but remained isolated and alone at school because it was generally acknowledged that I was the brother of the queer who lived with the child molester.

After stumbling through two years at City College, I transferred to Berkeley as Peter nostalgically advised from his exile in paradise. Of course, the campus was in chaos: the Vietnam War hung like toilet paper twisted in the knobby branches of the plane trees that line the campus. The teaching faculty was grateful for the few of us attending class, and it was a simple matter to slip through unremarked since so many of them had lost faith in the relevance of their own educations. Besides, I had a business to run.

Then, to confuse the matter (as Peter later liked to joke), I married our "mother"—rather, our "father's" wife to be. But, luckily, we are orphans. I did elope with Winnie on a whim right after I graduated from the university. But the truth is I married her to complete what I imagined was the next step in my life, to invent or reinvent myself. Lincoln didn't care. Peter never listened. Mary would grant me allowances all my life, of course. Only Wick might have understood.

Winnie and I met as I was trying to complete a graduation requirement, "Physics for the Elementary Mind," its only requirement, attendance. The teaching assistant took the roll at each meeting before televising the lecture. We were seven hundred plus students in assigned alphabetical seating. Three unexcused absences meant repeating the semester, general malaise, earthquakes, and the turmoil of the student demonstrations and rioting not withstanding. Winnie and I sat way in the back as the teaching assistant read off six Wongs in a row, all strangers, the FOBs and the ABCs assiduously ignoring one another. As soon as roll was taken, Winnie did her accounting sets and I read *Playboy*.

First impressions have always been my strong suit but I usually ignore them. I took Winnie for one of those older immigrant grad students from just another Chinese diaspora, from Malaysia, Singapore, Hong Kong, or Taiwan, a tigress hunting for a green card. Who else would wear makeup and perfume to school? She met my nods with the traditional contempt the authentic save for their ethnic doppelgängers, double nothings, neither one nor the other. She disguised her quick appraisal as the roll swept by, raising a tissue she kept woven through her fingers to cover a smile. She was, however, attractive to me, in the way that an older woman is, her stippled eyebrows, her aromas, even her condescension. I would not have to explain myself, and I could always offer up my helpless dilemmas, my hapless naïveté that Chinatown girls my own age found typical and profoundly unattractive. I find solidity, studied patience, and the confidence of experience very appealing. I always have. And makeup, the flat matte of a uniform complexion artfully painted with lip gloss, mascara, cheek blush, even the aromas these oils and unguents exude made Winnie's anonymity, her nearness in the dark of the upper balcony, even more intriguing. During the interminable roll call I would watch her little rearrangement of books, her arm on the armrest, the flash of pale flesh between her fingers, the crease where her forearm joined the elbow. I began inventing stories to explain her presence, a fantasy employing details gleaned from Peter's gay lexicon.

Just after April midterms there came a lull on campus, a strange quiet. The sirens, the helicopters, the chanting demonstrations suddenly ceased. With spring break in the offing and the promise of relief from the relentless clouds of tear gas wafting from the eucalyptus groves, a stinging aroma I associate with the campus in that time of turmoil and unrest, Winnie and I started seeing each other. We'd waded through the debris of paper and twisted sandwich boards up the stairs of Wheeler Auditorium for a mid-term. The hall was half empty. She finished her bluebook with time to spare and was reading my exam out of the corner of her eye. She kicked me, shook her head, and we quietly exchanged pens and papers. She finished my test, and I took her to coffee afterwards.

"What did you think I am?"

"You're someone I'd like to be."

"A girl?" She teased. She was always prescient.

"I think you're someone with a sense of adventure. You're from China, you speak languages, you're independent."

I'd never had the experience of an attractive Chinese woman who wasn't family flirting. And neither had I ever met an older woman who would lie to me. We exchanged a few pleasantries, but she cut through my adolescent chat with a scalpel's edge, spreading her life before me in pages sliced and fanned, cold cuts, hors d'oeuvres. She told me her father controlled a share of the export market in tapioca and cautioned me that she had several brothers in school in Europe, Japan, and the States establishing pied-à-terre in case the currency market wobbled, the native nationalists got restless, or a boy got fresh. She was destined to return home after graduation to care for her grandparents and was promised to some son of a family friend in banking. Those were all lies, but appropriate lies for a new acquaintance. Or so she thought. Winnie's never mentioned it, but my youth, my innocence must have been attractive in and of itself, allowing her a certain release. I was younger than springtime and gullible. As we became more familiar, we invented lies together.

"Do you ever get homesick?"

"You're a romantic person, Chris. It's not hard to wave good-bye to a stinky duck pond."

She was the mistress of a drug warlord, his hostess in America, kept for the entertainment of nefarious associates. I would be her American fling, that headlong flight into oblivion, strangers in the night, tourists. I saw her face superimposed on Miss February.

"A village in Toishan? Rice fields washed by a summer monsoon, moon gates?"

"I mean China, ducks and pigs. You've never been."

I'd never been anywhere, other than the gambler's special to Vegas, to Reno. When I was forced to fly to Hawaii, Peter and his friends kept me on a velvet tether, airsick, drowning in orchid perfume I thought they flaunted, not realizing it was simply in the air. As a homophobic adolescent, I tried to shrink, become invisible in their public company. I avoided them entirely when they visited the city. But I had absorbed something else from Peter, whatever lay beneath his hauteur and bravado, a fatalism, a resignation that some might find darkly attractive in someone as young as I—or simply hapless and naive.

"Your brother is on television and your auntie has property, a travel business for you to run. So you refuse to travel, and you pay rent in Berkeley. You never want what your family wants. The older you are, the more what they want is not important." She tried to imagine what that might be like. "I'm like that," she lied.

"I have a very odd family." I didn't know how to explain the whys of my family. "I know I'm being cared for, but I need to do something on my own, have a reason for it, something they can approve or disapprove of before I've even done it."

We talked, she counseled. "Why not? You can't die of disapproval." Fortunately, Winnie has always been a quick study. Unfortunately, she was caught in the heat of my moment, or so I liked to imagine.

The first time we met, I saw a Chinese girl, someone who looked like me, who looked like all of the sisters of all the friends I ever had. I'd never had an inkling that there might be more than what I could see of myself in them. But Winnie really was a Chinese girl, not like me at all. When we first slept together, that first time in a residence hall during a warm afternoon when her roommates were out shopping or playing volleyball in the court below the window, we knew nothing about each other, and I knew nothing about what she wanted from me, save perhaps the moment, to finally complete what began as a light touch, a tentative lock on her wrists, a kiss, the back of my hand brushing a breast through her cotton T-shirt. (Winnie doesn't have breasts in the American sense of the word, knockers, bodacious chachas. I don't think tits are encouraged traditionally.) Foreplay consisted of pushing the right buttons. Later, much later, I would never be angry, never humiliated by her affairs, all those meetings with old friends of her "brothers" that were revealed as we grew closer. Auntie was right to keep her. Winnie outlined all my inhibitions, all my limitations. Auntie understood that Winnie would make a far better mother for me than a wife.

On the other hand, I still firmly believe the very fact of our marriage struck something deep inside her. When we were together, she couldn't work, her own ambitions disappeared for a while, a dentist detected her first cavity. For the first time in her life she developed a serious opinion about the division between the People's Republic and Taiwan, prompting a sharp long-distance exchange with old friends that precipitated a deeper social isolation. Her telephone stopped ringing.

I was responsible for her irrational behavior, her uncharacteristic malaise. I was younger than she, at least ten years, as best I can now estimate. When I met her, unmarried at twenty-eight—or was she thirty?—away from home for nearly three uninterrupted years, she still wore red hair ribbons and lived out of her luggage, trying to coordinate her business suits and sweatshirts to match the casual attire of the native student. She lived as if she hadn't been in the country long enough for any of her clothes to be worn down or frayed. With everything perfectly matching, perfectly arbitrary, she was dressed for work or the beach, or perhaps a long walk in the park, but nothing in between. She would sit in class wearing a black sheath dress with earrings, makeup, a jade bracelet, and a gold chain. The morning after our first night together, she changed into my wardrobe: oxford-cloth shirts with torn cuffs, faded turtlenecks she found at the bottom of my closet, Levis rolled up to her knees, my torn sneakers.

One evening during spring break, we shared a bowl of noodles in Chinatown. Then, as we walked by the travel office, we saw the Gray Line bus to Reno parked at the door. I grabbed Winnie's hand and dragged her aboard. We spent the night in a motel room in Reno, surrounded by strangers, sex in exile. We married just as dawn lit the glass of the twenty-four hour wedding chapel and were in time for the gambler's special breakfast, ninety-nine cents. We thought it was very romantic.

But there I was. What do you do when you graduate from the university with a lifetime's experience as kitchen help, poorly read student, and travel agent who's never traveled? I was looking forward to becoming a nothing in the family's eyes, the unacknowledged son of an anonymous mother. I might have looked forward to the freedom of being nothing, but at the last possible hour, when there were no convenient institutions to send me to, there she was. And there I was, some might whisper, a green card, or a green hat, some would later giggle, a cuckold, a convenient immigration opportunity.

I never thought twice about our marriage. What else did I have in mind? The lease on my student apartment in Berkeley was up. I didn't want to move in with Auntie Mary go or back to Chinatown. Instead, Winnie and I moved into a one-bedroom condominium in Crown Village south of the city, one of several Auntie had bought for visitors from abroad. We were ten minutes from SFO, so convenient for friends and family. And not much later I would be providing shuttle service to the rest of the North American continent as part of the travel business.

Crown Village had its own recreation facilities—gym, swimming pool, and sauna—and a two-level underground garage with an elevator to protect us, mornings and evenings, from the jet streams of icy wind-driven fog that spill over the Pacifica ridge. The plastic pennants that flew from the fences surrounding the two tennis courts overlooking the freeway suggested a yacht club on the Bay. At dawn and at dusk they flew east, then west, caught in the ebb and flow of wind and fog. The apartment was completely furnished with Danish-modern modulars that Winnie had bought at a discount from the management. The kitchen was all electric, although very small, which suited Winnie because she never cooked. She didn't have to. We were a freeway stop in either direction from the international fast-food emporia embedded in the vast shopping malls that separate Chinatown from Hong Kong. The location, the food courts, suited us, the all-you-can-eats where we could indulge her taste for pizza, ribs, fried rice, and lumpia, an ocean of fruit-flavored juices and colas in refillable plastic containers with swizzle straws tipped with cartoon figures she recognized from the television cable systems she had watched from everywhere she had ever lived—the Pacific Rim, one electronic universe.

That first week, she had to fly to Hong Kong to consult with her family, or so she said. There remained the fiction that it would be Winnie who would save the family, another Madame Golden Flower sacrificing herself to an alien for the good of China, for the good of her family. And I looked Chinese enough to pass muster for the ancestors, who, practically speaking, had been dead, deaf, and blind for centuries.

Because I hated to fly, she took my picture along as evidence and proxy. There was a banquet with her friends in Hong Kong in an album of photographs, a bright red tome bound in gold she clutched to her chest all the way back to San Francisco. And, of course, money to invest, which was entrusted to Mary. A marriage broker engaged at the eleventh hour assured her convenient older brother that both Mary and Lincoln suitably represented filial older relatives who looked after the interests of their nephew. More important, there were assets, formal and informal, attached to Mary's name. The fact that we were already married was ignored. The absence of her parents was excused.

At home, I even found approval, acceptance after the fact. At least I was some good for someone was the consensus. Auntie Mary said, "It's not a marriage of convenience. She's not pregnant. This is a convenient marriage. It's good for everybody, ah?"

Of course, we weren't able to earn any kind of real income. In the bad old days, if she had a family, we would have been given a room in the family compound and she could have gone on being her family's youngest daughter. I would have been be the nameless son-in-law, young what's-his-name.

Instead of giving us a honeymoon, Auntie Mary let it be known that I would run the travel office and she would continue my allowance until we found what we wanted to do. We knew only how to go to school, so, our university degrees useless, we quickly reenrolled at City College, where I might learn a skill and Winnie could practice her English. I tried Accounting 101 and, still playing the dutiful bride, Winnie enrolled in a psychology class to gain some understanding of her Chinese American husband, or so Auntie advised. She told Winnie that men like Ah Lung Gung and myself, even Peter, were not like her brothers, her father, or any Chinese men she'd known before. It wasn't bad advice all around, in retrospect.

I don't know what else I expected from the first Chinese woman I ever bedded. In a moment of unrestrained passion I might have found myself looking for some anatomical difference, some angle I could compare to the few girls I'd had before. Sliding between her thighs, I crossed that bridge that ties her navel to her spine; I always found myself on the other side of where I'd been before, but never as often as Winnie enjoyed. I lacked the curiosity and imagination Winnie required. I was a kid. Screwing was an athletic event as far as I was concerned, fifty meters and the shot put. I was energetic but never a real student of anything. Winnie wanted more of me than there was. She thumbed through my entire collection of *Playboy* and *Penthouse* magazines in a week, highlighting the advice columns and asking me for further definitions for words her dictionaries only glossed over with their lists of synonyms. We struggled through an illustrated text of the *Kama Sutra* and spent our first month of marriage with the *Joy of Sex* that Peter had sent us as a wedding gift. But as my interest in the mechanics of sexual expression waned (it happens), hers did not. She surprised me in the bathroom with Miss July early on a Sunday morning, and she immediately incorporated this activity into our lovemaking for the next few nights until I just couldn't perform for her any longer. Somehow the private intimacies I imagined for myself had lost all of their heated immediacies with Winnie looking on. I had reached the end of my rope and she wanted to tie another knot.

It must have been soon afterwards that she seduced an old friend whom she had first passed off as a cousin. I heard them screwing through the paper-thin walls when I came back to the apartment early one afternoon. I didn't know what to do. I stood leaning against the blank stucco, the exterior wall of our bedroom, and listened. Then she let my fantasies unravel. How did all this come to pass, this guilt-drenched ménage we played back and forth, entwined in an affair that would continue even after we'd divorced, even after I married Melba, even after Winnie became my father's wife? Their sweat gleaming, eyes locked, the invisible clenching, betrayed by a sigh, a sound, her eyes closed, head back, snapping from the crack of her hips as her sweet sex opened wide, the tide, her ebb and flow. It was never so sweet.

"Do you always eat toast for breakfast?" Winnie asked me the following morning. She always had *congee,* a loose rice gruel she flavored with hot pickles, brine shrimp, and shreds of dried fish, a taste she acquired one summer at a finishing school in Taipei which provided her with a veneer of the Mandarin dialect and manner, more appealing to American Sinophiles than her Cantonese bluntness.

"Yes, but that's only because I never had someone to cook for me in the morning, sweetheart," I say, helping myself to a heaping bowlful of the warm gruel.

"But do you like *juk* in the morning?" She was dunking yesterday's lunch into her rice porridge, bits of a leftover pepperoni frittata from her doggie bag—which passed for groceries—one of several that filled the tiny refrigerator stacked with two-liter pop bottles from the corner gas station. She had even frozen the leftover macaroni and coleslaw in their paper cups.

"No, frankly, no. I like it in the evenings. But if you want it for breakfast, that's fine."

"I make you toast. I just don't like to eat it, not every morning."

"Babe, that's fine. I can even make my own toast. It's simple. That's why I eat it."

"Yes, I know it's easy." She stopped eating.

"But?"

It was hard for Winnie to confide without a confrontation, very difficult to take anyone into her confidence, especially not a man, never a man who couldn't speak her language, especially not a husband, never a husband. She would have had only her father as a model of a husband. And she would have only heard him tell her what to do at the dinner table, never privy to the conversations adults share when the children are out of the room.

"But nothing." She bit off the syllables and let them digest between us.

"There's something you want to say. Please, I want to hear."

"What do you want me to do?" Her question, the abruptness of it, its clarity, surprised even herself.

"What do you mean?"

"Don't ask me that all the time. What I mean. That is what I mean. What do you want me to do, for you, as your wife? You don't tell me so I don't know. We have to talk. My class, the group discusses this issue every time. You have to say what it is you want from me, so I can do it." She softened her tone slightly. "My friends said it in class. Communication is very important for everybody, and for you in particular." She was stuffing her book bag with taco chips and a cold fishwich.

"I agree, I agree. I want us to communicate. But why me in particular?"

"He says that Chinese Americans like you, the ABC's born here, don't know how to say what they want because they're always waiting to hear what American society wants from them."

"That sounds like an oversimplification," I responded too readily. She was right, of course. "Besides, we're not antagonists. We're married." I still wince when I hear myself say that so clearly. "I don't want to tell you what to do just like I don't want you telling me what to do."

"I don't ever tell you what to do. I help you, but I never tell you what to do." She slammed her teacup on the table, spilling it on the new tablecloth she had bought, complete with napkins, napkin holders, and a plastic cover she used as a mat for the house plants, another bargain, another sale.

"No, no, sweetheart, you misunderstand. I didn't say that. Not at all." I take her in my arms, hold her with sincerity, with as much conviction as I could muster.

"Why do you say it that way then?" She's teary, but her anger stiffens in my embrace.

"I'm sorry, sorry. I didn't mean it at all. Sometimes I say things that sound stupid or wrong to you. I know that." I hear Peter and Wick: no common language, no common speech.

She resists. "Don't you have to go to work?"

"Let's skip today. Let's go for a walk, go shopping." I press her close to me. "Let's make love."

She pushes me away. "No. I don't want that now. I have a headache. Talk first, communication first."

"Of course; I'm sorry." Of course, I'm not. What could we talk about? Shopping? She couldn't cook, so there was no buffer, no easy topic without disclaimers. No common appetites. No shared sensibilities. "Tell me about your class. What does your professor suggest to encourage communication?"

"It's not for me to communicate. It's you."

"Just me?"

"You, just you. I can talk to everybody else."

"Uncle Peter?"

"He's not my uncle. He's your cousin or brother or something, I thought you said."

I'd adopted the title because I'd been taught to introduce everyone who was older as "Uncle." I said it without thinking. I didn't even know what she had in mind at the time. Fictive family titles, the "Uncle" and "Auntie" the young bestow on those who might or might not be relatives, on friends of the family who are not relatives, on strangers whose favor you're asked to curry. The honorific slips through before I hear the patronizing curl that Winnie hears very clearly, that she has learned to detest. When we spoke, when we went shopping, ate, fought, even when we made love, I resorted to the kind of linguistic pablum my family used with me. We have no common tongue.

"Yes, stepbrother Peter. Half brother. Whatever." What did it matter?

"How is he your brother? And why does Mary stay friends with that Wickman? Are they married together? You know what they say? You know that?"

It's a test. It's the final and I've overslept again. "Our mothers were sisters? And you already know about Wick."

"How were they sisters? Peter says he was born in Hong Kong and you were born in some little place here."

"Lompoc." It's a little joke in the family. Everyone likes to say the word because it amuses them to hear it in all the accents the family employs to describe me and my blunted history. But I never lived there. It was Peter from Paradise, and Columbus from Columbia. My mother died before I had a memory of her, and I only had a story for my name.

"You know what people in Chinatown say about you guys?"

"Yes, of course. We're all homosexuals because of Peter."

"Not that part. About your family."

"What? Tell me. I'm all ears."

She looks at me as if I've called her a horrible name, as if I've sworn an ugly oath, spit on her mother. "You think I'm a joke? That what I'm saying is funny? That you can laugh at me?"

"No, no, you didn't understand."

"Everybody knows. I understand and you don't. Everybody knows that Mary and Wickman lived together. And all the stories about him. But they don't know where you fit. Who are you to them? All your ears don't hear anything, don't understand anything. Nothing. You hear me?"

I start to laugh, then hold back. I know how she will take my laughing. "What should I know that I don't? I don't know. What's the question? Who am I? Where did I come from? My father? My mother? I told you, I don't know."

"People say that white man, Wickman, that's who. Didn't you know? That's because you don't act Chinese. You don't even look Chinese."

I might have asked her to explain further or offered some explanation of my own, but at the time I knew any further talk would only fall on deaf ears. "You're right, I know you're right. I always wanted him to be. But he's not. That doesn't make me look like him, or act like him, or

Peter or Lincoln or any of them, for that matter. Nobody can explain why I am what I am."

"I have to go away now. You don't need me. You're just a kid." She bit hard on her lip to stop its quivering. "I made a mistake too. You're too young. You don't want to be married, at least not to me. I know how to be a wife, but you don't know how to be a husband. I'm too Chinese for you. Right now, all you want is to be unhappy with yourself, do nothing, waste time, waste your life. I can't do that. I want more. I can't waste any more time." Winnie's expression suddenly softened. Her raging, her frustration with me, with herself, melted away, such a quick study. "I'll tell Mary. She can explain it to everybody else." She'd made it all better. At least the part that she could touch.

Of course, she was right. My most immediate regret at the time was the disapproval I would experience when I told the family that my marriage was over—humiliation more than regret.

She had her ski jacket zipped and her book bag over her shoulder. Her car keys slammed against the front door as she stepped to the suspended walk leading to the stairs down to the car which had been her fictive cousin's wedding gift that she would drive to his flat where they'd been fucking.

The odd Italian North Beach neighbor, swimming against the Chinese tidal wave, in his thick black wool suit over a heavy cardigan with his sweater cuffs extruding the fashionable two inches beyond his coat sleeves, ready for the fog, will still wander through the door, ignoring the neon fresco of Pan-Pacific Travel (Columbo's boot long gone), stop short at the counter, then retreat to the street shaking his head. But now Grant Avenue north across Columbus Avenue teems with new immigrants, North Beach a Pacific littoral, latte and dim sum, Bohemia and the garment bazaars, the sewing factories. Columbus Travel: discover America, discover the world, the world just outside your door. It's only the younger generation that takes advantage of the business. The rest of the family, the immediate descendants of immigrants, no longer travel, unable to imagine where on earth they might go. Converts, early or late, they understand that paradise is here.

More often, among the passing silhouettes I spy a middle-aged Oriental around Peter's age, Chinese American by his suburban uniform—alligator golf shirt, khakis, windbreaker—a little heavy, balding—peering through the silvered plate glass at the bridge spanning the Pacific. I keep a transparent mural of the Golden Gate Bridge beneath the original pastel and the coincidental business name, Columbus Travel, with a Chinatown skyline, pagoda roof, in red, gold and green, the colors of good fortune to encourage wealth and a healthy self-interest. Repainted, the Nina, Pinta, and Santa Maria are junks traversing the Bay from the Oakland Mole, a small historical addendum from a postcard in Wick's collection of Chinatown memorabilia, a trompe l'oeil he offered when the family bestowed the management of the travel agency on me after Wick and Peter moved to Honolulu for their upside-down honeymoon (as I once overheard the phrase whispered in Cantonese).

I wanted to talk to them, tell about myself, high school, college. In the twilight of my marriage to Winnie, Peter would call in the middle of the night, a bad connection, Wick moving out, a rambling confession, new friends, a new passion, Twig. I wanted to tell him about my failing marriage, but instead I had to listen. It was always his dime—*WokTalk* syndication, Chi Bars, and Twig. Twig was a beach boy, a musician, popular in the discos that catered to the newlyweds from Osaka, Seoul, Canton, Ohio, eking out a living with day jobs with the Korean vendors that lined Kahala Boulevard facing the sea, flat-faced and squinting from the darkest corners of the sidewalk bazaars at the languorous parade slipping between their silk-lined shoals. By night, he was a jangly disco queen and dealt a little on the side.

"It's an exciting time to be alive, Chris. There's revolution in the air. I hope you're not feeling bad about your marriage breaking up. You're free, you're young. You can start over. Right?"

"And start right over again."

"Do that in five, bra'. But listen. I've made a friend. We met at an antiwar demonstration in the park. He's a musician, a rail-thin rock 'n' roll star, beach boy orphan."

"That's great. You finally found a friend your own age. So where's Wick?"

"Very funny. You must be okay. The last I heard from Mary, he's in Atlanta. Back and forth. She wants him on a tight leash but he's out to save the world again. There are all sorts of new missions working with refugees coming out of the DP camps in Hong Kong, Thailand, the Philippines. They're here in the Islands, too. I see them hand in hand learning to pull bedsheets and scrub toilets in Waikiki. It's that never-ending story."

"It's his calling."

"Right. Recalled again. My friend, Twig, tells me that his fondest memories have him losing a wrestling match on the floor of a church annex in Honolulu to Father Wong Dong, arms spread to imitate the crucifix."

I didn't know what to say. I thought they were never coming back. There'd been mild surprise at my sudden marriage. When he offered congratulations, Wick had told me he was glad someone in the family wanted to settle down. Peter's schedule kept him in Hawaii, but he sent us matching aloha shirts. I wanted to stay close. I needed them more than ever after I discovered I'd been tricked or tricked myself into marriage with Winnie. But they were spinning away from me. Whatever anyone else thought of them, whatever they thought of each other, I could hold only to the thought that Wick was my counselor, teacher, my father, after all. And Peter, my brother, despite all.

Peter and I grew up sharing our Auntie Mary, mentored by Uncle Lincoln, when Peter was still "Heyman," his first English name, and Wick, the "father." Wick named him Peter, in Paradise, just as he named me Columbus in Columbia. When I was young, my family referred to Heyman as "older brother," the first male of the next generation, a convenient role model that I might follow. There were no other boys in our extended family to carry Lincoln's paper name. Uncle Lincoln, Ah Lung Gung, was my paper uncle by marriage, or so we were taught. And Heyman, my half brother, was therefore a cousin, whom I was taught to call "big brother" in Chinese or Peter in English. When I was young, it was a convenient coincidence that in English we shared last names: Wong. In Chinese letters, the differences are clear, however illegible to me. My religious training, my less-than-basic Chinese skills, made it easier to lie to me. Peter, a decade older, had been schooled at the Kuomintang-sponsored Chinese Language Academy. He could quote Sun Yat-Sen. By the time I could confirm that Jesus loved me, Peter had his doubts.

We were raised in post-Exclusion Chinatown right after World War II. The community my aunties led me through during those years was English-speaking. The bakers, butchers, and produce clerks spoke English to me. I was groomed for assimilation entirely. But almost overnight, with the retreat of the Kuomintang from the Chinese mainland, Chinatown became a foreign enclave with new arrivals sounding a familiar but distant linguistic clamor around my ears. I date this sudden change—was it the fifties, fifty-two?—to the end of the Chinatown lottery and nationally syndicated radio shows, to Uncle's return from his brief service as a cook on the *Luraline* to Honolulu—that and the coincident purchase of our first television set, to which I retreated. Peter, Auntie, Uncle, and I were family, separated perhaps by the unique circumstances of history, of language, but fused by a common sensibility where age meant nothing, and television, the movies, everything.

As soon as I was old enough to appreciate his ridicule, Peter exploited our similarities and differences unmercifully. His Cantonese sensibilities intact, he loved to bully American me, aping my speech and language in his eclectic jabber, picking, teasing, sounding the coils of the unresolved sensibilities the children and grandchildren of immigrants embody, tearing at my smooth parochial-school American accent with shrill Hong Kong profanities.

Peter always understood me better than I understood myself, at least that part of me I didn't want to admit that we shared. Peter always told me what I felt because he felt the same. We understood the linguistic absurdity of our family's curses down to our very names, the hostility they feel toward the next generation, the danger we represent, to them and to our own unimaginable offspring. We could barely hear one another.

But Wick listened. Despite the scandal that drove him from the directorship of Shepherd's Haven and the two of them into exile, or at least out of Chinatown, the good Dr. Ted Candlewick was and remains an excellent scholar of Chinatown lore. The son of missionaries, raised in Hong Kong, he fell into that special category of *fan gwai* who spoke the local dialect, that special white man who spoke adolescent Cantonese, the *lup sup* dialect the kids manufactured in Chinatown, a white demon from whom no secrets could be kept. The ghetto holds these linguistic chimera in a paradoxical embrace, openly admired, secretly despised, envied, but especially attractive to the American-born of the diaspora. Shepherd's Haven, a nineteenth-century settlement house for fallen women and orphans, kept its lofty perch above our Oriental settlement by preserving Chinatown artifacts and rituals while holding to its mission to provide a message of salvation and acceptance to Chinatown's children. It was a simple message that resonated especially deeply in the

American-born, more deeply than the expressions of loyalty and honor issued by their parents, who secretly felt that they had abandoned family, home, country. Jesus loves you. He loves everyone, but with a special regard for children because they are innocent.

Uncle Lincoln scoffs. "Everybody. That's the problem."

At a very young age, I understood that I would have to bridge such divides.

Wick's public zeal for the artifacts of Chinatown's historical presence, the material accommodations the early settlement created to secure itself on the margins of the city's frontier beginnings, another formula for self-acceptance, also infects a legion of fellow enthusiasts for the nephrite opium jar, chinaware, teakwood, for the generation that survived World War II. His lectures on the importance of preserving Chinatown's historical narrative parallel an abiding preoccupation Chinatown's native scholars also pursue. Together they provide a foundation upon which subsequent generations of young people might construct the facades of their cultural identities as Chinese Americans, balancing the illusion of acceptance against the reality of their exile. Even after the Board of Governors ordered his suspension, the Haven kept the logo Wick designed: two coolies with shoulder yokes supporting the Golden Gate Bridge. His contributions to the institution are everywhere, and not easily erased. The old glass bookcases in his office that belonged originally to the Haven's founder, Dame Sidney Shepherd, still hold all manner of artifacts he rescued well before ethnicity and its cultural politics became popular. The original Genthe postcard photographs of pre-quake Chinatown, a collection of early restaurant menus with the daily specials printed in purple ink from stencils carved in beef-bone aspic, boiled brown sugar-lump candy distributed at the funeral of the notorious hatchet-wielding Little Pete, a raffia hoop dyed red and marked with the number four from an early Bomb Day celebration in Marysville, and a peddler's wooden clapper sitting on a scroll of song describing the lamentations of a Gold Mountain widow for the husband who would never return from his sojourn across the sea—they all provide color, an authentically exotic history, a provenance rooted in charity. These artifacts and the historical sensibility that prizes them are a far cry from the graduation photos of rescued prostitutes returned to China with which earlier administrations lined the foyer. It was under Wick's direction that a sign painter adapted the Bayscape from a pre-quake magazine to include the Chinese fishing vessels that were once the Nina and her sisters of my namesake onto the office mural when Uncle Lincoln bought the travel agency from Columbo Francescati's family. That, in addition to the two gilt letters, *u* and *s,* in the window put us in business.

The entire decade that is marked by General MacArthur's failure to wreak nuclear havoc on the newly founded People's Republic of China, the decade of my boyhood, gave rise to yet another missionary renaissance when all manner of Protestant sects—in pursuit of the traditional Salvation Army and YMCA, new Baptists, Anabaptists, Methodists, Fundamentalists, and Charismatics from Chinese diasporas across South and Central America, even Chinese Mormons from Honolulu—waded through a fresh tide of refugees gleaning new converts. There remained those few poor souls who were kept running by the immigration police while the House Un-American Activities Committee was sifting the Cold War Asian mix. But for the children whose native tongue and accent were solidly American, acceptance was a sacrament, especially for those who demanded as I once did to offer grace, with Wick beaming proudly as the waiter was slopping soup into our bowls at the old Neon Moon, embarrassing Uncle in front of his cronies, Uncle chatting loudly to the waiter ladling the steaming birds-nest *congee* while Peter prompted my blessing. There we were, in public, where everyone could see, mumbling grace, my head bowed over my rice bowl, Peter wearing his pastel lavender blouse with the embroidered sleeves he'd done himself, blessing the table, waving one of Auntie's ivory cigarette holders.

I was Columbus when Mrs. Francescati, Columbo's mother, delivered ravioli and tomato sauce door to door. I wore corduroys, a maroon V-neck sweater, and a white shirt to St. Joseph's Catholic School for the tongue-tied and undecided children of the neighborhood. My fingers dampened, I touched my forehead, genuflected, confessed the intricacies of Chinese disobedience to the Irish fathers in this Italian neighborhood until puberty sent me to the all-Chinese gatherings for suitable mating and sex education the Haven sponsored on Saturdays, where we learned to dance in the dark and Wick let us star in the movies about Chinamen in the West.

Mary hid us in the Catholic church to minister to our Chinatown accents. Incidentally, we were taught to expect love in all of its western expressions: God's embrace, martyrdom, the relief and unifying perfection that comes from confession. Following Peter's footsteps, I was sent to catechism on Thursdays and required to attend confession on Saturdays, mass on Sundays. There was Catholic school to distinguish me from any confusion with the rice Christians fleeing the Communists as the bamboo curtain fluttered once, twice, in the typhoon that swept the Republicans from the mainland and the UN from Korea. And as early as I can remember, there was Wick at our table, providing us instruction in Protestant notions of fellowship and singing "The Hit Parade" with gusto. He was the palpable half of the absent Uncle Lincoln, our father.

I hear tapping against the window. It's Peter, white ducks and orange camel-hair sweater, chipping delicately at the glass with his Rolex, then extending his index finger to remind me of our lunch at one, our appointment at six—or is it a friendly obscenity for the staff? He backhands a farewell with a soft fist that makes the plate glass shudder as he disappears into the pedestrian slipstream. Or it's Wick, balding, robust. Tall in Chinatown, over six-foot-four in his prime, black windbreaker with the collar turned up to hide his ministerial yoke, black shirt, white ducks, and pennyloafers with soft soles. Always hatless in a neighborhood where old men wear hats, a gray fringe that reminds me of the Capuchins but so unpriestlike, so imposing a figure, a white man of heroic stature who spends his days and nights in Chinatown.

Wick was lean when young, then heavier as he grew older, jowls darkened by the pubic shadow that made his jaw blue. He had hair everywhere, especially heavy on his arms, hands and fingers. Despite this aging, thickset, middle-aged body, he kept his upright posture, allowing only the warp that extra padding forces. He grew sideburns in the sixties, dewlaps, wrinkles around his eyes, thickening brows, all the details of an elegant pre-earthquake mansion, a San Francisco Victorian with dormers and a secret room, a rice room with a dark corner for Chinaboys.

Wick was always there to listen and advise, to be a go-between for my divided self. At the time, I thought only he could save me, listen to my confessions. Not even Auntie would sit for the whole story without inventing her own. And Lincoln, never.

"Shut up, why don't you?" he says, not unpleasantly. If Lincoln's generation did not have full control of their English vocabulary, they could at least control their tone. His generation loathed confession. He would have to claim us eventually, paterfamilias, but in the meantime, he left the fiction of family to invent then reinvent itself without unnecessary comment.

Seduced, then abandoned, I take comfort in Peter's kitchen. His pied à terre on Telegraph Hill has the industrial look: open stainless steel shelving, maple-topped chopping blocks, steel drain boards, an industrial range with a wok burner capable of generating 100,000 B.T.U.s, enough to crackle the ectoskeleton of an Australian prawn while leaving the meat tissue tender and succulent, shrimp meat wrapped in a natural potato chip, the crustaceous antennae and surviving appendages curled and crunchy. The perfect salt-and-pepper prawn vehicle. A stainless steel wine keeper, two refrigerator-freezer combinations, and, running the length above the long sloping counter to the double sink, wire racks to hold dishes, wine glasses, and silverware, air-drying, exposed. Two dishwashers. The ideal kitchen in which to discuss Uncle's finally marrying Winnie.

"I guess he could adopt her. But you don't suppose—?" Peter deveins prawns with a fine tweezer, mindful, always mindful of the flesh. "Was there a ceremony?"

The dining room, his occasional classroom, extends from the kitchen, a long glass-topped table with the centerpiece holding napkins, bottles and condiment dishes, wooden serving spoons, individual cooking baskets for hot pot, aluminum skewers, napkin rings on a dowel. He hadn't been teaching lately, and the wooden folding chairs were stacked in one corner, leaving us a broad empty space to hear my confession.

I'm on a ladder wiping the kitchen down with a bucket of something hot and industrially chlorinated. We haven't been back in a while, and the place has accumulated the city's effluvia. The air ducts, when not forcibly expelling, become passive receptors.

Eventually, Lincoln would have Judge Wong marry them, he and Winnie, in his chambers. Mary and the judge's secretary, Teanna, were witnesses. "You remember her, Peter. She graduated from high school with you."

"I've known her since the third grade. She married Hoover Mak, post office."

From Peter's window, I can spy a corner of our childhood, the Washington Square playground where the shadows cast by the spires of St. Peter and Paul lay a gridwork for the tai chi ballet in the mornings and where the newly retired from Hong Kong shelter their incomes in town houses along Columbus Avenue.

Peter wants to invent dinner. "Did Mary tell you we're going to refinance this building? The real estate market is hopping. Buy in the 'burbs." He watches me peel broccoli stalks. "I was remembering all the times we used to fish the Bay, go eeling, chumming for rockfish."

I remember too. That was Wick. He would take us across the Golden Gate Bridge to go pokeholing for monkfish in the rocks at low tide. He taught us to glean like real Chinamen, Wick did. Those thick eel-like fish had the most ferocious teeth snapping at number-two bass hooks. Once impaled, the hooks were left as hangers that stayed until the head was cut off, and even then, their postmortem spasms were threatening. Skinning the monkfish, I fought revulsion at the touch of it, the live trembling flesh, the muscle curling against my knuckles as I nailed the head down, then carefully peeled the skin off, flayed alive, then carefully filleted the livid flesh from the spinal cord and dumped the offal into the rocks where the gulls fought for it, diving, snatching.

We'd both seen him after Peter took up with Twig. Peter had even put him up in Honolulu. Wick had aged. He had begun to resemble a marooned beachcomber: faded Hawaiian shirt, angry red spider webs mapping his cheeks, gaze fixed to the rhythm of the white surf line breaking across the moonlit water, too many evenings in paradise.

I remember the face of the boy who was Wick's first accuser. I had known him, a classmate of Peter's in school, the set of his mouth especially, fleshy, a rounding chin that disappeared into his neck, head bowed. He would have been Peter's age. I wondered if Twig was Peter's revenge, some early childhood jealousy.

Peter turns to me. "What could be worse than to skin a writhing monkfish, to flay and fillet? And what could be better eating? A little salt, garlic, ginger, soy, sesame oil, a sprig of coriander, a bowl of rice, a Riesling."

I still see kids fishing the warm Electro Turbine generator exhaust that empties out at Third Street.

Peter has his own suggestions for Winnie. "I can send her to Hong Kong, for as long as she wants. She can stay or lose herself in a mall. She can become a manager for a deli franchise. They're marketing pastrami, turkey, roast beef, and cold salads." There were new appetites in the colonies, teased and shaped by the promise of western acceptance. Peter jeers at the British cafeteria slop Winnie loves. "Baked beans on white toast, sugared tea and boiled milk, the desserts whose names more aptly describe a sexually transmitted disease, a flesh-eating macrophage, necrotizing fasciitis."

Peter also spits at Wick like *love look away.* "I introduced him to Spotted Dick and he's never forgiven me."

Peter laughs like *can't we be friends.* "Now take my new pizza, it's Emmenthal and god knows what, turned in butter to disguise rapeseed oil, seasoned meats, probably chicken, could be turkey, piped onto an indifferent but multifunctional crust. It has a shelf life, refrigerated, of better than a month, but we rotate every three weeks. Reheats in the oven or microwave, fifteen minutes. You waddle away knowing that you have had the gourmand experience."

"And the gourmand says you ate too much," I can ad lib.

"And for two dollars more, that's the bargain. Stauffer's, Swanson's, Campbell, PepsiCo, cost less. But two dollars more? People will be drinking fifty-dollar wine with my products. No problem. Just take a bite of this orchid wrap."

Peter prepares ravioli, a gigantic pillow filled with ricotta and fungi that includes egg yolk and shredded prosciutto de parma. He rolls a thin sheet of pasta onto a chilled marble pastry board with a glass rolling pin filled with ice water. "This will be served in a béchamel. I'm also thinking about what to do with this white truffle. A friend of mine from Rome, a Filipino steward for United, is connected to a culinary mafia that hijacks truffles from the Mediterranean into the U.S. That, and Canadian bear paws, lynx, wild game, horn moving back to Europe, my God, it's like the Spanish Armada, it's the sixteenth century all over again, nation states carrying cargo around the world. Slaves, opium, drugs. And you know American customs wouldn't be caught dead with a pig at the airport."

"A pig?"

"To smell out truffles."

"Right. They even look a little silly with the bomb-smelling beagles."

"Right." He flips the sheet of dough and continues his pressing. "Big sign: Working Pig?"

The table has become a forest of wine glasses. "What are we drinking now?"

"I thought something very light. I bought a few Gewürz and the new May wines. We'll let the truffles carry the melody and the wine will just hum along." He swirls the amber liquid in his glass. "What fruit do you taste?"

I pour again. "I thought we were going to eat something from the village."

Peter scrubs the garlic skin off with his hands. "Village fare. What? Dried tangerine peel? Thank you, Mr. Science, no thank you. Christopher, you should go for the show but there's nothing worth eating, or what there is isn't worth the effort. Lincoln loves fishgut puddings and the worm frittata, but such a chore, mental as well as physical. There are reminders of the good old days all over, the wooden wheel the locals hang around your neck when caught fornicating with materfamilias. I think the villagers call the prostitutes eggs, fresh eggs, or pullets. From twelve to twenty-two. It must be the water and the sun, the aroma rising from the ponds, rubbing up against Ms. Chicken or Mr. Pig. Hair with the shine and color of new licorice, eyes glittering with curiosity, and rural physiques, hard, tough little bodies, and hard little bubble butts, my, my."

"And the family homestead, Peter."

"Yes, yes. Placards stamped with Uncle Lincoln this and that. Love 'em but leave your lust at the door with Grandma. I could understand the concept of new bride as plunder. She's a very disturbing addition to the household, a new temptation that needs tempering by the fire, a slow warming in the sunlight by the window. I see her squatting on newspapers, skinning ginger with the backside of a chopstick."

"Ah, China."

"Or preparing a meal, something kidnapped from the open market abattoir, that zoo. My God, the freshly flayed and filleted." Peter rags on, his tastes, his appetites in pursuit of the sins of our fathers? Lincoln? Wick he left behind, but we would all remain loyal to Wick, not just for Mary's sake, not just to conceal him in our silence. Watch me, Peter declares. I dare you.

Of course, no one wanted to watch Wick strip in public. I see now that he was always a little too willing to bathe naked in the limelight, his mea culpa sounding more and more self-serving. Even the newspapers suppressed the detailed confessions he offered to the synod. They were fantasies not unlike the possession narratives of demonic enslavement and incest rocking the Church at the same time. Wick's tenure had been so much a part of the Haven's entire pastoral mission in Chinatown, there was nothing to be done. Leash him to a chain staked in the backyard, feed him scraps, call him Lucky, and he would live a long time, like the turtles in the tubs, the gourami in the flower pot.

Mary's brothers took Peter at his word when he publicly declared himself gay. There was enough distance between Mary, Lincoln, and the rest of us to ignore any curse left lingering.

Attitudes have changed over time. It wasn't as if they were competing for attention. Peter, when asked, might joke that he would never have been molested unwillingly. He took every opportunity to declare that he was born gay. He wanted the limelight to keep Wick in the shade. Maybe he was angry at Wick, too. Whatever. So they were Peter Pan and the Fairy Godfather.

"It was wild, I know, but you know, freedom in the air and all that crap. Of course, it's all just disco now, baby." Peter put everything on a low boil after the charges against Wick went public, continuing to commute from his Hawaiian exile. Wick's name finally disappeared from the newspapers. Then the curtain was raised and Peter arrived in San Francisco with Twig in tow, both looking like harpies, brocade on their shoulders, heroin chic, razored profiles. The two of them and their emaciated tribe—too edgy for the Honolulu locals—had been making the scene in the punk palaces flourishing in the Philippines, on the Orchid Road in Singapore, in San Diego and LA, at the Balikbayan gardens in San Francisco.

Then Twig made Peter crazy, becoming another lost lover Peter had collected off the beach at Waikiki, his latest stateside companion, another dangling appendage, but this one with attitude. They were a pair. Peter admired Twig for creating his own legend, borrowed from the mokes, the has-beens, wannabes, martial arts masters, a soupçon of every Oriental myth and bullshit the beachcomber culture of the Pacific Rim features: a silk pillow, upholstered and tasseled for the Siege Perilous, the iconic graffiti history, Saipan love, tradecraft in the pidgin the exiled, the marooned invent, waiting for the next victim to wash ashore.

"So, who's Melba, Christopher? I want to meet the next one before you elope. This one, she speaks English?" Peter bullies me unmercifully. But who can I turn to? "Christopher Columbus Wong, you feel inadequate because you are inadequate." We could be shouldering our way through a food bazaar looking for freeze-dried tofu. "Did you find it? There, there it is," he points to a bin. Peter loves to pluck the innerspring that sits at the heart of the parts cut away but livid in my memory. "It says so right on the package, *'Dow foo gon,'* right?"

"Yes, that's it."

When I complain, he echoes my complaints, the litany of each successive wave of new Americans. "You understand people speaking Chinese. But you can't speak Chinese. I know that. The Chinese words you understand are felt experiences, not just words; they're feelings, sensations, all taste and feeling, all your aunties and uncles, all the dead and living." He thrives on my most heated and intimate confusions. They both do, Wick and Peter.

When we're together, I tell them, "Sometimes, I dream about knowing. I can hear people speaking Chinese. I understand what they're saying, but when I try to talk back, I can't come up with the words. I keep talking to them and they see through me, they can't hear me."

Wick reminds me. I hear him lecturing to us. "The ABC's are infantilized by language. When you speak, you're five years old again. You can't grow up, not in Chinese."

I speak enough Chinese, damn it, I complain, whine, petulant, sneering, which used to delight Peter when we were very young and his advantages were new weapons. He and Wick could raise a glorious clamor from the choir, a tumultuous harmony, a crash of voices that flooded my ears, my eyes streaming, and my nose would go soft and wet.

"When Chris speaks Chinese, Chinese mothers lactate. That's why," Peter continues, "you have such a way with these older ladies."

What is it that comes before me now, laughing hysterically, a nightmare robed in an off-white evening gown figured in inked counter-clocking swastikas, hexagonal mirrors hanging from his belt, catching blinding bursts of sunlight off the brilliant street, fly swatters tied to his wrists, his fingers weaving a secret code to watchful initiates while his arms widen to embrace the glorious explosion of a Cantonese opera, all voices, all instruments singing the same melody? It was always very confusing, and I needed escape. No one listened.

When we were kids, Wick made sure we saw more than Chinatown. He took us all over the city. We could do anything with him watching over us. Lincoln couldn't or wouldn't. With Wick we went camping, rode bikes in the park. We even went to the SPCA kennels to play with the dogs and cats we couldn't keep at home. We caught fish at the city piers or sat on the rocks above the city's utility exhaust pipe where hot water steamed into the Bay, turning the water green with algae, a rich soup that drew the rockfish. We pretended to be characters in English movies and we memorized vocabulary to make our accents invisible. Wherever we went, children would gather, drawn by our songs, our games. Try this one: "A revolving fragment from the Paleozoic gathers no cryptogamous vegetation." Or: *Rex regnat, sed non gubernat.*

I could never let Wick go. And neither could Peter.

The first week I imagined witnessing Winnie's adultery, Mary let it be known that there was an urgent message from Winnie's grandmother who was in the hospital and not expected to survive the summer. No such calamities would be necessary once the routine of return, time passing, the excuse of a month's sojourn had been established. Of course, she never went home. She would eventually move in with Uncle. Winnie would wrestle with my family on her own terms as a cousin, perhaps as an adopted daughter, and in the end, as Lincoln's wife.

That evening was patchy with low fog bordering the coast. Oyster clouds washed by the falling light were shrinking over the East Bay skies. There was a heat in the air redolent of eucalyptus and molding oak bolls as a late spring wind pulled the curtain of leaves aside and insect wings beat a tentative balance on their perches. A rainstorm hovered and the clouds turned into a ragged curtain drenching the scrub pine and oak groves that dot the hillside. Pretty from the mall parking lot: the sky washed in light ink, darkening where the mountain impales tendrils of fog, a Chinese painting, Sung.

I had Winnie's car that day. She'd lent it to me to go shopping. Now I know that I'd been her too-willing accomplice, that I'd been had by my own fantasy of a Chinese girl, a latent mania.

It is after she has informed me of her liaisons, almost Christmas, when I imagine myself slipping unannounced into her "cousin's" apartment and quite unexpectedly discover her fucking him. The first thing I see is his lank hair hanging almost to the floor, as he lolls nearly somnolent across one arm of the couch while his legs dangle across the other end. Without looking up, I turn and move quickly through the adjoining door, quietly past the hanging pots and pans, the boxes of paper plates and plastic utensils this FOB buys by the case. I let myself slide into a dark corner, paralyzed. I know she will leave. I would have parked her car at the curb, right in front, a miracle in itself. And when she passes by, she will know.

Where jealousy, paralyzing rage, the hollow ache that starts in the belly and slowly sinks to my loins will loom soon enough, it's the fact of their knowing.

I hear her once through the padded wall: "Don't hurt me."

Now I hear myself, my own song, a hollow note from where I stand, in the hall, around a corner, behind a door. Or is it Peter I hear, or Wick and Mary? I am a child. I crush my hands against my ears and hear my anxious breath.

It is my attentive imagination prying, rubbing my hands over their embers, inhaling the fetid steam rising from their glistening, their twists and thrusting, their trembling, inconstant motion. Now he hunches between her legs, the pale flesh of his ass shaking left and right. Winnie holds him with her legs wrapped tight around his waist, his hands tucked securely under her buttocks, grinding his pubic bone into her sex. Her fingernails dig into his shoulders. She mutters rhythmically, cries out to him, "Please don't hurt me! You make me so crazy!" She hooks the waistband of his elastic briefs under his testicles so they sit like purple jewels at the base of his swollen pink tower. She measures it with her palm and marvels at the head which extends a full inch past her thumb, comparing the crystalline drop at the slit of his pulsing cock with the tease of spit at the tip of her tongue. She kneels over him now, both hands gripping his helpless sex like a baseball bat, and, kissing each testicle in turn, rims the head of his cock as if she were removing wine corks with her pursed lips, pumping his shaft, plumbing for his sweet spill.

Is it with him, now, that I see her perched at the side of the bed, thrusting her sex to his mouth, her head thrown back, her hands caressing her breasts? Her tongue flicks back and forth across her upper lip, mirroring his lapping. He lips her swollen rosette and she rolls her thighs around his neck. She utters meaningless words to match the flooding spasms, rhythmic waves rolling effortless over her body. "Oooh, I want you to do that to me, kiss me just like that, yes."

But, oh dread, she spies me. Her lips move, and I see his broad skull graze, then whirl like a slow dervish at her sex, and I hear her demand as she holds my gaze, "Watch me, oh, watch me."

As I sit here in the dark, I feel a dampness, a wanton emptiness that needs filling. So I imagine them together, all of them, the family together.

We divorced after we'd been married for almost a year. Winnie stayed with Mary for a while, then began to accompany Lincoln on his business trips. I knew by then, like Wick, she wasn't going to go away. So I also wasn't all that surprised when she appeared again. She and Uncle had just returned from a buying spree in Hong Kong. Uncle had entered into China proper, leaving Winnie at the Peninsula Hotel, where travelers can shop in the comfort of their own suite without leaving the hotel premises—the loot's delivered to the airport properly tagged for U.S. customs. Immediately after their return, she'd called the office and left a message that she would be coming by the apartment to pick up some things. By then, Winnie's departure had become a prolonged affair where I would discover one day that her underwear no longer appeared in the clean laundry I sorted on the weekends. Shirts I hadn't worn in months reappeared, her perfume lingering, a trace of her eau de cologne turning heads in the locker room at the gym, mingled with my sweat, leaving the unmistakable impression that someone had recently savaged the sale shelf of toilet water at the Drugmart. I'd made a clean sweep of the icebox, the frosty containers of Caesar salads and frozen dressings, butter and dinner rolls still wrapped in their airtight pouches, their plastic knives fastened by a rubber band, a straw nailed to a frozen cola drink. She'd carefully gleaned the closets and her drawers for necessities, seasonal clothes and shoes. But she'd left all of the stuffed animals she had carried to our first shared bed. She abandoned her books, a collection of the semi-technical texts which her business major required, but, republished annually, she reckoned worthless for trade or cash. She did keep our wedding album.

I vacuumed under her collection of plants which I otherwise neglected and in a week or less collapsed in the central heating. I never realized the fastidious care her collection of delicate ferns required, especially her maidenhair dappling the gray light coming from the window over the kitchen sink. The constant pinching and misting, the sandy grit in the tub, were testaments, evidence of a tenacious will that required more than I or the life she could imagine with me would ever provide. She needed more, wanted more, and I was not unhappy that our fictive family could provide because I cared about her as I imagine I would have cared if she were an older sister. Of course, at the outset, I was always bouncing back and forth. I confess relief, but relief punctuated by waves of jealousy and misplaced rage. She wanted a real Chinese husband, or so we thought. In the end, she built a bridge between us all. She was more in tune with the family than I could ever be.

When she first came to visit what she'd left behind, she smelled like someone entirely new. She and Lincoln were already traveling to Hong Kong together, and she was living in Lincoln's apartment. She'd done something with her hair. At school she had worn it indistinguishably straight, that fierce, athletic bob her schoolmates favored for team sports. In the marriage photograph I have of her in my mind—bright red lips, a bright green broach at her throat, the red Chinese wedding dress—she has a permanent wave, a starched net of curls making her appear older, almost grown. But now she'd had it cut asymmetrically short, inventing a cultist look entirely her own, the angled gamin that suggested cheekbones where none were visible, casting the suggestion of a shadow across one side of her face. I hear her key chain rattling, immediately followed by her tilting head at the door.

She looked terrific. She stripped off her new raincoat to show me her latest look, a viscose and elastic matte tube dress, a clinging peach jersey that hugged her nipples and the dimples of her buttocks as she preened for my admiration. I could see the outline of some transparent lacy chemise attached by spaghetti straps tied like shoelaces around her slight figure as she scurried through our tiny apartment exchanging her worn items for new from the well-ordered inventory in the closets and under our bed. "I brought you dinner too, old times." It was a Hofbrau collection of sausage and potted meats, sauerkraut, coleslaw, and potato salad in the familiar Styrofoam boxes I'd come to associate with our marriage. "Uncle won't eat carry-out food with me, but I know you must miss it," one of our many misunderstandings that, now she belonged to the family, made her dear to me.

It had been Auntie who told me that Winnie was keeping house for Uncle. "Best for everybody," she said. Uncle behaved as if nothing unusual had occurred, that the exchange was appropriate, suitable, a domestic matter, family, and thus the province of women, governed by a female logic beneath our notice.

Sipping the Coke she drank with her pickle, Winnie confessed to missing our little dinners together. "Remember we used to buy one dish from every restaurant in Stone Village, Mexican, Chinese, pizza?"

I can't say no. (When I confessed Winnie's eating habits to Auntie shortly after our marriage, she immediately asked if she might be pregnant, a happy suspicion that spread through both families until Winnie doused their fire with a detailed description of birth control pills and her intention to remain childless.)

"The most I missed is enchilada sauce and pork kebabs. But Pancho Sancho was closed tonight."

I count my blessings. "French fries and catsup."

"With mayonnaise, with salt and vinegar." She settles on the carpet, hiking up her dress and kicking her shoes under the coffee table. "And sugar." She nibbles at the sauerbraten. "And Del Monte fruit cocktail," she adds with a dollop of potato salad. "Uncle couldn't eat anything in Hong Kong. Jet lag. He slept all the time and didn't go out at all. Just toast and tea." She reads minds too, and laughs at me. "We didn't even have room service because he didn't want to watch me eat."

She scoots a little closer to the table and carton of sausage and purple cabbage. Tucking her dress around her waist, she spreads two napkins across her pantyhose, looking up at me, swirling the meat in the coleslaw.

"I love to watch you eat, Winnie."

"I know that's a lie, but I think that's okay. We used to be married, so you can lie to me like old friends. Just sweet lies, though. That means you miss me sometimes."

"I miss you now."

"How can you? I'm right here."

"I mean I miss what we had together."

"That's not what Peter said. You don't tell me, but everybody knows already. You have an American girlfriend." She mops a spill from the table. "You don't want to talk about her?"

"Peter told you?"

"No," she draws herself up. "Wick, first, then Auntie, and even Uncle Lincoln. Then Peter said yes, but I knew already. Did you think I'd be jealous?"

"No, no. It's just that we haven't really talked together for a while. I didn't think you'd be interested." I was so transparent. Everyone knew.

"Another old friend lie?"

"No, really. Why would you care?"

She waves my words away as she carefully slips the covers over the food we've only touched. "American girl, Christopher. You don't like Chinese girls anymore?" she purrs coyly.

"I have always liked all kinds of girls. I happened to fall in love with you." No answer is always the best answer. Winnie likes to lead now. She has brought two tailored silk shirts and insists I model them for size, a collarless straw yellow and a turquoise with rather lengthy lapels and a pattern of frogs embossed into the fabric.

"It's special present."

They both fit beautifully, weightless and cool, but the turquoise number has no collar button and opens to my sternum. "I'll wear this one when I buy an Italian sports car."

"No, no. You have to wear them for your new girlfriend. She'll know a mysterious lady bought them for you. She'll get jealous and love you to pieces." Winnie plucks at my shoulders to keep the shirt from slipping any further. "Just don't slouch or you will catch a cold." She peeks round me as I stand before the mirror. "And don't put your hands in your pockets." She slips past and begins gathering odds and ends to accommodate her new wardrobe: a sweater, shoes, a harmless black slicker she bought when we were caught in a sudden downpour at some Peninsula mall. We spy on each other through the looking glass as we used to do. The narrow mirror hung on the closet door affords little space and we bump and jostle for a look at ourselves as we are now. She slips her jersey off to experiment with a different ensemble and demands the shirt I'm wearing to match the black vinyl raincoat over the shoelaced silk chemise.

"Sexy girl," I step back, refusing the shirt.

"Let me try it," she demands, hands on her hipless waist, thin as a ribbon. Her chemistry demands constant nourishment, but she never gains an ounce. The only turn of a curve on her frame to distinguish her from a fifteen-year-old boy is her tight little behind, a momentary hindrance as she drops the ribbons holding her chemise from her shoulders and allows the garment to fall at her feet. It's her ass, not the little raisins above her rib cage, that suggests her sex. She kicks the chemise in my face and snatches the shirt away. I gaze at her through the diaphanous slip as she tries to cover herself in my shirt, giggling at her exposure, a décolletage that reaches well beyond her navel, and at the ludicrous spectacle of myself in the mirror, draped in her silk bunting.

"Don't we look silly?" I offer.

"Silly?" She postures for the mirror.

Words have always failed me in her company. Our most intimate moments turn cold at some misunderstanding over language. "I meant me."

"You don't know how to talk to girls." We're staring at each other in the mirror. There's a look of serious concern in her face. The playful, achingly familiar heat we used to share, before there were words, only the desires our illusory expectations played on one another, freezes. If ever I were the man for her, the lusty, sweat-drenched heaving force I made myself against whatever her illusions about me she may have had, the lover, the husband, all such fragile imaginings dissolve with a single word.

"I know. I meant sexy." But that's a lie. What are words worth when I must never speak them spontaneously, without that patronizing curl she knows too well? Even with the rich stink of Winnie's new perfume in my nose, the pleasant ache still swollen with wanton expectation, I hear the easy chatter of Melba sweetly beckoning.

"Peter says we must say what we mean, every time. You better do that with your American girl, Christopher." She turns from her reflection and gently removes her slip from my head. "You have sex together?"

"Yes. Wonderful, glorious sex, as often as possible." Glib lies, lies I can tell without guilt, lies for old lovers, ex-wives. Three times, almost four. Sometimes, she says no, makes me wait. She lights candles. There are evenings I suspect that she spends with another, when the phone goes unanswered. There was a day. We met late in the afternoon, a slow walk through

North Beach, a lovely dinner. I talked about work, about Winnie's diet, my Uncle Lincoln and Winnie, the family, everything I could remember about myself. She was quiet, seemed attentive, drew me out.

"How come Melba's not here, then?"

"Well, it's not always possible. She has other friends."

"Other boyfriends?"

"No. Yes. I don't think so." I don't know. "I don't know. She's an artist. And she meets with others that are interested in the same things she does. She's very independent." And I would never ask.

"Girls are like that. I want to be an independent person myself. And you don't care now?"

"No, I like her independence." It's too hard to explain. I would give Melba all the independence she desires if only she would come with me, choose me, finally.

"You didn't like mine." Winnie kneels on the carpet and prowls under the bed searching for her other wardrobe. "You don't care if she has other boyfriends?"

"She does have other friends. Boy friends, girl friends. It doesn't matter."

She's found her box of sweaters and begins to try them on. "How many times do you see her?"

"She lives near the office, so I see her all the time. Lunch, dinner, we go to the movies."

"No, I mean how many times do you sleep together?" she challenges coyly. "Every day? Lunch? Dinner?"

"Yeah, sure. Whenever opportunity knocks. Why are you so curious?" But I already know why. Winnie wants to trade, a fair exchange, old love and new love, two loves.

I could tell her. At the bottom of the stairs, I had kissed Melba lightly. She held me back. "I don't want you to come up tonight," she said, turning her face aside. "I can't be with you tonight."

"What? Sure, sure. Is something the matter? Something I said? Headache? Heartache?" I kept talking, kept smiling. "I mean, it's okay. I'll just stumble to the office and sleep on my desk. No problem."

"Okay?" she gently probes.

"Definitely, absolutely, one hundred percent yes." I didn't move a step. I couldn't let my arms drop. I held her.

"Chris?"

"I know. I should go now. But I can't let you go." I didn't mean to say that with such wounding passion. I felt tears running down my face. I wasn't crying; I had a smile on my face, I could feel it straining against my ears. At the same time, I wanted to leave right then. But Melba pressed herself against me, then, and led me up the stairs to her bedroom where we undressed in the dark.

"Your friend is shy? She makes you beg? I want to know if it's different with an American girl."

"No, of course not. The plumbing's the same. It's just the shape and size that's different."

"She's bigger in the chest, I bet."

"A little bit bigger all around, actually." But it wasn't Melba's parts I wanted. I told her I loved her, that I wanted to be with her forever, that I wanted to marry her, all the declarations I had held back the entire evening came in a flood of tears and weeping. And even as she bid me enter and spend myself in all the hurt and heat of my need for her, she kept herself apart. And when I was done, she slept. I did not.

Winnie is attracted to the passion of confessions. "Do you talk about us?"

"Of course." That was a lie.

"Everything?"

"Everything she wants to know."

"Yes?"

"Every romantic detail, tops, bottoms and all the in-betweens. Do you mind?"

Winnie steps over the clutter and back to the kitchen. "I don't mind," she calls from the fridge. "I'm eating all your food again."

"I don't mind." I begin to dress slowly. She's plopped on the couch in an old sweater and panties with a sandwich. "What are you eating?"

"Salad and meat. It's good. You want a bite?" she offers, pulling her sweater off.

Of course, I do. I lick her skinny chest up and down, tasting the pickle juice and Russian dressing she lets drip without surrendering her sandwich.

There was a change in Winnie, a sense of style, a quicker gait. Uncle had given her permission to have purpose, a direction, indulgences. Auntie was teaching her to cook. I became her younger brother, the kid. I was not expected to lead. Now, with everyone's encouragement, Winnie could also take charge of me. With Winnie's encouragement, with her fresh interest in me, I remade myself, changed my entire appearance. She dressed me for work at the travel agency—short-sleeved wash-and-wear Dacron, button-downs, a loosely knotted tie, a safari jacket she found on sale at Abercrombie's, with aviator shades, amber tints, hanging from the epaulets on my shoulder. There I would sit in a glass-framed window plastered with posters of exotic destinations, deserving and desirable.

Auntie still used me to fetch and carry, to engage me with the chores near at hand, while Peter orchestrated the end of his scandalous exile, with Twig in tow. But we all had to be watched. After all, left on my own, I'd been snagged by an American beatnik, as Winnie called her.

"Your new friend is an artist, a weaver? What does she make?" Auntie and I had just finished with a jewelry purchase from a friend of Uncle's, a twenty-four-karat gold chain he'd delivered with a stern lecture concerning its softness. The old man had draped the chain across the backs of our hands and gently pulled it across our skin, attesting to its friction-less extravagance while warning Auntie about its inherent tensile fragility. And right next door sat Melba's art. I'm sure Auntie knew, not about Winnie's visits, but about Melba. They were all curious.

When first we met, Melba was nursing a tepid latte over a stand-up lunch at Alvina's Cafe and wrapping a slice of pizza. She stopped me, hooked the back pouch of my jacket as I inched past with my espresso and brioche. She'd recognized me, had spied me through the window of the travel agency. I turned, and there she stood, staring directly in my eyes. Nose to nose, brown curls, a sprinkle of pale freckles, like the cinnamon dissolving in the white foam in her glass, pink, so pale, and my life suddenly changed. Rather, my life changed again. At least, I thought that I had caught a glimpse of what my life might become if I could escape as Peter had escaped, into a different world.

Melba was like new air. She stood so close when we talked I was afraid that if I took a breath on the wrong syllable, I would inhale her.

Melba freelanced original macramé wall hangings to interior designers from her studio apartment quite near my office. She wore samples of her knots in her hair, a complicated cap she invented with colored fringe and beading that made her every gesture dance. Her major source of income at the time came from wholesaling Bolivian hemp bags that her ex-companion, Milo, an anthropologist from Indiana University, sent from a cattle station at the edge of a rain forest. He'd gone there to complete his dissertation and wound up opening a slaughterhouse to market the local beef he butchered into familiar shapes for the crews of an American oil company. He and his former companions, each in their turn, had taken in native children, the latest an adopted Chinese baby girl who had been twice abandoned, most recently by the wife of a Peruvian Airlines pilot, a friend of Milo's, when she discovered herself unexpectedly pregnant. Melba had done the whole number, changed her name, fallen in love with the local textiles—jute and vegetable dyes—and had finally been frightened away by Milo's involvement in the burgeoning traffic in cocaine. She kept a snapshot of the two of them with his kids and a flock of vultures perched patiently on a galvanized fence, Melba in surplus fatigues in the foreground, the bearded Milo in a leather apron holding a baby and surrounded by a group of naked children of various ages and hues. "I called myself Maya, very earth mommy. The vultures made me a vegetarian," she said, "and the kids a firm believer in birth control. Milo uses the kids like puppies in the park to catch girls, to stimulate the maternal reflex. He thinks the children keep us in our place."

"And they did?" I examined the photo carefully. "Very exotic."

"That's Asia Milo's holding." A baby with bead-black eyes and ink hair, a braid of beaded string around her waist, a feather in one hand, but otherwise naked, Milo holding her almost too casually against a blue, cloudless horizon defined by a curtain of tall unkempt palm trees. "For a while, it did. Orphan Chinese babies have that effect."

"Yes, I've heard that. But something's funny there."

"Where?"

"Well, she doesn't look Chinese."

She began to erupt. "Well, how could she?"

I held my breath as she cocked her head.

Her smile, then laughter, emerged from behind a beaded curtain, small shakes and rattles as she actually laughed at my joke. She'd been listening behind my own display of baubles and bangles. It was my finest moment. I felt immediately comfortable with her. She even took my hand, my wrist actually, to check my watch. She had to run an errand. I had to return to the office. She had a question for me. Was it cheaper to buy a ticket round-trip to San Francisco from Bolivia here or in La Paz? Her touch was firm, deliberate, certainly intimidating, and wildly infectious. She knew instinctively her power over me, that I was only waiting to surrender. I was sure she could feel my pulse.

"Milo's pilot friend found Asia in a Baptist orphanage in Cuzco. They called her Meiling. Her papers said Maria something something of course. I found a Chinese grocery store owner in Santa Cruces who was willing to give her Chinese lessons before I left. We were learning a song in Fukien dialect."

"I can count to ten," I offer.

"So can I." She scrapes the bottom of her cup to capture the sugared lees of her cappuccino and licks it off her spoon with the tip of her tongue, slowly. She's not embarrassed when she sees I'm staring at her, watching her. "It's my sweet tooth. You probably speak Chinese, Cantonese, too."

"Just the family's local dialect. I stopped speaking when I started public school," I said. "My ex-wife's from Hong Kong, but she refused to listen to my attempts to recover the vocabulary of a five-year-old." My glib explanations tidy the stage, lend a little authority to my image. Let the chorus of voices be gone. Because she wasn't actually leaving, Winnie's explanations to Auntie, to Peter, to the entire family on the verge of our divorce were layered with a kind of linguistic contempt that all of them understood perfectly because I didn't.

"Ex-wife? Aren't you a little young to have a past?"

"Like Asia, I guess. It's a long story. Arranged marriages. I was a child groom, wouldn't you know."

I amuse Melba and she humors me as I offer up the litany of growing up in the neighborhood, from Uncle Lincoln's takeout to Peter's celebrity chef, a little of Winnie and the family's need to care for orphan Chinese babies, the life of a travel agent who manages only to cross the Bay Bridge to Oakland. I feel I'm losing her, talking too much, giving her the tour. But I hold her attention anyway. I do this for a living and I'm still amazed. "California people get quite adventurous, gastronomically speaking. You know about monkey brains? Gourmet vacations are very popular. We have a spin on restaurant tours, an ethnic fast-food package that does lunch with a mini-van tour of the neighborhoods—a Tenderloin Vietnamese sandwich, hand-pulled noodles in the Richmond, the inner Sunset Korean barbecue, the big burrito we take to the park, sushi, hot links, and ribs. Or, I can offer you a discount for our bear paw banquet package, but we'd have to cross the border."

"Not bear paws?" She shudders gamely.

"Well, it's considered an aphrodisiac by some. Very illegal here, of course. But the Indians in Canada can hunt bears legally. We trade them imitation Bally shoes from Taiwan and arrange a feast in the woods, actually an aluminum double-wide at a fishing camp outside of Vancouver—bear paw, spleen, elk tail, antler, wild ginseng."

"I hate to eat and run."

"Rat on a stick?" I can't help myself. "No doggie bags?"

"I have to go, really," she says, tapping my wrist watch.

"Yes." I feel exposed, suddenly, vulnerable. "Time flies." I don't want to say good-bye. I will my wrist frozen to the table, the swizzle stick digging into the palm of my hand. Stay, please stay.

"I have class, then I have to meet someone. An old friend."

"Who?" My tirade, my sudden panic often induces short-term memory lapses, awkward rudeness, a rictus, drool gathering at the corner of my mouth, difficulty swallowing. This must be love. It feels like death.

"He's bringing me dyes from Peru."

I am smitten. "Oh, right, right. Maybe we could see a movie, have dinner?" I hold my breath.

She bags the pizza in a jute bag dyed the color of beets. "I like the movie part. Sure. Call me. Or listen, I live so close, I'll knock on your window."

All right! Score one for me. I watch her cross the café, sunlight streaming through the curtains, the grimy plate glass, at odd angles through the motley of faux Tiffany shades and hanging chandeliers, her figure ducking in and out of newspapers among the crowded tables. I follow the back of her head bobbing and weaving through the smoke of roasting coffee, flies spiraling in the sweet steam from the espresso machines. At the door, she peeks back through the afternoon din, her face a lightbulb left burning in the daylight.

She fixes me with a smile, waves. "Ciao," she mouths and exits.

I cannot believe it. I look around to see if anyone has been watching, search under the table for something she might have left behind, evidence that she had been there. Out of habit, I bus the table, the dregs of her latte in a thick glass delicately laced with dried milk foam, the plastic spoon her tongue has touched, her rumpled napkin. For the first time in my life the smell of cooked milk seems vaguely attractive, and sweet, so sweet. There's a small pile of dead white moths like tiny dried leaves clinging to the heavy black table base. Seduced and abandoned.

The next day, she stops by the travel agency. It's a Wednesday at the end of July, when my occasional temps, my kindergarten classmates Felicia Lee and her sister, Helen, finally have the office under control. Typical wet city morning, fog congealing on telephone wires, windows, the ironwork on the buildings, the fire escapes, flag holders, a sticky rime redolent with the smell of the bakeries, the coffee roasters, the aroma of wet chickens wafting from across Columbus Avenue. Melba in her Afghan shepherd's jacket, Peruvian mohair cap, and granny glasses peers over the front counter.

Felicia, wrapped in her electric blue suit, sets a half-eaten almond croissant on her brown paper doily, dabbing at lipstick on her front teeth, smiling involuntarily at the sight of a white woman her own age, a mature adult, dressed like a hippie, and remarks in Cantonese to her chubby sister that somebody has lost a sheep.

"Was she laughing at me?" Melba asked, amused herself.

I tried to lie. "No, no. Private joke." But she knew.

I'm locked up late at the travel office trying to peddle some non-refundable tickets to a German consolidator who's packaging a week in the fleshpots of the pubic triangle: Taipei, Olongapu, and Bangkok, but with a twist. King for a day, emperor of the night, there soon will be trips marketed to upscale warrior-lites as the War collapses into re-runs on late night TV. A reunion with Miss Saigon, a riverboat ride on the Mekong— chopper to a restored hill tribe camp with a Hmong scout played by a Huynh cousin, a Wong by any other name, whose family Uncle Lincoln sponsored to the States. Imagine the final evening, a parade of Amerasian children down a dusty boulevard, burning hooches outlining the old French city, cuddling with someone small, dark, and aboriginal, civilized by a smear of lipstick.

The travel business isn't the same. The office subscribes to a sound loop that plays airline ad music. When clients look up at the ceiling trying to locate the melody, they see the azure expanse of the oceans spotted with 747's crawling across the map on golden threads across the red stripe marking the international date line from which Neptune guards against Chinese dragons paddling on the other side. Everybody wants to fly, to be embalmed in an aerosol can, elbows locked against the padded armrests. Rebel consolidators capture a block of tickets and go bankrupt before the passengers reach the gate. There are airlines that refuse seat reservations, that refuse to fly if there aren't enough seats sold. I do better with ship tours, better with the train. I can hold a seat on a bus. And I hate flying, hate the feeling of my skin turning into Teflon, of my inner ear crushed against my sinuses. Melba and I had this in common. Her own determination never again to set foot inside an airplane came from her year of plunging across the Bolivian Andes.

That first afternoon we meet, she beckons to me with one of the cards I leave on tables wherever I lunch in the neighborhood, bright red and green illustrations of travel portfolios with "Columbus Travel" splashed in gilt. "I have a friend who has to fly from La Paz to Los Angeles?"

"A fate worse than death."

"His bad karma." She combs strands of hair with her fingernails over her right ear, revealing a pale splash of freckles running down her neck. "Is it cheaper to buy in La Paz? He wants me to reserve the ticket here."

I chatter knowledgeably, filling the space between us with food talk, with how I hate to cut a single ticket from South America, how it's easier to send her to a bucket shop, wondering who "he" is. "Ask for Mohammed or Rocky. Fly Equatoriana, Aerlinea Argentina, Aero Peru, Pan Am—they all have wholesale blocks. Better to avoid TACA, which as often as not kidnaps whole flights, promising New Orleans, but landing in Houston."

"I hate to fly. I'd rather walk, even from Bolivia," she says.

A week later she raises the same dilemma. Who is "he"?

"His plans changed? He wants Cartagena, now."

"Columbia? Is he a drug dealer?"

"He's an old friend," she shrugs. "An ex."

I make the call.

One evening, Melba arrives in a new disguise. A familiar chipping against the plate glass above the hum of the telephone in my ear, Montovani looping, pulls me to the front window. It's my sweet, sweet Melba flattening her face against the glass with her shocked hair dyed bootblack and smeared across her powdered white forehead like a violent Richter scale, black eyebrows plucked to a fashionable stipple, cherry red lipstick—a punker in black Levi's and a padded blue silk vest, a bandit Chinese princess.

"Hi, Christopher Columbus." She alertly polishes the window glass with her sleeve before stepping in.

"Hello." I tug at the industrial staple in her ear, recalling my particular horror at such acts, even symbolic, of cosmetic mutilation. "Does that hurt? Are you by yourself? You wanna eat?"

"Not hungry. My friends are eating down the street. We're going dancing at DNA."

"What's that?"

"De-oxy-ri-bo-nu-cleic-acid."

"Who?"

"It's a club. For the genetically disturbed." She smears my cheek with face powder and scrubs it vigorously with the tip of her finger. "I've rubbed off on you."

"You don't want me to feed you."

"Nope. You look busy, anyway."

"Yeah, I am. You don't want my company."

"Sure, always." She plopped into the swivel chair, lifted her knees, and spun slowly, orbiting the office.

"A ride?"

"Two, please."

"Poke in the eye?"

Folding her arms, she spins to an empty work station. "Didn't you say that one of your relatives had bound feet?"

Why do I have to tell Peter, tell Wick, all of us sitting in Peter's kitchen? I am being so insensitive, so naive. Wick is probably packing for Atlanta again, slipping Auntie's collar because Peter is waiting for Twig to come through the door.

"From bear paws to bound feet, now barefoot in the bedroom, Bravo, Christopher," says Peter.

I tell them. Melba finally invited me to spend the night one evening after she'd put her weaving to bed. I'd fixed a leaking drain pipe under the kitchen sink and she'd made dinner. It was restrained, resigned, inevitable, long overdue. I spent the night, but we were full of apologies. "Is that all?" "My breasts are too small." "Was it good for you?" We made love again in the morning before her alarm clock rang. I couldn't sleep. I lay beside her listening to her breathe. Then we had breakfast together, both of us a little sweaty, anxious for a shower. I watched Melba wrap a sandwich for an excursion she had to make that morning. I wrote "Melba's lunch" on the bag, which she thought was a little corny, but sweet. She gave me a little conspiratorial wave, the Italian hand, that looked like her cupped fingers around an imaginary castanet. "Well, good-bye, ciao. Just lock up when you leave."

"What if I want to come back?"

"There's an extra key hanging by the back door in the kitchen."

Wick's propped against the new countertop steam table, a little too attentive, too well-meaning. I can see that it's not about me.

I tell them, "We've been spending time together. You know, she's off to school, breakfast dishes in the sink, her work, all that jute and yarn warming in the sunlight in her studio. I have a job, a business that I can walk to, down the stairs, across the street. We make love after lunch. She took me to see an Italian movie with English subtitles. I know this sounds dumb, but I'd never imagined before where all the Italians came from. It was a Frederico Fellini retrospective. We saw *La Strada*."

"Of course," Peter never tries not to be dismissive.

"You've seen it."

"Of course." He can't help himself. "Giulietta," he says with a sigh over the accent.

"Stop, Peter. Don't." Wick always intervenes. "Peter's in heat, Chris. Just ignore him. Besides which, Peter, Frederico is quoting Offenbach's Giulietta." He began to hum the theme to the second act I remember from the solarium of the Catholic daycare.

"Like I've lived my entire life with your petty jealousies and insecurities. What makes you so contemptuous of others? Why do we have to live our lives this way?"

"Maybe it's the *lo fan* folks, the white people we imitate. It's instinctive, a survival skill, little brother."

"That's good, Peter. At least I'm good for something," Wick says.

Peter ignores him. "Turning the other cheek, interracial loving—did you nap through catechism and the movies?"

"It's not about race. She's not like that. She sees past all that, Peter." All I knew was she was most decidedly not Chinese, not Chinatown. So far from the manipulations, the constant negotiations that made my relationship with family so flawed. With her, I felt for the first time in my life acceptance, pure, total, all embracing. "She laughs at my jokes, really laughs. And I think she likes me."

"God blesses lovers, Christopher. Be a lover," Wick responds.

"Or be a clown."

Peter always catches me playing the fool. I do it so well in imitation of you, dear brother, dear father. Everybody plays the fool.

And they never mentioned Winnie.

4

Mares eat oats and does eat oats
And little lambs eat ivy.
A kid'll eat ivy too.
Oh, God, more food.

Auntie and I frequent a dim sum palace near the Pacific Ocean, on a residential boulevard in a suburb that declines gracefully to the sea, perennial gray light, a neighborhood that's been annexed by the most recent immigrant wave, a shopping mall that's become a cornucopia of restaurants, bakeries, and a supermarket with a deep fryer that can accommodate a whole tuna. Butane-fired mobile steam tables parade the aisles, wheeling around large banquet tables at which they dock with a glance from the oldest male or a chorus from two or more women. We've started late, after one. A smoked tea, a glass of wine. The sweet succulents seem a bit tired. Not that Mary ever has an appetite. Still, she relishes a meal, its display, my company.

"Eat, eat." She divides a sticky rice tamale with the string that binds it in a ti leaf and puts both halves on my dish. "Go on, look," she says, poking at the stuffing, a smoking morsel of pork and peanut. "This is excellent, so fresh."

I can always manage a bite for Mary. "Peter called yesterday. He says hello to you."

"Well, good, hello back. Why doesn't he call me? Is he going to take me out to dinner?" She swirls a shrimp pastry in soy and vinegar and nestles it next to the sweet rice.

"He was in Honolulu again, Winnie too."

"I know Winnie's in Honolulu. She called me."

"Then you know already. Peter wants me to go with Winnie to Hong Kong." The shrimp's a little tired, but the rice, the rice is always good.

Probing a pillow of rice, a splash of sauce, dividing the flesh of a softened peanut in a glaze of oils, my appetite stirs.

"For business. I know. We might buy some property."

"Peter wants me to go to the trade fair. He has business in Rome."

"Is that where Twig is hiding himself?"

"No, Amsterdam. He has a new band." I look up and a cart with a tower of saucers stacked with egg tarts, sesame doughnuts filled with sweet bean paste, and a large thermos of tea confronts us. The waitress looks at me, shrugs, then asks Auntie in Cantonese what I want.

"More tea? Winnie said Melba might go to Amsterdam too."

"Ask if there's any chicken feet left in the kitchen. I heard that too."

"Take your time. Eat." She pours tea for herself, sips at the steam creeping over her glasses. "I can't keep up anymore. Amsterdam? What's that? Peter sent me a picture. His hair's all red and he wears earrings and eye shadow."

"Holland. You know, where the tulips grow, wooden shoes. Where the little boy put his finger in the dike to save the town from the ocean's flood."

"Danny Kaye. I remember that movie. He used to visit Chinatown. Did you know that?"

"Danny Kaye?"

"Yes, Danny Kaye. He liked Chinese people. There's a picture of him cooking Chinese food at Johnny Kan's restaurant. The movie actor guy. Very nice."

Wrong movie, Auntie. "I didn't know that. Not Gene Kelly?"

"No, no. I told you before, but you forget. Nice man, but no family."

"This was Gene Kelly?"

"No, no. Danny Kaye. He used to shop in my friend's store. Buy five of everything. He wanted me to tell him what to buy and I told him silk jackets were an excellent bargain. For his wife, I said. Then he told me he didn't have a wife. He bought five jackets anyway, for his friends."

"When was this?"

"Before you were born, probably. Peter would remember. They shook hands. He was a gay boy too."

Even after she relocated to the Peninsula leaving everything in Winnie's care, Auntie never moved beyond the confines of the family, of Chinatown, in her mind. But Chinatown has expanded well beyond any distance she could walk to shop the greengrocers, the fishmongers, the butchers, the bakeries. She can't cover it all. But she's always been transported by the movies, television. "There's Chinese people in Amsterdam?"

"Sure. Japanese, Chinese, Vietnamese, Filipinos."

"That's why Twig's there."

"Partly. He's popular in Europe." And, of course, the drug scene is international.

"Before, when you were just a baby, they thought we were spies."

"Who thought?"

"Europeans."

"Spies? Chinese spies?"

"Yes. Not from China. From Chinatown. They were looking for Communists."

"What would they do when they found them? It's legal to be a Communist in Europe."

"Marijuana smoking is legal in Amsterdam." Auntie knows best. "I saw it on *60 Minutes*. We used to keep all the doors closed and burn incense all weekend just like they do now."

"What are you talking about?"

"It was to make the smell go away when we made *bak jow*, Chinese wine, my mother, my father, Lincoln too. The smell told everybody what we were doing. When they roasted coffee beans next door, sometimes the baking bread smell and the incense helped. Or when it rained. That helps. I bet it rains a lot over there. 'Singing in the Rain.' That's Gene Kelly."

"I think it rains and snows a lot in the winter. The ocean freezes."

"I could never live there. I'm too used to the weather here. No snow. Summer's not too hot." Her tea has settled nicely, and her face seems warm and friendly towards the spread of lunch steaming in front of us.

My clearest impressions of childhood are of watching and being watched over by what I first imagined were Indians. I was, I'm sure, always wrapped in Aunt Mary's warm custody, not exactly in the bosom of her embrace, but secure. There were the odd times when I was very young, the summers with Uncle Lincoln. But if asked, I said I lived with Auntie Mary and my older brother Peter. When I stood behind Peter, I felt protected from the curious eyes of Mary's brothers, their constant scrutiny fixed on him as we were sent from one household to the next. But there were always Indians, always present, appearing only as shadows, wallpaper intaglios, chiaroscuro figures, plotting, deciding, constantly observing Peter, me, and Auntie Mary busy with another orphan child Lincoln or Wick had dropped at her door.

I was the Indian, a papoose, the orphan Indian child. Uncle Lincoln once planted that suggestion in jest, and once he did, I took great comfort in the attentive observations offered by these invisible ancestors. In recollection of the times, of the place we inhabited, I now recognize the careful scrutiny the country focused on our existence, our well-being. Another Asian war was ending, and we were, again, the hapless victims whose confessions earned our place in America, just as it has always been in the family where everyone has a place, a role to play.

For me and Peter, for Lincoln and Wick, orphans, in-laws, and their extensions served to swell the crowd at weddings and banquets, traditionally a show of influence, of force. The immigrants of the diaspora had to be practical. Families had been isolated by famine, war, and immigration. The ties of filial duty through marriage provided a strategic opportunity to muster allies in bad times. And women were the keystones to a culture in exile where customs and accommodations evolve. Women as wives favor their own families, avoiding their mothers-in-law if any exist, as often they did not in the truncated extensions of the time. A mother is a nostalgic, always painful reminder to both husbands and wives of duties versus deeds. For a son, she is a duty left undone, an unkept promise to return, to China, to Chinatown. For a daughter-in-law, the figure of her husband's mother standing guardian at the door next to the umbrella stand—one eye watching American game shows, the other marking entry as well as exit— is the traditional filial nightmare. Sisters become other men's wives and mothers, their filial duty done at birth.

Another Asian war had passed. Only Auntie Mary was left. Her sisters had become other men's wives, while Mary, who nearly died from fever before her fourteenth birthday, who refused all arrangements of marriage, who faithfully tended our grandmother's lotus feet, remained, content to share the seat overlooking Portsmouth Square, growing herbs in the window box, listening to the rise and fall of the ocean of voices, the tides of the city come washing past her perch, tending China's orphans. Finally, with Mary's grandmother dead long enough to heal the legal disposition of the ancestor's estate beyond the statute of limitations, Auntie's brothers sold the building and divided the profits among themselves. They complained that Peter was grown up but still joined at the hip to Mary—worse, to the reputation of Wick. At least that was the reasoning, that public knowledge of their relationship would force our eviction, scatter us for good.

On a warm spring evening Peter and Wick assembled a farewell supper for our lost home, our Chinatown flat.

We were met beside that lotus-covered door once more.

We were bereft, especially Peter, who had made Auntie's third-floor Chinatown aerie a laboratory for inventions of all sorts, indulged, secure. He remembered Lincoln teaching him how to cook, and Wick as Mary's constant companion. I was too young to understand then that it was the only home Peter would ever remember, where our exile began.

Why is this night different from all other nights? I'm dressed, or undressed, playing St. Stephen as Little Beaver, an elaborate outfit I've assembled, a chest shield I'd made in crafts class with beads and colored plastic straws, Mary's gift of a sleeveless suede vest, and soft moccasins lined with plush.

I was the last of the ten little Indians, the naïf, the savage. I was her foundling, an Indian child left on the doorstep in a reed basket. The Indians were my real guardian angels, not the sisters at Catholic daycare. They watched over and protected me from afar, peering from behind the bushes in the park, from the dark corners of my bedroom, their shrouded silhouettes on the wall on cold evenings, silently minding me.

I am stripped to my breechclout and moccasins. Wick mixes body paint made from ink sticks, powdered tempura, and egg white, and ties feathers to my hair. He has brought me armbands, bracelets, and bells I could wear round my ankles. "Unmentioned, but untamed, a mighty hunter, undeniably good-looking and strong."

"He is probably the last." Peter stands at the dining room table dicing bitter greens for a quick soup with chicken feet, a few dried beans. "There's not much left in the wigwam. Long time no see buffalo, Kimo Sabe."

"Perhaps the Great Spirit should be asked for takeout?" Wick suggests. "There's one salted duck egg left in the icebox. Unless Peter can perform a miracle."

I was always ready to perform in Peter's miracles. "Should we say a prayer? Ask God to bless our journey?"

"The eviction," Peter calls from the kitchen. "Our exile." Always fearless in the kitchen, Peter loved to improvise. And this night is no different from all the other nights we'd spent together—except that it is.

Dear Peter has reached his majority, and he determines that it is the pursuit of love that is life forever, the endless opportunities that will keep him eternally young. Peter, slim as a knife, swims at the Y, shuns the kung fu studios, but loves the tai chi dance that Auntie joins in the square early in the mornings with a small group of elders. I see them from the window seat every morning, watch their figures emerge from the drifting gray fog that rises from Kearny Street fronting the park up the terraced knoll. Their bodies are centered. Their arms and legs move to the cadence of the metered amber traffic lights, blinking metronomes. They dance on a cloud with ribbons of light cast by the red neon sign in the window of the bar adjacent to the old city police station.

Peter is dressing for class, a day at the mythical campus across the Bay, splashing me with aftershave, exuberant, affectionate, beautiful with his Ivy League crew cut, brown loafers, white chinos with high cuffs, cotton paisley shirts, three-button collars, pullover V-necks in charcoal gray, in orange. Peter is blessed with very high, very pronounced cheekbones and the suggestion of dimples, which almost imply birth defects in an Asian face, a face of famine and catastrophe become somehow fashionable. Too pretty, some suspicioned. With such a rich wealth of detail, such unusually flawless skin, it was easy to predict he would attract a crowd, a camera eye that loves him. Was it on the first day of school he would preen in the mirror, "I'm early, but I want to be first."

Wick would add, "The last shall be first, Peter."

"But very old," we would chorus.

With a thick calligraphy brush, Wink paints chevrons and circles on my chest, arms, and legs in egg tempura as I watch myself in the wardrobe mirror. The wet paint glistens so.

Auntie, Peter, and Wick fought for my soul, my salvation from Auntie's brothers, who early in my education offered me up as a sacrifice to the

Chinatown missions traditionally charged with the care of orphans. I began instruction with a contemplation of *The Ascension* by Michelangelo or a photograph of Bernini's *Virgin,* immaculately aglow on her backside, while I napped on a pad in the solarium, memorizing the blue Flemish renditions of St. Stephen's martyrdom, a paean to anatomical excellence, his leg flexed and caught by the arrow piercing his upper thigh. I was fixated on the symmetry of the cherubim spiraling upward, their perfect limbs, their curls, the discrete fall of their silk swaddling, wisps woven from clouds discretely winding between their legs.

Wick lifted us out of the convent, the swaddling, the tapestry, and taught us fellowship with gusto. He cultivated our natural curiosities in our bodies with his own routines of physical culture and exercise. To lift weights, go to the gymnasium, to swim, to climb mountains was American. Peter was a confirmed disciple, indoctrinated into the regimen of weight lifting and bench exercise. I watched them working out in the evenings. These routines were for a lifetime. We would be Americans. The anatomy of the soul became explicit, became the iconic American Indian, Charles Atlas with long hair wrapped in a headband, with sculpted deltoids and pectorals. The languor, physical perfection in repose, was foreign, exotic. God was the Indian brave, stiff, upright, the next transfiguration of male grace. And Wick was Tarzan. See him swinging by a laundry line through the narrow alleys of Chinatown, every morning leading a small group jogging past the hidden basketball courts, the terraced volleyball pitch. He leads by example, where rugged individualism, a straight back, and vigorous posture are encouraged, rather than the fetal prawn of confession, digestion, and absolution so favored by the traditional Catholics of Washington Square, who see in the raised cross and the ascension a familiar hint of the Chinese loyalties the family wishes to instill in their American-born children. The subtle difference requires that we be naked.

With the language absent, there is a contemptuous familiarity in the religious practice of the Catholic church the immigrant martyrs require of their children. "To accommodate the world that surrounds us, church and family, you only know what it is to worship from the knees," Wick would thunder. Here was the other side of it, independence, self-reliance to challenge the herd loyalties of vertical descent so favored by the church and family tradition. "What the ABC's don't need is discipline, subservience. You need gusto." That old rugged cross, the camp songs sung with gusto, frank talk about domestic and human plumbing, and a bilingual joke about semen. He had no patience for traditional reticence or the inhibitions created by a childhood under constant scrutiny, of constant imitation, to recite, memorize, internalize the catechism of acceptable behavior. Candlewick, Wick to all, boundless, enthusiastic, overflowing, reaching out with all of the vigorous love and affection openly expressed that was utterly absent in the Chinese diaspora. Shunned, in fact.

The lanky figure of the young Dr. Ted Candlewick of my memory sits perched on a leather banquette right outside his office door at church camp. His long legs shoot out straight in front of him. We were always being trapped by his legs in the narrow corridors, the tiny rooms of the Haven. There were always cartons of fresh oranges and apples in his office, as well as his infamous mix of dried fruit and cereals, nuts (largesse from the Nut House), and wheat germ, gummy with honey, that we passed around in cookie tins, paper cups, a handful in a shirt pocket, which he touted for regularity, for snacks, for allergies, for long legs, for whatever might ail. We were fed like guinea pigs. We even called it pet food. But we ate it just as he ate it, leaving a trail of cereal grit and raisins wherever we went. He always wore the same blacktopped sneakers, imitation leather and crepe soles he bought in carloads for the boys' and girls' basketball teams. In our eyes, he was the virtuous man strengthened by sacrifice, a man to imitate, a father figure who could stand tall in tennis shoes.

Not uncoincident with our eviction, Wick was forced from the directorship of the Haven by a crescendo of rumor and innuendo. The homophobia that rests just beneath the idealization of men in fraternity, apostles, idolatry as an enterprise, also sent Peter to his Hawaiian paradise. If there was Wick the predatory goat, the pedophile, to be banished, there was Peter, Wick's special assistant from the time Peter began attending events at the Haven. By the time Peter graduated from high school, he was one of a small group of young apostles who all fell under the suspicion that if one were gay, all must be; that if one were a pedophile, all must be. At first, when the rumors and then charges concerning Wick's sexual behavior became public, there was barely a ripple. His special relationship with us, a Chinatown family, was well known and fidelious. I'm sure Mary and Peter would have been prepared to testify in public if anyone—including even Wick's accusers and their families—would have allowed such an airing. I think that Lincoln always knew he and Mary were conspiring with a lunatic—all idealists are martyrs eventually. Wick had been preaching to an equally lunatic choir that relished self-sacrifice, martyrdom—confession first, some spectacle equivalent to public execution, public suicide. The public seemed determined to avert its gaze. So the scandal remained in the shadows, however much the Reverend Dr. Candlewick was willing to perform his penance.

This spectacle finds a broader and more obvious parallel in the fall of the Ching Dynasty, the appearance of that selfsame millenarian spokesperson who applies that same charismatic succor to the benighted, the wretched, the poor. He fails gloriously, or in Wick's case, ingloriously, trying to invent the new man, a chimera to challenge traditional injustices, to cure the incurable, speak the unspeakable.

In America, Wick and his kind invent the cherkenduce, scattering granola and fresh fruit at the flock. Demographically segregated by the Exclusion Laws, we are condemned to an indigestible assimilation. The traditional homeopathic regimen of our ancestors is denied entry at the Angel Island immigration station. We are poisoned by the four food groups, our chi exploding out our butts in a miasma of indigestion fueled by lactose sugars. It begins with food. Out of the settlement houses, the English schools, the citizenship classes, the fight is joined to reform the diet of the Chinatown bachelor society, to exterminate all vestiges of the high salt, sugar and lard, polished rice regimen we are told will inevitably stunt our growth. We see in each other the evidence of our beginning as well as our end.

I think it began that night, the night we celebrated the eviction. Wick and Peter refused Auntie's suggestion to order takeout, pointing out that we had no chairs. We had avoided eating in public since Wick's story had appeared in the Chinese newspapers. Of course, I had no inkling. We had always eaten alone together in a fashion that simply assumed we were surviving in a hostile environment.

Peter and Wick were in the kitchen. They'd been to the gym, been fasting, a regime Wick had introduced for his apostles. Peter would have had a light broth simmering on the stove. There were the soda crackers I always dissolved in canned tomato soup, but there was no tomato soup. In an otherwise empty larder, there was that last salted duck egg and a cache of Wick's pet food in a brown bag perched in a litter of cracked seeds and a dusting of soy powder they had poured into a crock. We stood on the fire escape above Washington Street, with a view of two small family banquets in progress in the restaurant across the street, with candles guttering on the dining tables, appealing to our sense of ceremony. We lounged with our bowls of broth, soda crackers, some shaoshing wine, as we blessed the tourist pedestrians and fed the rats and mice below us with the dry slurry that slipped through the iron rails.

Some kids attending the banquet slipped out onto the balcony of the restaurant to throw fortune cookies at me, while I ducked behind the ancient jade plant and pitched its fleshy petals. Both sides were out of range, and resorted to pantomiming. Two of them were firing from the second floor balcony. They were armed with rifles, Winchester lever-action .30-.30s, judging by the deliberation of their hands locking the receiver after each shot. I had the advantage of height, but armed with only a bow and arrows, I knew that eventually I would be shot and I would die wonderfully, the anguished cry, *aiiieeeee!*, sprawling, clawing at my wound, my horse's trailing rope just beyond my fingers.

Resigned, I stood erect with my bow fully drawn as the two boys fired ridiculously, unimaginatively, impatiently ripping the ironscape with a hail of buddha-buddha-buddha burp gun hellfire, recoiling as they danced back and forth waiting for my decision, who would take the arrow. I glanced up to face the night sky, my ancestors, the invisible stars, waiting to receive me. And then it happened. A third rifleman had slipped upstairs to the darkened third floor and made his way to the adjacent balcony directly across from mine.

Now I see him, and he knows I see him, and he knows I hear the soft explosion as he rears back, simulating his weapon's powerful recoil slamming into his shoulder, into his cheek.

I was fully drawn, could feel the steel flange of the arrowhead pricking my fist. He was anchored by the iron railing, point-blank. His pantomine described the heft of a long gun, a buffalo rifle, .50 caliber single-shot, and he jerked backwards slightly, imitating the kick after percussion. He was very good. He didn't shout. He simply mouthed "Bang." I let fly the arrow and watched the arc of it pass harmlessly into the sky. I let the bullet take me in the stomach. I bent slightly, clutching myself, then bent lower, bowing almost to my knees, then falling to my knees, raising my head to acknowledge my killer, ignoring the two below who insisted on a stream of imaginary fire too anachronistically silly to account for. I died for him.

From the street below, I hear a shout. "Goddamsonuvabitch!" Was it Uncle Lincoln come to rescue me, to take me for another month in the country? "What are you guys doing up there?"

Lincoln was prospering by this time, a small-time investor piecing a share of this and that business opportunity, a restaurant, a dry cleaner, his gambling shares. There was also the manufacture of immigration opportunities as thousands fled China throughout the fifties. Uncle could finally sell the Barstow trailer takeout and leverage his investments. He became a silent partner in several enterprises, certain pai gow tables all over the state, a small office building in the Italian North Beach neighborhood with an Italian travel agency, the nearly eponymous Columbo's, which Mary and I would finally inherit. In fact, he might even have bid on the family's apartment house for spite. With the wrack and ruin of China's post–World War II reconstruction and its impending cultural revolution, immigrants were everywhere, opportunities, legion. Uncle knew two brothers who had bought what had been a bottling plant built over the artesian wells on the steep climb up Jackson Street where they manufactured and distributed bean sprouts and tofu. They were being sued by their father, who had returned after abandoning his American family and retiring to the village a year before. The father had two young wives and each had two children, so he was trying to reclaim his assets. Lincoln financed the sons' side and won a silent share, as well as a silent stare and the baleful moan of filial tradition twisted in the agony of change.

"Lincoln, come up," Auntie beckoned, "the door's not locked."

"Hey, Peter. Tell Chris to put on some pants. Everybody can see you guys out there."

I looked across to the restaurant's dining room, but the balconies were empty. The third-floor double doors were dark, shut tight. The doors on the second floor were open. I saw white people among the milling crowd, still seated, while all around them leftovers were poured into white take-out cartons, the cartons put into brown paper bags. I could almost hear the familiar ritual of division, the refusals, the excuses, the abrupt acceptance, the bounty of leftovers given to the oldest for the benefit of the youngest. I wanted to stay on the fire escape to watch the exiting guests, their scale from my vantage so adorably small. Then Uncle's words struck me and I realized that it was time to move because everyone could see me, could see all of us.

As we turned the corner and left the old Chinatown aerie behind, Mary, almost fifty years old, was still an ivory wand in a silk quiver. Lincoln, a few years older, set an easy pace up Grant, across Columbus Avenue, into bohemian North Beach, the aging Italian neighborhood, a longtime haven for the hipsters, the Beats, becoming topless a-go-go. How do I remember our leaving, how do I remind Auntie of how it was for me?

It was like a movie. Auntie's favorite film star was Rosalind Russell, but Auntie herself might have passed for Peter's favorite, Anna Mae Wong. I wondered about Uncle Lincoln, about Wick, and Mary. In my movie, I imagined that Mary was at one time secretly married, first to Lincoln, then Wick. That Peter and I were their unacknowledged children, the paper sons of an illegal marriage consummated after a Mexican divorce. Or was it Reno? Las Vegas? When I was a boy, anything was possible. Chinatown was a warren of immigration loopholes, gambling syndicates, FBI listening posts spying on both sides of the bamboo wall. And between the two of them, the four, then five of us, I could imagine foreign intrigue. Perhaps they were spies from opposite sides, two Chinas, bound by race, divided by politics, lovers at a distance. Lincoln disappeared for months on end. Auntie raised Peter and me in the illusory shadow of family cast by Uncle and, of course, Wick, who captained the steamer sailing for open water, pursued by heathens, Chinese in feathered headdresses, our two Charons, the native and the white stranger, to ferry us across the wide boulevard, across the rice paddy, to swim the harbor to freedom.

Lincoln was in the kitchen eyeing the mucilaginous goop that came from the camp mush mix Wick's crew of disciples served to every camper from their first church camp breakfast to the close of every activity, church service, and fellowship retreat—with milk, with fruit juice, or straight from the container, a handful at a time. Wick was especially adept at flinging bits of the shake at the inattentive, punctuation to break up a dull peroration. A continuously evolving recipe, the mix was dependent on the marketplace of foodstuffs distributed to charitable institutions. A high-octane concoction had found its way to the Haven, dried fruit and berries, seeds, and nuts, without artificial colorings, flavors or sulfites, and flavored with fruit juice concentrates of Swiss manufacture, gleaned from the warehouse of an outdoor recreation distributor gone bankrupt. Peter and Wick always carried some to the gym to fuel their workout.

The paper bag had been carelessly set in a puddle of white lightning Auntie had been pouring into teacups. Peter finally found a mixing bowl, but by that time the bottom of the bag was saturated.

"What's this stuff?" Lincoln scooped a small handful, ate a raisin, and guessed. "Mush?"

"It's pet food, Uncle Lincoln, for the mice." We knew each other best in the kitchen.

He laughed. "Thanks for the warning. Wild Indian food, kid. Put on some clothes. Hello, Wickman." I imagine them staring at one another, standing around a table with no chairs.

"Lincoln."

"What are you feeding everyone here?"

"Breakfast cereal."

"Too sweet."

"We mix it with fresh fruit, milk. Dry, it stores forever."

Auntie Mary stepped tentatively into the kitchen, alien territory this night. "We were having a little farewell ceremony, saying good-bye to our view of the park. Are you joining us? There's spring in the night air, Lincoln. The fog never materialized. Shouldn't we be planning a trip to clean the graves?"

Lincoln pinched a bit of the wet cereal and let it sit on his tongue. "You left the door open, right? Besides, you and Chris," he looked at Wick and Peter, "you have to move. You have to get out of town. I'm here to show you the way. We'll go get something to eat, and talk about where you want to go. I have a friend who might have something for you. I did him some favors. He owes me one back."

"Another favor for a friend." Auntie was looking at Wick and Peter. "How exciting."

"Not this time. It's really a favor for me."

"Intriguing, so mysterious. Let's get dressed, Christopher."

Auntie insisted that I run a bath and wash the paint off, and by the time I was dry and dressed in my parochial corduroys and sweater, Peter and Wick were seated around the table, watching Lincoln, his jacket on a kitchen stool, his sleeves rolled up, his hands covered with a thick slurry of cereal. They'd opened an ancient paper carton filled with herbal medicines in apothecary jars and had emptied the various tinctures of ginseng suspended in oil into the mix. There was a paper envelope of cinnamon sticks and strips of hawthorn, cloves, some chrysanthemum root. Here they were again, the sorcerer and his apprentice. Sweet tinctures of flowers that had crystallized were scraped into the original recipe.

"What are you making, Uncle?"

"A mess." Peter kept tasting as Lincoln added dribs and drabs, asking, "What do you think?"

"It's very sweet, herbal sweet. Tastes like a cough drop."

"There's a little milk in the icebox," Wick suggested.

Lincoln shook his head. "Don't make us fart, padre. Chris is allergic."

"Right, of course. Lemon juice?" He held up a plastic lemon squirt.

"Little bit."

Peter held up a clear glass vial with what looked like a newly formed child floating in amniotic fluid. "Korean ginseng. Who's the spy that brought this?"

"Yeah, hot stuff, Peter. Chop it up real fine. Don't want the government catching us with contraband in the closet." Uncle brushed past with the back of his hand encrusted with oatmeal. "What do you think, boy?"

I poked at it, and a large glob gathered on my finger, which I was determined not to taste. "It feels like warm cement. What's it going to be?"

"I don't know yet. A secret weapon, maybe the atomic bomb, okay?"

Later, reimagining the story, Wick would remind us of all the immigrants who had transformed the world, clever and inventive agricultural scientists who crossed fish and fowl, animals, flowers, the Bing cherry, the white lightning distillers, the applied agronomy traditionalists among the many immigrants who saw America as a laboratory of opportunities, the aquaculturalists who routinely planted carp, crabs, snails, and watercress in the park lakes and reservoirs. Lincoln had spent that very day agreeing to invest in the expansion of the bean sprout and tofu plant in an abandoned brewery built over an artesian well.

"There's *mui heung*," Lincoln added over dinner. Uncle had ordered a feast that even allowed for my own prejudice for eating a single dish at a time rather than spearing from all the dishes set before us. I had my own serving of paper-wrapped chicken. "Where do you think that came from, right? Salted fish in oil from Monterey, where that Lam woman made her fortune exporting dry fish to China. Chinese in China love that stuff, coming all the way from Chinatown. Her daddy was a scholar who wrote the poem on the package, all that feng shui stuff about the wind and water magic that dried the American fish she hung on a clothesline. No more laundry after that. Cheap to make, and pretty. *Hai peng, hai leng'a.*"

Wick reminded Lincoln of the dried squid caper.

"OK, sure," Lincoln began. "The Chinese guys started shipping dried squid to China. Nobody could figure out why. You know, squid is common in China. But they had a trick. They put a few squid for show in a big barrel of salt. Then they sent it past the British collecting tax on salt. Salt was easy to gather on the coast, but it was taxed when it moved inland from the sea or overland from the salt mines. One squid in a barrel of salt. *Hai peng, hai leng,* right?"

It was an evening of conspiracies revealed. "Success is a momentary, a fleeting event, don't you think, Lincoln?"

"Just like life, padre. Momentary and filled with fleas."

Wick added sincerely, "The successful manufacture of dried fish depended on secrets that kept the flies from laying their eggs on the carcasses flapping in the wind. The maggots could devour the entire catch in a week. The shifting winds limited the amount of fish that could be dried because of the smell that could engulf the entire town. So their strategies, their tricks, were for survival only."

"Not looking for acceptance, padre. One guy's perfume, another guy's stink. That's America."

Peter interrupted. "I still love the perfume of *mui heung* steaming in a pot of rice. It always reminds me of Grandma. Or steamed pork hash."

At the mention of the old woman, Mary smiled indulgently at Peter's fond reminiscence and downed the entire contents of her teacup. "The smell of old feet."

"The oils and fats will kill you all by themselves, Peter," Wick added.

"What's the secret?" I wanted to know.

Uncle scoffed. "Insecticide. Fly spray. Big deal. Everybody knows."

"The mineral salts, like arsenic, make for a lethal gourmet morsel," Wick said, winking too broadly at Peter, then me.

"Yep. That's why you want to eat everything, try everything, kid. Before you croak, right?"

Mary watched them experiment in the kitchen, dressed in a prewar Derby suit, a gray pinstripe complete with a faded silk handkerchief in the lapel pocket, pants with enormous cuffs as if they had been rendered at the knees, and button shoes. She'd gathered her hair beneath a soft matching cap. "Stop playing with the food. Shall we go?"

Peter whistled. "You look like Betty Hutton. Auntie, get your guns."

"Okay, enough." Uncle dumped his experiment on the chopping board and began washing up. "Enough, let's eat."

Peter added a final touch, shaping the cereal patty into a thick loaf, and set it on top of the stove. "You can paint it when it hardens up, Christopher." He grinned at me as he fingered a final dollop. "Last chance?"

"Last is first," Wick added.

"Very old," a chorus of voices.

I cherish the moment, one of those whimsical recollections. My rapidly fading Cantonese leapt magically to my tongue, and I said in perfect dialect, "Thank you, but I've just eaten." It was wonderful. I'd formed the absolutely perfect repartee and made everyone laugh. And now we would go to a restaurant well after my bedtime and I would never be sent from their company again, listening alone to their elusive banter from the next room.

We eat at the old Neon Moon, where an enormous lantern hangs from the ceiling, its carved wooden architecture intricately depicting an ancient Chinese city on the banks of an ocean teeming with fish and coiling serpents. Men with fishing poles over their shoulders, women with babies tied on their backs, houses mounted on foundations of bamboo, young boys washing water buffalo against a border of temples and pagodas, two- and three-eyed saints and bodhisattvas inlaid with bits of glass— all are lit by the tri-colored neon glare from the window, bathed in the glow of a waning moon. In my imagination it is almost dawn when the quartered oranges and fresh tea are laid. We are concealed behind cherrywood in a private booth with a curtain drawn, vestiges of the private act of public dining, none of which exists any longer. I don't remember Wick's blessing although I know he was with us at the table.

Auntie passes the fruit as Uncle speaks to us. I see him there, next to a younger Mary, a younger Peter. Their gray jackets hang on the chairs behind them. Lincoln's words seem to come from Mary, cool, reassuring, measured, even though his face is flushed from straight shots of Hennessy he sips from a teacup, his forehead, his upper lip damp with an oily sweat, his entire body bent to the table, his face hovering over his plate, his rice bowl, already old, nearly gone.

Auntie touches her lips with a corner of a cloth napkin she'd dipped in hot tea, nodding as he tells my future. He has bought a building on a street named after me in the Italian neighborhood. And that's where I'm to live with Mary forever.

Peter wants to leave. He knows better than to ask.

Lincoln shoots a look at Wick. "Go where you want. I'm not your father," he might say.

In the apartment we were about to leave forever, Peter's future was brewing. It must have sat there in the oven curing under the spot the pilot light kept warm. By the time we returned, the stone loaf Peter had shaped that evening had expanded before the outer crust had dried, leaving a fissure where the gas had escaped. There was a certain symmetry to its shape, like a gourd or a hairy melon, swollen round at one end with a long, thin neck at the other. Wick later speculated that there must have been yeast in one of the ingredients Lincoln added to stimulate the rise.

"There's lots of sweet stuff to feed the sponge," Peter said. "Or wild spores, the kind that make sourdough. Why not? Nature's own, creeping out of the open crocks of Chinatown's waffle batter, mothers brewing since the gold rush."

"Maybe you just forgot to wash your hands," Lincoln suggested.

Whatever it was—the original recipe was never duplicated, nor was it necessary since it was only the form, the idea of it that was important—that dried-fruit herb mortar became the first brick laid in the foundation of Peter's success, the Chi Bar, the first food product that he was able to market successfully. Of course, it had been Lincoln's experiment in the kitchen that made it possible. But it was Peter who had stuck it in the oven to cure it. And it was his idea to slice it hot, when it was still penetrable, and to bake it again.

"What is it?" we ask in unison.

"Taste it," Peter replies.

"Peter, it's hard as a rock," Wick speaks for all.

"It's an Italian cookie. Mrs. Francescati used to make them. Biscotti."

I say, "It's like eating grit."

Peter was certain. "Nibble a little bit off at a time. It's sweet, it's got fruit, sugar, cereal, herbs. You could carry it in your pocket, in your gym bag, it can't spoil, won't melt. It's indestructible, but easy to digest when you need quick energy, a healthy energy snack."

That night at the Neon Moon, he had been less sure. "Uncle Lincoln, Auntie knows already, but I should tell you now that I want to find a place of my own." Peter looked at Mary, avoiding Wick.

"Sure. You graduate from college. You find a job. Great," he said flatly.

Peter would never say, I want to thank you, say how grateful I am. I know you gave me everything and I can't give you anything in return, not yet, anyway.

Wick will never say what no one wishes to hear.

Lincoln always says, "Let's get out of here." The kitchen staff, the waiters, the busboys, the dishwasher are starting their meal. "Those guys want to go home."

We move into the well-lit but empty street. Lincoln leads the way, holding my hand. Mary waits for Wick. Peter has already gone away.

"Do what you want. I told you already. I'm not your father."

I'm running late.

A new Chinatown surges west of the Broadway Tunnel, surrounding the Tenderloin. Nightclubs; parlors for cosmetic surgery and massage; hair and nail salons; exotic delicatessens with a whiff of Hunan chili pepper and lemongrass soaking in rice vinegar; the ubiquitous Vietnamese sandwich, a baguette with headcheese, pâte, cilantro, and a slice of pickled daikon; and that come-hither-have-you-eaten-rice-already smile, the rice paper cartoons of the fifties, silk-wrapped parchment skin, head akimbo, eyebrows drawn to a fine stipple, lotus blossom lips. We are Madame Butterfly; we are the King of Siam, as another Asian apocalypse laps at our shores, of flood and famine, stories of revenge, whispers of fratricide.

I wave at a familiar greeting, "Thank you, I've just eaten." I watch myself appear gleamingly reflected in plate glass framed by stainless steel, as I pass the food shops sandwiched between the multilevel garage and

the urban park. Here is the molten core of us, the Mongolian grill vent-
ing an aromatic miasma thick enough to eat: sesame oil, chilies, lime,
fish sauce, the diaspora becoming the smoky fields from which our ashes
spew, hallowed be our name, Wong, Huang, Wang, Tran, Huynh, Nguyen
drowning the call of the ding-dong bells of Old St. Mary's.

We'd abandoned the city. Lincoln was back and forth to LA on his final
glide path, with Winnie holding his heart in her hands. Wick was listening to voices from the refugee camps in Thailand. Peter was commuting
to Honolulu to host a cooking show. I was living in Berkeley, and Mary
had moved to a waterfront condo, a cell in a Babylonian ziggurat on a
Bay slough south of the city, where she could observe riparian fowl, listen to the honking resident geese, and kill an occasional pigeon with her
slingshot frozen peas.

From the freeway the complex resembles a modern-day pyramid, recalling the Pharaoh's final resting place on the fringe of Luxor where the
Fellahin live in ghettos that were once funereal, where Little Egypt has
retired. Auntie's cell, a one-bedroom, one-and-one-half bath with an eyebrow balcony and double-glazed sliding glass doors, winks at the salt marsh
condos across the slough. Each side has the other to view, protected by
the sun's glare in the day, but tiny jewel boxes of life, a voyeur's confec-
tionery assortment twinkling in the evening. The building itself is sinking, and by the time it reaches Auntie's third floor outlook, she will have
been dead for a century. How easy then simply to fill the apartment with
concrete, an instant burial chamber as well as a firm foundation for the
next construction. "Some condom, ha?" Auntie jokes.

Auntie Mary and I share the couch where she wants to finish watching a rerun of *Sayonara* on morning television. "Did you know that I
was a production consultant for the Pocket Opera? I was consultant to
the Puccini Festival productions of *Turandot* and *Madame Butterfly* in
1957." We meet beside a lotus-covered door once more.

"Winnie and Lincoln called," Auntie tells me. "They stopped here on
their way from the airport." The family is gathering again, this time to
adopt Melba. "And Peter called too," she adds, to be fair, to acknowledge Twig. Auntie likes to remind me that she is still watching over all
of us. We always gather to multiply. Even Wick is drawn in—or, more

likely, told when to lend his company. After our exodus from Chinatown, Auntie keeps him staked in the yard or behind a curtain on a long leash where he can listen but is seldom seen, rarely mentioned in her company. Wick slipped in and out, finding steady work with refugee organizations managing the growing exodus from Southeast Asia.

"I talked to them, too. Winnie came by to pick up some things. Peter told me a funny story about having snake for lunch in a market in Toisan. He's investing in a goose farm in the New Territories. And his boyfriend Twig is making a record in the city, in a studio near Golden Gate Park." Wick had also called me, but I deleted the item from the list. Auntie and I are spending the afternoon together, a dim sum lunch in the city, after all.

"Snake? What's so special?" She's dismissive. We are transfixed by the screen, where Hana-ogi once again explains to Marion Brando why Miyoshi Umeki wants an eye operation, wants red buttons for eyes, for her Raggedy Andy-san.

Auntie explains. "Chinese people eat snakes in the winter. Lincoln used to drink snake whiskey, *bok jow*. We used to make it. The hard part is catching three snakes. And one has to be poisonous. You can do it by drowning three snakes in a bottle of white lightning, but we used snakes that were already dead and whiskey we made ourselves. The hard part is the cooking. We had to lock all the doors so the smell wouldn't get out. Nobody can leave. Or nobody can come home. Or find a place like this, in a condom with a window that opens to the sea. Uncle made it and sold it in Chinatown."

"Condo, Auntie." We both laugh. "Lincoln was a bootlegger?"

"Everybody made it. My father was an herbalist. He taught Lincoln how to make it. It was perfect with the restaurant business and all. You use leftover rice and you need one poison snake. Two ordinary snakes and one poison one to make the whiskey right."

Mary is distracted and threatens to thaw frozen coils of noodles in the microwave for our lunch. She imagines herself reflected in the light shimmering off a flooded rice paddy, a river bank, the Bay waters. "We eat the gall bladders." She rarely ventures beyond the Oriental garden of her imaginings.

But we don't have to. "You forgot? I'm taking you to lunch."

"I just talk about it and get very light in the head." Auntie, alone, indulges herself in her fanciful flights. "I can only imagine that's right. I never tried it. Not for girls," she adds coyly.

"Are you ready to go?"

"Look," Auntie points to the commercial on TV, the familiar cartoon figure of the kung fu fighter stripped to black tights battling the dragon which collapses in a heap as the warrior whirls around the stricken serpent, coiled in knots. A voice with an English accent and Chinese syntax describes the multiple benefits of herbal snack bars as the fighter ministers to the exhausted snake. "Chi Bars, a nutritious food supplement filled with the traditional ingredients of the Chinese apothecary to stimulate the regenerative reserves of the body. For men, for women, in eight delicious flavors. Try one today."

"That's Peter," Mary guesses.

"Maybe his voice. It looks more like Twig."

"Tell 'em 'sayonara,'" Brando drawls.

"Let's go eat." We should eat. We do eat. It's something family does, the way that introducing Melba required a dinner at the Neon Moon.

Melba was doing macramé when I met her, twisting, knotting rope, string, yarn, and soft wire into rough textured belts, rugs, and wall hangings, imitating various tribal designs, at odds with Auntie's generation that grew up swaddled in Chinese export silk—clothing, embroideries, scrollwork. "That's hers, Auntie." I point to a piece Melba has hanging in the gallery next door to Wong's Gold Shop (no relation). Right around the corner from the office, Upper Grant Avenue is a warren of Chinese grocery stores, Italian butchers, the ubiquitous head shop, espresso bars, Auntie's dry cleaner, and a friend's Chinese gold shop next door. "It's made from dyed African jute." It is already marked sold.

"I know who made that mask. I talked to her before."

A face emerges from the nest of twine and jute, with wooden dowels piercing the earlobes and nostrils, shocks of hair delineating the long skull, bushy brows, the beard, with the lips rather cunningly, I think, rendered in thin strings of the same material shaped around a laughing mouth. My arms ache clutching the dry-cleaning and I can feel sweat dripping as the plastic bags form a tight seal against my chest. Plastic grocery bags hang from my fingers. But I want Auntie's approval, so I can be patient, watching for her reaction in the glass as she eyes the face eyeing us. "You've talked to Melba?"

"Yes. I like that mask. When I saw it, I thought, well, now, it's very clever. I see the face laughing and the pot belly."

"She had it hanging at the Art Institute show and won an honorable mention."

"Yes. It's like a big mask made from all kinds of stuff. That's your friend's weaving? Her macramé?"

Melba had titled the mask "Ho Tai in Africa" after I'd mentioned the face reminded me of the porcelain figurines of the jolly, pot-bellied icon of good cheer that appear in every souvenir and art goods shop in Chinatown.

She had seen the resemblance immediately. "Ho Tai's a name?"

"I think, literally translated, something like 'good looking' in Cantonese."

Auntie says, "I told her it looks like Lincoln, that flat nose and the belly."

"It's a little expensive for a joke." I'm thinking of a different sort of house warming for the new arrangement. "Besides, Melba already sold it."

"I know. I'm the one who bought it, for the new condo. I'm making an investment, original art by a young artist. You found such a talented girl."

"She's almost thirty." Auntie's being clever again. Now I won't have to buy Winnie and Lincoln a gift. "She just looks young."

"Oh, so old." She lets her voice crack. "Listen to me, you have such good taste, and it's all from me. I've taught you to appreciate older women, haven't I? Winnie's almost the same age. In Chinese years, your friend's almost exactly the same. They can be sisters."

At the time there was still a question about whether Lincoln would marry Winnie or adopt her. Sisters, Auntie Winnie—I was anxious the family wouldn't concern themselves with the coincidence, the propriety of another scandal. Of course, it was hopeless.

I am by this time perspiring noticeably. Melba's past a major hurtle. Auntie and Winnie will become allies, for they have me in common. Everyone must have their role. Winnie guards Uncle's door. Auntie likes to test her lately evolving fragility on Winnie just as Winnie learned to lean on Auntie's advice, even after she left me.

We make our way across Columbus Avenue to the garage under

Portsmouth Square, so I can drive her home, Mary listing the chores stitched with the latest gossip, Lincoln's decline, more business, her own macramé to weave my newest identity into the fabric of the family.

Winnie positions Melba's mask in the entry hall of Uncle Lincoln's new Embarcadero penthouse to face the front door.

"That's better than the mirror, Winnie."

"The mirror guards the door. Do you know about feng shui, Chris?"

"Cold water?"

"Wind water." Mary and Winnie, they laugh together as one. "Never mind."

The flat is filled with the usual Chinese teak and rosewood, marble table-tops and split bamboo Auntie has taught Lincoln, then Peter, and now Winnie to shop for, to buy for a song in Asia and ship in a corner of a container filled with Uncle's various enterprises: locks and keys, shoes, whatever the import market will bear. And its position among a collection of porcelain vases, the riot of cloisonne and brass figurines from Thailand, the rough fiber mask seems appropriate. Among her most recent collections, Winnie keeps a farmer's raincoat, made from straw, that hovers over the dining room table and a handmade broom in a stained wooden bucket she rescued from a paddy-water fisherman who used it for bait and fertilizer. Winnie appreciates handmade crafts, the utilitarian aesthetic, has an eye for the disruptive confluence of east and west, as her furnishings suggest. She and Auntie share a love for very heavy, very dark rosewood furniture that reminds me of institutions like Shepherd's Haven, of waiting rooms filled with decorative touches arranged in chronological order: from Neolithic arts and crafts through the ages of iron, bronze and copper, natural fibers, ceramics, and the scrolls to honor calligraphy. Peter, rather meanly, describes the almost museum-like order of Winnie's aesthetics as neo-Hyatt Macau. But he likes to think he's seen it all. As yet another cultural revolution turns China into a huge garage sale, Peter and Lincoln lend their jaded eyes, their cash, to the undiscriminating vendors. The novelty of an artist actually producing something original must be amusing to them. But Auntie and Winnie understand.

"So, what do you think?"

"I think you and Auntie were absolutely right, Winnie."

"Yes?"

"It looks exactly like Lincoln, but more. He guards the door."

"We'll see. Wild, wooly stuff in his smile. I'm making tea?" Winnie brushes away a bit of jute from Melba's mask clinging to her sleeve. "I hope you don't mind. I'm not interfering with your new friend too much?"

I nod as often as I can to make her comments appear seamless. How can I explain to Winnie the way Melba gnaws at me. But they have their ways. All of them do. Winnie has the habit of watching my expression. When I appear confused, she stops abruptly, searching for a new approach, a new strategy. We're so much closer now, better as siblings than as spouses. It's Auntie's influence.

Auntie's aging, but she still keeps an eye out for me. "I don't know how you two stayed together at all.

Winnie asks, "Mary said your new friend was married before? They had a Chinese baby? How old is she?"

"Almost five, now. She was adopted by her former boyfriend—not husband."

"Never mind. I'm too nosy. We just want you to be happy." She pauses as if to apologize. "You know we both take care of you now."

I nod. Winnie always needs reassurance.

"Everybody's glad that you're not uncomfortable now," Auntie says. She leans on Winnie and takes her by the arm, leading her into the living room. "You're not feeling mad?" She sits close to me. Winnie returns to the kitchen and we're alone for a moment. "Winnie must marry Lincoln. Her immigration status requires it. Have you talked to your brother? Peter's so busy. Now he has this new boyfriend. But he came anyway to meet your new friend. I want to show him that Winnie and I are close. She's like a real daughter to me. We can say anything to each other. Peter should be an older brother to you, but he doesn't act like one. I don't know what he's going to do with all his boyfriends. And Lincoln, I know. He never tries very hard."

He never had. Not for my sake.

I'd begun to notice that Auntie seemed to repeat what we always let pass without saying, probably for Winnie's sake. But Winnie already knew. We'd been married. I don't need to mention Wick or Peter. I don't need them now. I had never felt so oddly confident, suddenly secured by Auntie's open expression of loyalty, her need to repeat our unspoken confidences, passing her mantle of responsibilities to Winnie to share.

Auntie loved me when she held me back from the traffic rushing past the corner, when she fed me, dampened my bruises with Seagram's, took money from her brothers' pockets to send me scurrying down the stairs to school. Rarely, if ever, do we say "I love you." I had to be coached to utter such phrases, and only when some immediate reward, some tangible exchange was at hand. "You love me" is self-serving. "We love each other" is a weather report. But "I love you" was always submissive, a bribe, obsequious.

Auntie's called a cab. "I have more shopping to do. Stay, finish your tea."

Alone together after Mary leaves, Winnie takes both my hands in hers. "Even if I marry with Lincoln, I'm watching out for you, Christopher. Like Mary." Her breath is sweet in my face, her lips close enough to kiss. I want to wrap my arms around her, crush her in my arms. I'm wanting what can't be, of course—certainly not in Lincoln's new apartment. But there is an ache in the physical space between us that Winnie fills, that is different, that doesn't touch Melba. I feel heat radiating through her hands. "I can't call you 'Auntie,' Winnie." I lay my offering at her feet and look at my shoes.

"Think of me as your *'dai day.'* You know what that means?" I feel her hand on my face.

"Older sister. I know. Thank you." I can't look at her any longer or I will do what I know is unseemly.

Suddenly, she lifts my face to hers and kisses me, a warm seal of approval, of acceptance, that my own delirious confusion makes vaguely erotic. I hold very still, a momentary compression. It's no brushing of lips, no playful teasing, no prelude, I'm being kissed conclusively, held firmly, I can feel the tips of her fingers touching my ears, her warm palms under my chin. Her lips, tissue-soft as they touch mine, are pleasantly tense and immediate as she lingers a moment before moving my face back an inch to stare into my eyes. I'm frozen in place. I can even taste her lipstick. It's as if I've been caught chewing the host at Holy Communion. In my father's house.

She grins. "You have to be a good kisser for your girlfriend. Are you all right? Christopher? Close your mouth." She's laughing and I laugh and we have the rest of the afternoon to draw us together. "Just sit there. I have some fresh peaches we can have with some smoky tea, if you like."

Always food to fill the breach, to heal, to hold me in place until I can speak again.

I move closer, aroused. I try to catch her hand across the coffee table, but she locks my wrist with her fingers and turns me aside. "We can't here." She smiles. "What do you tell your new friend about us?"

"Nothing. I can't. I could but I don't have to. She'd understand. She's had others, ex-husbands, friends, who knows?" Even as I sit back on the couch, I hear in my tone the asinine petulance under my attempt to be worldly. Winnie lets it pass, lets the old friend's lies pass without remark. She skins a peach while I help myself to a plate of peanuts and strands of dried cuttlefish, a staple of a distant memory of an old woman who seldom spoke I called *Ah paw*, who used to bag these snacks for the Chinese movie houses on Saturday afternoons, red ginger, dried plums, salt and sweet.

"The little casino where I was a dealer kept the dishes filled for the customers. Did I tell you that already? You never ask about me anymore."

"I want to apologize. I can't make the same assumptions about us any longer. I'm really trying. It's just that Melba makes me feel not quite substantial enough, like I'm too young." Winnie watches me carefully. "Like I'm too young again."

"You're a catch, Christopher. You have a business, you're not so young and foolish. So your new friend has a little girl, an adopted Chinese baby?"

"I told you. They weren't really married, and it was her friend who adopted Meiling in Peru."

"That's the daughter's name? Meiling?"

"It sounds Chinese, don't you think? They probably took it from the movies."

"Or a brothel. In Peru. You're getting peach juice on your shirt." She dabs at the drip with a paper napkin. "I'm glad you found this one. You need some one to take care of you."

"No, I don't want that." She listens. "I want to look after her. We've both lost something. Does that sound strange?"

"No. I know that feeling. I already had it when I met you. Now I have Lincoln who needs taking care of. This one and that one. We're all birds of a feather. More tea, Chris?" The dried squid is very salty, but it does make the peach taste so sweet. There's something triumphant in me, something I want to savor.

"You'll bring Melba up to see where we've hung her mask?"

It's Melba. It really is Melba. How clear it all seems. "I will. You'll like her, I mean, I hope you'll like her as much as I do."

"Mary already knows her. Isn't that a coincidence? She wants me to arrange the dinner."

"Yes, of course. She already told me."

The family met Melba under the Neon Moon.

"I'd love a garden again, and grow vegetables, pick ripe fruit, squash bugs. I had that in Cielos. In Bolivia?"

I stood by the door watching them. Melba was perched on a stool between Peter and Wick. She was wearing a silk dress with a high Mandarin collar, turquoise, with matching frog fastenings from the neckline to the hem, an antique in perfect condition she discovered junking in the neighborhood. The sleeveless design left her arms bare to a single jade bracelet on one wrist, and something silver, probably Mayan, on the other. "We lived surrounded by tropical rain forest. I don't need jungle. But I like dirt." I'd never seen her so elegantly appropriate, in the company of my foppish cousins. She was even drinking a martini, the stemmed glass rolling expertly between her fingers.

I'd found them in the new bar of the old Neon Moon waiting for me. Winnie's message said eight, and they'd been prompt.

The new owners had demolished the place, the cheesy lamps-of-China motif with its multitiered pagodas illuminated by winking Christmas tree bulbs, the tapia-cloth wallpaper and split bamboo molding, the plaster pagoda dogs crouching by the moon gate, the arched bridge over the wishing pond, the laughing Bodhisattva nicked by coin tossers chasing fortune cookies—all gone. Thick translucent plastic studded with television monitors and light fixtures ran from floor to ceiling, laminating the entire room. The ceiling, walls, even the bar glowed with a shifting spectrum of light playing over the reflective surface. The TVs looped Japanese disco videos. The dance floor was a mirror framed by the same translucence that would magnify the frenetic strobes hidden in the ceiling, a black light that made the dancers glow in the dark when the music and lights were synchronized, pulsing to a disco beat. Later, we would watch the spectral Twig become a skull and skeleton in the glow of the Neon Moon.

By no coincidence, Wick was there. The two of them, Peter and Wick, had dressed for the occasion in matching white suits and vests and the customized aloha shirts—made from the menus of the old steamship companies that traveled between Honolulu and San Francisco—that Peter had worn on his first TV broadcast in Hawaii.

Peter was tipsy, showing off his shirt. "I have the wine list and dessert menu on my back."

Wick waved his cocktail in the air, watching it turn a deep shade of Neon Moon blue, already deeply involved in his discourse. "In the Islands, we only see things from the fortieth floor of a condo. Golf courses and the pakalolo patches take up any serious horticultural endeavor, and that makes dirt very expensive. Of course, there's the aquaculture the native traditionalists have started. But niches for new immigrants, first-wave Chinese diasporatics, then South Vietnamese military and government, everybody who can get out, got out. You've heard of the Cambodian butchery.

"So it's business as usual in the land of the free. We hear the pitter-patter of cheap labor and free enterprise in sandaled feet shuffling up the boulevards."

Peter waved. "She's lovely, Chris. Stop eavesdropping. It's safe."

They turned and their smiles turned neon as some loose spectrum of light caught the enamel in their teeth.

"I love your family, Chris." I felt Melba's hand slip comfortably inside my jacket, her thumb against my spine when I bent to kiss her.

"You're drinking?"

"Your brother is a bad influence. I haven't had martinis in years. They were a six o'clock ritual for my parents. Go ahead and take a sip. It's making my lips all numb."

We eat a fixed menu in a newly renovated booth. The rosewood panels are gone as are the curtains that once gave dining a dusty privacy. Diners are here to be seen in the new venue. The tabletop is a series of three revolving concentric circles, each smaller by the width of serving dish, made from smoked glass. It is a meal with a variety of finger foods Melba can fold or roll to her liking, Winnie's indulgence, an easy test, true and false, yes and no. Is she vegetarian? Can she use chopsticks? Is she a finicky eater? There are no challenges here: a soup steamed in a melon etched like an urn; parchment-wrapped chicken; minty pork, cilantro, and pine nuts she could gather in a lettuce leaf; a sweet-and-sour rock cod, deep-fried with green cherry eyes and a maraschino between its gold blistered lips, a puffed smile, curled like a comma on a bed of tomato, pepper, and crisp white onion shells; a bird's nest woven from fried bean threads filled with mushrooms and quail eggs; a tea-smoked duck with steamed buns Melba can mop hoisin with; and a cool almond Jell-O for her dessert which she says smells like hand lotion, which it does.

Winnie points to the head shots of Twig on the sandwich board by the bar. "Peter, what beautiful tree did you cut Twig from? He's too pretty." Winnie watches Melba and Uncle carefully. Melba is a little distracted by drink, but never Winnie. The boys are bent, however, and testy.

"He's an interesting example of the lush windfall you find all over the Island." Wick sits uncomfortably between Auntie and Lincoln.

"Wick's jealous. Hates it when I pick up fresh fruit off the sidewalk."

"I didn't know you were in Honolulu." Auntie will always know where Wick is, but not often why. It was painful for her to guess, I suppose. "Business?"

"Creative enterprise absolutely, Mary. We have in tow a group of Miao tribespeople who served with American military units and are now warehoused in camps in Hong Kong, Bangkok, and Manila. Some have made their way to Honolulu, but most are right here in Oakland. So I'm looking around for ways they can start earning a living."

Peter waves his lettuce wrap at Winnie. "Do you taste the coconut milk, the rich finish it gives to the sauce?"

"Of course. It's your recipe. I gave it to the kitchen for tonight. Auntie and I tape your lessons."

"Auntie's cooking?" Peter teases. "Where's my invitation?"

"She's teaching me. She tells me everything to do."

Peter watches as Wick passes samples of bracelets and necklaces strung with tiny animals and familiar totems carved in what looked like discolored ivory. "Aren't these clever?"

"What are they made from?" Melba smiles. "Some sort of animal bone. Teeth?" Her tongue flickers across the profile of a tiger.

Uncle sees this and smiles approvingly. "I'm not sure. Whatever was left over from dinner."

"*Hai peng, hai leng.*" Winnie fingers the carving with an appreciative touch.

"They're using whatever material they can get their hands on. They all do craftwork and the women sell whatever they manufacture while the men collect recylables of all sorts. The church has a center in Oakland." Wick's eyes glisten with enthusiasm. "War's not over yet."

"How are you, Lincoln?" In their drag, Wick is always edgy around Lincoln.

"Better than I look, padre, comme ci, comme ça." He waves at the pulsing lights leaking from the bar, coloring their white suits in electric pastels. "The light shaking like that makes me seasick."

Peter shoots back. "Bad sailor, Uncle?"

Auntie isn't listening anymore, so Winnie engages Melba in her version of food talk, safe talk, to fill the breach. "We never eat here since they changed." Winnie begins to list the reasons, but she needn't have bothered. Melba lives on vegetable broth and egg whites. But for the show, for the challenge she's braced herself with a second martini. She splits the fish cheeks with Lincoln and tells him she thinks the eyeball he lays beside her green cherry tastes like drawing paper.

"Uncle Lincoln," she puts a half piece of fruit on his plate with her chopsticks reversed, "I think they cheated you on this one. It tastes like a dyed grape." She rips at the lips and pulls the crackling off, sucking at the glutinous jaw. They eye each other respectfully. "I love fish heads, don't you?"

"Now I love little girls who know how to eat," Uncle beams. "They always use those dyed grapes for decoration. Nobody eats 'em."

"That's silly. They should use lichee or kumquat, something fresh."

"Well, next time you and me'll have the kitchen do something special."

"Like what?"

"I don't know. Have you had snake before? Frogs?"

"When we lived in Bolivia, we butchered beef, so we were always looking for a trade. Bet you haven't had armadillo. That's good."

"Armadillo? Oh, sure. I get that in Texas when I'm visiting Houston. Hang 'em to dry out a bit, then soak 'em in bourbon. Very tasty."

"Monkey? Fresh monkey?"

"Yep. Tastes a little like elephant, more like elephant foot."

"Guinea pigs and puppy dogs' tails," Melba slurs. "Rats. Chris told me about rats that feed in the rice paddies."

Peter wants to claim the most exotic. "That's my story. He doesn't know. Get those skewered on a stick for the bus ride just outside Canton City. Yessir, fresh dragon eyes and rat meat for the road. You always look for one with a thick tail. Meatier."

Auntie pats Melba's hand. "You must not encourage him. It's really terrible for everybody else's appetites. Lincoln's why I never like to cook."

"Bugs?" Lincoln insists.

Melba tries to subdue herself, holding the question in the air. "Well, I ate a caterpillar once."

"Really?" Lincoln challenges. "With hair?"

"With feet." She giggles uncontrollably. Uncle and alcohol will always have that effect. "It was an accident. Fell in my salad. Does that count?"

"If you remember, it counts, sure." Uncle's voice falls away.

Melba turns to follow his gaze. They emerge, exotic Indians with bandanas knotted around their heads, a troupe of kung fu warriors in silk jackets, fresh collar and cuff linings gleaming white against the black silk, their faces painted in Day-Glo pastels. It's the band. A figure nods at Uncle, who raises and lowers his head in an exaggerated greeting. For that moment, we are set aside for another, more pressing business that holds our entire attention. It's Twig passing in the night. Twig with his Yuon groupies, Laotians, Vietnamese, Cambodians, migrating from Phnom Penh to the Shekou transit camps in Hong Kong to Honolulu, to San Francisco. He's a bit taller than his companions, still bone-thin by American standards, but with the compressed bulk in his upper torso all these street warriors achieve by pumping iron in camp, in jail, worshiping Bruce Lee. Their faces are so young, so featureless, like a clutch of newborn mice. I can't tell the boys from the girls as they glare out from their moving pack, their litter, eyes narrowed to slits as they move by extending across space, a pulsing amoeba.

Twig's magnetism is not lost on any of us, even as we hear their voices break, the street patois, almost fey, in their stabbing chatter and haughty posturing. He greets Uncle and Winnie, kissing the cheek Auntie offers and winking an eye done in purple eye shadow and lead-white brows at Peter. They're on tonight. Twig has his performance hauteur cinched tight, tighter than his pants.

Wick turns suddenly despondent. I know why. He understands here and now that Peter is free.

After Melba left me, I was always asking Auntie what I should say. She would sigh a little impatiently. "Why do you ask me now after she's gone?"

Mary is never angry with me, only impatient. After Lincoln's death she would never be never quite the same. And there would always be Wick to worry over. I'm sure in her mind, Winnie and I might have married again. After all, just as she'd managed Winnie's departure, she'd managed Melba's too, then tried to coach my response. "You and Melba are all finished finally?"

"We're not divorcing. We want a trial separation."

"Not more practice?"

"Auntie, I'm not mad. Why are you?"

Auntie ignored the question. "Is it because she's an American girl?" She reached for a piece of duck with chopsticks gripped at their base, maneuvering across the table for a fat piece with a thick rind. "You should eat something." Auntie's generation remains endlessly curious, fascinated, perhaps even attracted to the ease with which the next generation dissolves their marital unions. But then, Auntie's generation says "American" when they mean "white." Peter, on the other hand, makes a point to say "white" when he means "white," except on TV. For Auntie, Melba's an American girl; for Peter, she's a white girl.

Melba, my white American wife—red hair, pale skin, freckles, green eyes, an authentic nose—has really left me. I speak of our separation to Auntie with a facsimile of grace, honor. I love her still, but we have agreed for the while to live apart. Wick's the only one I can tell who can absolve me in confession. And nobody else cares, not Peter, not Winnie, and really, not even Mary.

Melba still calls as if to let me know she needs me. But it's me. I can't let go. It's a far cry from our first months together when she took to dressing herself in a black silk padded jacket, snap-in white cuffs and collar with padded buttons. In her shades, her brunette curls ironed straight and dyed ink black, she wound up looking a little like a tong moll. She even dabbed Tiger Balm as a perfume. It was a time.

"You're back, from Mexico City? Sure, that's great. Tomorrow in the city?"

"No, the bookstore at the landing. I'll take the ferry. I don't want to drive."

"The ferry doesn't go from Berkeley to Marin. You're going to take a bus to the city?" Somehow I couldn't imagine Melba on the bus, never mind walking. "We can meet in Berkeley, if you like. I don't mind driving."

"No. I bought a bicycle, a mountain bicycle. I can BART the bike to the city and ferry to Larkspur, then bike to Sausalito for the ferry back to the city and BART back." In the San Francisco Bay Area, that's what passes for mass transit.

"I haven't been inside a car since I got back. I hate the polluting traffic mess, the stink, the fumes. God, Chris, get out of it once in a while, smell the air. Don't add to it. I don't know how you do it. You cross the Golden Gate every day, gorgeous monolith that it is, and you spew carbon monoxide all over it. The mouth of the most glorious bay on the West Coast, and it tastes like an ashtray."

We meet for brunch at the Artichoke, grazing on sprouts and sirloin-shaped grilled tofu with a pat of parsley butter.

"I'm making money, you'll be happy to know. The microgarden." Melba had become a Berkeley foodie and joined the backyard tenant farm industry. Her raised beds deliver freshly culled organic toy tomatoes, peppers, arugula, and baby lettuce daily to one of the glitzy gourmet restaurants overlooking the mudflats.

"Too many lunches with the Wong people." I study the menu. "I was in Long Beach with Winnie. Mary's in the hospital again."

"I'm sorry." She pokes at the salsa with a blue cornmeal chip. "Long Beach?"

It is no coincidence. "A heart specialist Winnie has always had eyes for. Buried Lincoln."

"An old friend, right." She holds the waiter's gaze, a young blonde boy in whole wheat all-cotton coveralls, a turquoise choker, a winter tan, conspiring lunch. "Ciao, bello. The vegetarian mixed grill?"

"Excellent choice; arborio rice or Mayan groats?

"Groats, and the Arctic mineral water."

"Sir?"

"The burger."

"That's a quarter-inch sirloin of tofu marinated in tamari and ginger grilled in a bulgur crust."

"Bulgur?" I'd left my reading glasses. "And tofu?"

"Yes, it's a soybean product."

"I know what tofu is."

"Yes, sir. And to drink?"

"Coffee."

"Pero?"

"Si."

She laughs for my effort. "Not your style, Chris. Sorry. But I can't even smell meat these days. I hear that even Peter's experimenting these days, Amsterdam light."

"No problem. You're both right. At my age with all this grass around my feet, I should be grazing lower on the food chain. So, how's you?"

I love to watch her play with her food. She tears off a piece of a warm whole wheat tortilla and fills it with salad, picking green bits, a carrot curl, a bit of tapénade, then takes a careful first bite, stuffing stray bits of alfalfa spouts into her mouth. She's wearing loose cotton pants and a jacket the color of fresh oats, over black spandex. Melba became a vegetarian after successive vegan, mucous, macrobiotic, and fruit experiments, all leaving their indelible imprint on me. "You must be hungry" is the only thing I can ever think of to say to her when we meet.

"Starving, famished." She's learned to brag about her appetites. Hidden behind the menu, her reading glasses propped owlishly on her nose, Melba scans the terrace.

"You look terrific." I say that with all regrets. I remember her best at the commune, in the summer, deeply tanned. She would cinch her denim cutoffs from behind, hooking her thumbs in the belt loops, hitching them higher, the frayed cuffs riding her thighs, revealing a band of white skin, protruding hip bones, her brown torso muscled and drawn deeply at the midriff. The aroma of coconut oil and poolside chlorine, and something else—she would have been chewing cloves with her latest boyfriend— would curry the air as steamy clouds rose over her shoulder from the hot tub, looking like some exotic tureen perched in a tree house.

We married and stopped eating.

Older now, she's developed that flattering, inviting gaze nearsighted women affect, her peeling sunburned nose, her large green eyes quiet waters, a myopic shimmer that gives the illusion I have her undivided attention. She's colored her hair, a reddish hue crowning the darker brunette waves. And she's plucked her brows to an anorectic scar favored by the gelato punks who lounge about the town fountain to watch their fathers' trophy wives. She tells me she's experimenting with an all-fruit diet.

"I do, don't I? I feel good too. It's all the exercise." Her pale complexion, freckled but smooth, catches the warm sun, curves toward the bright lights thrown from the water, from the sky. "You've put on some." No prisoners. "Well, you know me. I met a guy from Santa Lucca in Belize, imagine."

"I don't have to." Food and relationships are the only safe topics between us. My food, her relationships.

"He's subbing for the assistant pastry chef at Trois Hommes, but he wants to open a small trattoria in Italy. Peter introduced us. He's quite young and I didn't even know what to say to him. I forgot that men, new men, strangers, actually look at me. I felt undressed. I couldn't tell if he was flirting when we talked about grit in the endive. I don't know how to talk to this new generation of men. I was afraid to speak when I was chewing. He pulled the chair out for me. I hardly knew what to do. You know. I sat in it. Then he tried to push me to the table and I was still too far away from the table to reach anything. He picked me and the chair up to slide me closer. So embarrassing. I still wanted to tell him to take his elbows off the table, to stop fiddling with the bread."

"Try to keep your weight on the balls of your feet when he pushes you in. You'll avoid giving him a hernia."

"He's a board-certified podiatrist but still a kid, twenty-five, loves Stravinsky, has a wonderful way with balsamic vinegars and oil, constructs fussy salads and all the garnishes. You should see them, Chris. They're corsages made from endive, escarole, impatiens. I could wear them. He's a fiendish bicyclist and doesn't even own a car. He rode across the entire country the year he graduated. I don't even try to keep up. He's up at dawn," her eyes shift momentarily past me, "riding trails or at the gym. Quite tall. Buff."

He loves women with big feet. And that's how it ends. So your feet don't touch the ground, you say. Loathsome view from the perimeter, a dread, a hollowness stalking about in my stomach. A lover with his feet caught in the spill of his pants taut at his ankles, semi-erect, proud sweet pound of meat weaving about like a pole axe. She masturbates for him and grins helplessly as she climaxes. The boor, the animal in the shadows is gorgeous, a narrow torso, abdominals darkening the sweet creases that climb to his iron-clad pecs, the vascular swollen black-and-blue road map. All buffed and polished in the dark, he leans back against the wall, his legs popping cables, his nipples stiff in my fingers, tensing at my damp caressing. I smell him, acrid, bitter, his sex.

She wraps pieces of tortilla around a smear of black bean paste, corn relish, grilled tofu, and fills her glass with glacial ice water.

"What's his name?"

"It's Ramdas, Ramdas Steinman."

I grimace. "What ever happened to Bob, Hans, Guido?"

"I know. When he told me, I made a rude noise, but he forgave me. He's very sweet, and much too young. When we first started to talk I thought he might be gay. My own stereotypes of course—a tall, well-mannered young man making small talk with an older woman."

"But?"

"But I like him. He's interested, passionately interested in the world, and he's got so much energy, infectious energy. And he's taught me how to take deep breaths, to really breathe and move, and to relax. We meditate together, sometimes zazen or watching a candle burn or we sit and watch the dirty dishes. He's very good for me."

Her hands wrapped around my neck, the top of her head lowered, buried in my chest, her hot breath against my belly, bent at the waist, her weight suspended, swinging, her tongue laving my chest as she lurches against me, impaled, her nipples caught between his fingers, she tells me over and over, her voice taut, explosive.

She's wearing me, her exotic beard, to see if anyone is staring. We look around cautiously as we pass mindless chatter across the table. The sparrows that live in the girders supporting the restaurant's roof drop to the patio, collecting small crumbs. The larger seabirds, the gulls, the terns, hold themselves at a distance, watchful, wary, eyeing the collective host we are as they watch one another. Tamari soy, sea salt, a verdant salsa, the slap of Bay water lapping quayside, the aroma of diesel fuel and tar, and words, singly, in a rush, the silent catch we've mastered for the unspeakable.

"Who? Who is good for you?" There would always be someone new.

"Ramdas, my friend? Pay attention, Chris."

Yes. She says, "Did I tell you I want to buy the house I leased? Winnie said to do it, stop wasting money."

I already knew what they wanted, what Melba wanted from me, what Winnie wanted. Auntie told me. "Christopher, you know. She doesn't need anybody anymore. She won't come back to you." Auntie had looked away as she spoke, staring past me, "But we have to help her anyway. And she trusts us as we have to trust her."

"This microgardening is right for me. I'm making enough from the garden to support myself and the house if I can put together a down payment."

"How much?"

"Not much. Winnie says she can work out a way to refinance this and that. It would be a final cash settlement. She thinks it's time we divorce."

I should have known. Winnie watches over me. And Melba—when I saw her eyes glittering at the sight of Twig that first night at the Neon Moon, I knew.

"Mahalo, people, you come dancing tonight, right?" Twig turned to Auntie and Lincoln.

Uncle Lincoln nodded. "Past my bedtime."

And Auntie nodded. "You don't need us now."

"We're gonna eat a little bit before we start." His fellows had already taken a table at the far end of the restaurant. Lincoln caught a waiter and ordered a bottle for their table.

"Now who says there's no such thing as a free lunch in America?" he snorted.

Melba raised her eyebrows at me, "Local bad boys? Are they a gang?" she asked.

Wick said, "No, my dear, its just rock and roll. Our new cousin and his band."

Auntie poured tea. "They only look that way. They play music. The Tree of Heaven, from Hawaii. That one is Twig Wong, Peter's friend. He was expressing his gratitude to Lung Gung. We found them work. Of course, Uncle thinks it's noise."

We all knew.

Wick added, a beat too late, "Lincoln likes to croon to Vaughan Monroe, Frankie Lane, ghost writers in the sky."

Uncle had had enough and interrupted. "I need some air." It might have been Melba who needed it more. "Ladies and gents, Melba and I are going for a little walk so we can finish our food talk and you can eat your dinner. Come on, girl, I want to show you a pickled cat in a jar."

"Can we taste it?'

"Naah, it's not finished soaking. Takes at least seven years." They squirmed past the extra chairs piled with our coats. "Don't leave without us. We'll be back."

Melba returns to the table alone. The Neon Moon is deserted, but we spend frenzied hours dancing for Twig's sake after Auntie takes Uncle, who has been in the kitchen talking to the cooks, home to bed. The figures on the bandstand stutter and disintegrate as the strobe lights blaze across the dance floor, tracers catching Winnie and Melba dancing with Peter in chromatic freezes, pulsing to the backbeat of the keyboard. The walls pant and writhe with liquefying hallucinations.

Back in her apartment, Melba excuses herself and goes into the bathroom. Over the running water I hear her purging, vomiting delicately. She takes a long shower. In bed, bright-eyed, flush with her bulimic effort, she sets herself adrift with talking, casting spells, the fantasies that touch her, that we might share, to tell me what I want to know, the important touchstones in her life.

I listen to the dark. It sounds like a Vespa, a little two-stroke engine whining from the bottom of Union Street, a steady unbroken keen in first gear that divides the silence of the night between the blocks of apartments and flats that climb Telegraph Hill, the keen of a buzz saw, the rattling stutter of muffler backfire at the Grant Avenue intersection, before beginning its next ascent. It turns at the top and the racket finally melds into the constant sea of respiring city sounds, a barking horn, a squeaky gate. I feel suspended by the anticipation of another, the first diesel bus muttering at dawn. It's Melba, murmuring deliciously, insatiable.

"I guessed that Twig is your brother's new friend, Chris, and I guess that Wick is an ex-friend, and I can't guess anymore. Do you want to guess about me? Nobody asked about me. Isn't that peculiar?"

"Everything they want to know is right beside me." I reach out for her. My hand slips between her legs. I feel her tense at my touch, then relax.

"Please don't, not yet. Talk to me. Make me talk to you, first. You'll just fuck me and go away. If that's what you want, it's okay." Her hands find mine under the blanket. "Don't you want more?"

"I want you and whatever else you need to make you happy. I love you. You know that. But I can wait, if you need time. Tell me what you want."

"I still see other men. I have one who's an old friend, who helped me when I came back to the States, who I'm especially close to. Do you want to know his name?"

"Is it important that I know?" She wants to tell me.

"Bill's an attorney, divorced. He's a friend of Milo's too, and helped us when Milo got caught transporting cocaine the last time he came back, one of the reasons Milo can't come home."

"If he could, if he did," I ask, "you'd go back to him?"

"No. I try very hard not to go backwards, and he's a step back for me. Bill's asked me to marry him, and I almost said yes several times. It would be perfect for us. He loves me, he's older, very steady, very stable, rich enough, and I really do think he loves me. He says so."

"But no?"

"Not yet, no. He's seen me through all of the hard times, and I'm grateful. All he ever wants is to marry me. He's very sweet. And I probably should."

"So what are you waiting for?"

"I'm not waiting for anything. I'm not like that. I'm not the kind that waits. Did you know that?"

I roll over to her side of the bed and bury my face at the nape of her neck, picking at the thin strand of gold Auntie had given her over dinner. "This is something for you," she had said, "a token. I love the mask you made. I wanted to know the face behind this wonderful mask." Melba had protested, but Auntie shushed her.

I run my fingers down the curve of her spine and she tucks herself against me comfortably. I kiss the tiny gold links into her skin. "Why me?"

"I love what you bring to me. You share your energy with me. I love younger guys. You volunteered." She cups my testicles in her hand.

"Go on. Blame it on my youth. It's all those Chi Bars Peter feeds me."

"I bought a box. I bet you can get them for me wholesale." She grips me tightly. "Listen to me. You have to know."

"Anything, everything, what?"

"I see others."

"I know."

"I never wait. If I want someone, I take them. I tell Bill, and he says he doesn't care. He still wants to marry me. Is that stupid and confusing?"

"I don't care. I want you." A fierce desire settles into me, a wanting that needs me to act, to quiet her, to turn her toward me.

"How are you so sure? How do you know? You never ask. I'm a little afraid of that part of you."

"All right." I massage her shoulders, working my thumbs behind her ears, follow the outline of her clavicle with the tips of my fingers, then slowly slip my arms around her to catch her breasts resting easy in the palms of my hands. "There's someone else you've been seeing."

"Yes."

"Are you sure you want to tell me?"

"Yes."

My hands find her moving everywhere my fingers touch, tracing a rib, her hipbone, the heated divide I can just reach as I stretch myself against her.

"He's very special to me right now. He doesn't want to marry me. But we're deeply involved. Passionately involved."

"How often do you see him?"

"Almost as often as I see you."

I know. I always knew. She begins to move against me, a sigh echoing a touch, her hands against my legs.

"Yes, no, what?" Tell me.

"We're together a lot." She rolls over and nestles against me. I feel her hands smooth against my chest. "We spent the day together, before dinner tonight."

I remember. When she came to dinner, she was freshly showered. Peter, even Wick, attentive, guiding us through the deserted alleys of my boyhood, had described the specialties of the businesses that surrounded us. Peter had Melba poking at the writhing produce sleeping behind thick glass. We'd spied an ancient gourami in a dark aquarium in the window of a store with no visible business to offer, a dark shadow resting beneath a thick layer of black moss. We could hear the murmur of voices floating past the open transom, gamblers softly at their games.

She kisses my chest. I feel her tongue making circles on my skin; spiraling down, her tongue snakes my swollen cock, and without willing I release and she holds me fast in her mouth.

Later, she comes to me again. "I made space for you, Chris. I'm so empty." She catches hold of me, urging me to enter. "Please, I want you inside me, please."

And I cradle her entirely, her back against my arms as she lifts her pelvis and lets me slip into her sex. "Do you still want me, really want me, Chris? Are you sure?"

I want to erase it all, this talk, and hold myself back for her, fill every space even as I feel her closing against me, pressing me. "I don't care, I don't. I want you. We can make a life together."

"I'm sorry, Chris," she moans. "But you have to know."

"Do you love him?"

"No."

"Is he a bad boy? Do you want him now?" She waits for me now, patient, attentive, breathless. "Do you?"

"I don't know," her voice catching as I find my inevitable rhythm. "How," she cries, "how do I know, when will I know, ever know?" she repeats.

"You'll tell me everything, always." I whisper fiercely in her face.

"Yes," she moans.

"Will you?"

"Yes, yes. I do. I will."

"Say it again."

"Yes."

"Again."

"I can't. Oh, Chris." She urges me forward. "Don't stop."

"Say it."

"Yes, yes I will, oh yes, and yes again."

"We'll be good together, I promise," I say as my passion subsides. "We just need to practice some more."

"Yes."

"Bad together, if you like."

"I like, I like." She laughs as I lick beads of sweat from between her breasts. "Again? Hmmm, so soon?"

In the dark before dawn the sound of electric breathing wakes me, holds me in suspense. Am I dreaming her urgent ministering, her hunger enveloping the numbness between my legs?

I forgave her. I could scarcely catch my breath. It was a new world, where confession was good.

5

Now I felt on the verge of control, of taking responsibility for myself. Auntie Mary had seen to my past and I had Winnie preparing my future. The world seemed full of possibilities. Melba was mine to woo and win. Her mask guarded the door from anything unforeseen from without. But I had to reckon with the past, still crowded with old loyalties and events of which I had no memory, over which I had no control, but which I couldn't ignore.

"Mahalo, son, and I thank you for the lift." On standby, Wick had caught the red-eye out of Atlanta. I was to connect him to an outbound for the Islands that wouldn't leave until that evening, an eight-hour layover—if United flew, if the fog stayed beyond the Gate. He could hide out in Honolulu for a day or a week, then go on to the DP centers in Hong Kong, Bangkok, or Manila, whichever would have him. I would have sent him directly to hell as Peter fumed when he found out Wick was again on the prowl. But Winnie had telephoned me, at Lincoln's behest—or was it Mary's—to book him on the midnight flight and provide sanctuary for the day, to hide him in our condo where I hoped I had changed the sheets.

"Are you still Columbus and is it still America? I can't tell anymore. Like your uncle would say, I'm getting too old for the trail, son. I'm saddle sore and plumb dusted." He was in bad shape, tired, with a badly infected accent, as if his mouth were stuffed with dental cotton, as was mine.

"You can call me Little Bo Peep." We shook hands gingerly. We no longer hugged. "Luggage?"

"I put it in a locker already. What's the matter with your mouth?"

"Extraction. Dr. Wong." I couldn't talk. "Toothbrush? Razor?"

"I have a kit in my pocket." He rubbed his eyes, squinting. "I'm an old hand, Christopher, and a hard-ass, I guess." We stood for a moment,

Wick holding me in his gaze, resetting the physical space between us that he could comfortably keep without having to bow his head any lower or my having to look up. "I'm not going to Mary's."

"It's okay. Winnie told me to book you through late."

I had been sent to fetch and carry. That message was clear. Wick had been caught doing something stupid, reckless. In the car I could smell the alcohol on his breath. "Now, if you can rustle up some breakfast, I'll eat and sleep and be out of everyone's hair by evening."

Once Peter took up with Twig, Wick had no reason to remain in Honolulu. So he simply slipped his leash when he thought no one was looking. After all, he had his calling, the same clamoring the entire world heard as the Vietnam peace echoed with the anguished cries of those who survived. When he wasn't fund-raising for his new congregates, he would attach himself to a radical veteran's organization mustering the American legions home. He had found a role for himself among the several agencies that had begun to work with the wave of new refugees pursuing the American withdrawal from Southeast Asia. With the capture of the South by the North, Chinatowns across the country had swelled with a new generation of Asian refugees. The collapsing diasporas in Laos, Cambodia, Vietnam, the Philippines, Thailand, and Hong Kong sent the ethnic Chinese packing, quickly followed by their tribal cousins calling for Wick and his brethren.

Wick had found a position with a resettlement center working with a group of Yuon evacuated out of Laos to Hong Kong, then Atlanta, Georgia, then Oakland. But he had dallied an extra day in Atlanta, drawn to a prayer rally for missionaries working the refugee crops in Asia. He had impressed somebody with his command of Cantonese and wound up speaking to a small group of lay counselors come together to consider the challenge of Amerasian orphans, their appropriate placement, and the adoption bureaucracy. Had he dwelled too long over the photographs? Somebody had recognized him, made a phone call, and three former Haven campers in suits had given interviews to the San Francisco newspapers, raising the old charge of sexual predation against the shepherd who raped them. Next we heard, the Atlanta police had arrested him.

"The Adventists objected to my lingering over their T-shirts. All very peculiar, actually. I was speaking to a young woman, in fact, about how easily a religious message can be misinterpreted. The simplest phrase, 'Jesus loves you,' raises unease and suspicion, becomes an off-color remark. And if we hear 'want' rather than 'love,' we ask 'Why?'"

Why indeed?

"When you're arrested, you can't explain yourself. I've learned that it's better not even to try. I left a message for Peter. I'm sure he's angry. It took two days for him to post my bond."

No lost lamb, Wick, the rogue, the senile discontent, and I, the assistant zookeeper, about to accompany the leashed beast into tropical solitary. "Better go?"

"Please."

Peter was the angriest. I thought then it was for Mary's sake. Now Wick had to be watched, had to be closeted away. But no one wants to put one and one together because the Haven still operates successfully and Peter was a TV star for a while. If Wick had just shut himself down, if he hadn't insisted, we would all have been free. No one wanted to be reminded. The newspapers ran the story on page one for a day, so I assumed that Auntie asked Winnie to ask me to provide a quick escape before somebody in secular or religious public relations put two and two together and saw Wick dousing himself with pomegranate juice or for that matter saw Peter with a Chi Bar up his ass. I just wanted out. But they were family, as even Melba understood when I called her for sympathy.

"Poor Wick. Was it a demonstration?"

"No. It wasn't about anything he did. Someone recognized him at a convention in Atlanta. I'm putting him on a plane for the Islands tonight."

"Poor Wick."

What about poor me? "Peter left him in jail over the weekend, and apparently there's been an argument. Mary's worried that the longer he's in jail, the more the publicity."

"Jail. So awful. Say hi for me. But you love him."

The arrest did shake us all, including Wick, who was more deeply disturbed than any of us realized at first. I didn't know then, but do now, that he never spent another night with Aunt Mary, never went home again. He'd had his chances.

In the car he babbles at me but I think it's from lack of sleep.

"Nobody listens. Especially the police. Nobody wants to hear. Everyone has their own little story. In the car with handcuffs on my wrists, it's TV. Officer Wong, no relation, no grammar, says, 'I ain't the judge.' They read me my rights at the station. The jailer was watching *Hawaii Five-O.* Imagine. Photographed, fingerprinted, I started to pay close attention to the brutes in front of me and behind me in line. They were reading the charges aloud. Mine, thank God, was for simply disturbing the peace. But I wanted to listen to theirs because I was afraid that one of them was going to be my cellmate. We laughed about it later because he was listening to mine."

I have my own problems. It's high noon. I'm gulping antibiotics the size of inflated leeches. Like everyone else, our dentist has moved across the Golden Gate Bridge to a shopping center in the suburbs, following a sublet Uncle Lincoln offered that our distant cousin couldn't refuse. I'd just gotten back to my desk when Winnie called for the favor. I was trying to visualize a wisdom tooth extraction, my mouth stuffed with gauze packing and a teabag to staunch the residual bleeding. The nitrous cloud made the sunlight beaming through the plate glass sparkle and spin. Winnie's call interrupted my latest meditation, one our Dr. Wong prescribed. To prevent infection from settling into the bone, I was attempting to promote the "dry hole" syndrome he discovered in the latest *Periorganic Review,* an alternative health journal that Peter had recommended on his ten-best *WokTalk* buys.

The Chinatown homeopathy is everywhere. Peter Pan *WokTalks* joined the macrobiotic movement with Chi Bars. Eat, eat healthy, be healthy. We've taken a giant step away from Uncle's takeout and moonshine. Uncle doesn't think so, of course, and Auntie Mary sees nothing new. We are reinventing ourselves, again. Ever the student, Wick likes to remind us that he dates his own afflictions to the abuse caused by his missionary father's interest in all forms of Chinese homeopathy—in particular, dentistry performed on Wick as a lad in the streets of Kowloon and Canton City where he spent his formative years. Our dentist shakes his head in wonder and disbelief at Wick's cautionary tales of abuse— the thumb-smeared amalgams, opium tinctures—but always includes some organic post-operative alternative. He recommends tea leaves to staunch the post-extraction bleeding.

"When prospective patients look past the smoked glass of my office and see a few Chinese, it makes it all the more authentic. Wouldn't you want to eat here?" Dr. Wong offers acupuncture and meditation along with liberal amounts of nitrous oxide as analgesics to what his assistant, the beautiful Leslie, laughingly refers to as "the masked and the gassed," his patients. He is especially popular among the rock-and-roll musicians like Twig who were migrating across the Golden Gate. Dr. Wong was making a fortune.

My day began with Dr. Wong spinning one of several pins he's stuck in me. "I want you to visualize a creek bed in summer. All rocks and shallow pools, dappled with water skates, dimpled with mud drying in the sunlight. Are you with us, Chris?"

"Rinse?" Leslie Luis whispers in my ear.

We've been together for more than an hour, cheek by jowl, the smell of his aftershave thick in my nose. It occurs to me that the doctor's quick black pupils have been sharpened by the nitrous oxide I exhale in his face, as my gas-fed fantasies dance from his aroma to the warm pressure of his assistant's breasts pressed against my left shoulder. Leslie's a trim young thing, a Filipina from Chicago with a Chinese grandfather, dark brown curls with red highlights framing the lovely arrangement of bones, perfect teeth, bright red lips, and enormous aviator glasses tinted pink.

As soon as the nitrous begins hissing, Leslie steps down from her wheeled pedestal, raising her chin, tilting her head, raising one perfect eyebrow. I feel a mild electric shock, and in my mind's eye, Leslie and I hold each other close, dancing to the Five Tops singing "Love is a Many-Splendored Thing." We rock slowly to and fro, tokens at an "Oriental Party" that the society columnist in the shopping news I'd read in the waiting room described as retro, fab. All the guests wear bathrobes and black wigs. With sharpened chopsticks for the famished but untrained in the art of eating with pencil stubs, they skewer "heavenly bites of morsels whose mysterious ingredients this hostess refused to identify."

"Dragon balls?" It's Peter Pan offering a tray of canapés.

"Now watch the puddle dry, Chris. The water disappears. The mud looks like mud." It's Dr. Wong. I smell his jasmine cologne.

"Chocolate pudding," Leslie breathes in my ear.

"All right, chocolate pudding." They both giggle. "The pudding skin dries smooth and tight. Underneath, it's still warm and puddly, yummy and solid. And what we want here is a nice, smooth consistency, all the way down to the bottom."

"My favorite breakfast is warm pudding, coconut tapioca. I had some this morning," Leslie chirps. In my shopping news fantasy, she wears a red and black teddy with silken embroidered frogs that rise and fall down her front. The karaoke plays the overture to *The King and I,* and I can read her ruby red lips telling me that she is Siamese if you please, from another re-run.

"It's the wrong movie," I say, gargling the syllables in my throat.

"Good, good. Now the important thing to remember in this visualization, Chris, no sharp temperature changes for the next, oh, let's say, ahh, twenty-four hours. No cold pop, no hot coffee. Or tea," he adds.

He's removing the needles. There's a fleeting glimpse of Leslie—a black wig skewed on black hair, red mouth smeared with chocolate pudding— as she changes the mix flowing through the mask to pure oxygen.

"Remember, now. Don't put the pudding in the fridge, right? Keep it warm and soft so the top skin can form nice and even, okay? Visualize the clot—warm pudding, right? Tomorrow, if you see a little blood, you can try this."

Leslie hands me an herbal poultice in a baggie and giggles when I ask, "Do I smoke it?"

On cue, Dr. Wong calls out as he washes his hands. "Some Goldenseal and a teabag. Just unwrap it when you get home and press it gently against the wound. Really works. I get it from a Chinese herbalist on Miller Road. Nice fella. Name's Wong, coincidentally. Hi to your folks and Peter."

"And Doctor Candlewick," Leslie adds.

I do not hasten to add that Dr. Candlewick's in jail.

The airport parking maze reminds Wick of his latest escape.

"The actual path to jail passes through the underground garage and up an elevator only the police and prisoners may use, away from the public. After I was photographed and fingerprinted, my wallet and keys were taken, but they let me keep twenty dollars for comestibles. I felt humiliated, but I wasn't frightened until I reached the last room before they put me in a cell. Strip, they commanded. So humiliating. It's odd, Chris, but we are all humiliated in the process. The warder who searches hates looking. He threw my shoes against the wall to see if anything was hidden in the heels. Shook out my clothes. His greatest anger came when he told me to bend over."

When Mary first suggested that Wick would be better off in Hawaii, she was persuading herself there was sound business sense sending a tanned Wick in a leisure suit and aloha shirt to peddle Oriental nutrition bars. Corporate could look him in the eye, hear him speak in English about yin and yang without the visual disconnect. They could put a Chinaman like Peter Pan in the counterculture, somewhere inoffensive, the *pake* in paradise, without incriminating a real Chinese.

Later, Peter angrily reasoned, "In a TV ad, Peter Pan can sprinkle a frisson of gay, but Tinkerbell cannot be an aging predatory pedophile. He thinks he's God's left hand."

Now, there's Winnie persuading me to be nice. So, okay, "Yeah, yeah, Winnie, I'm on my way." My tongue's still thick, numb.

"What's wrong with your mouth?"

I hang up. The girls are trying to rectify a consolidator the local chapter of the VFW wanted to sell to its members, some rebel tour Tahitian Air has invented, a visit to the Solomon Islands to relive World War II.

I have that mess and juggling figures from the Airline Reporting Commission after Peter sent me down a long, unromantic road booking tours then going bust for Twig's Hawaiian rock and country band, now on creative sabbatical in the wooded hills of Santa Lucca, curing in skunkweed from the Humboldt triangle.

I shift my attention. Now it's two days to Yosemite, the wine country tours, San Simeon, routing buses to the Napa Valley, rent-a-car packages, LA airlines, Universal Studios, dance voyages on boats for locals. Make nice, and telephone Melba.

So, hi, and what's happening?" I can be cool. "What are you doing?"

"I'm writing a story for Peter's organic newsletter. It's all about the garden, about composting. The soil's so poor in the jungle."

"I didn't know that. All those trees?"

"What did you say?"

"Trees, trees. All that jungle stuff."

"I'm making a book about tropical biomass and the sunlight trapped in the forest canopy. I'm making a collage from old photos and some drawings. That world was so magical for me. A jaguar teaches a little girl to spin liana vines and banana leaves into plant food."

We'd smoked some of Twig's outrageous weed the night before. I'm becoming a connoisseur despite the short-term amnesia that accompanies what's become a steady habit. She's still deliciously disconnected.

I want to lift and twirl her high in the air. "Listen, I have a miscellaneous charge order for a package to Maui, Kamehameha Travel. The sales rep has two first-class round-trips, an upgrade at the Princess Hale Kulani, and a car. Our discount makes it two fifty-two apiece plus change, a bargain."

"I can hardly understand you." I have her laughing, confused. She's aroused again. I have that power over her. "How's your mouth?"

"Terrible, I feel awful. You want to spend a few days in Hawaii? Leave tonight?"

"Did you say Hawaii? Now? You know I can't move that fast. I can't just pick up and go, anymore."

"Hey, we don't have to run. We can fly. I have Wick scheduled for an outbound and I thought we might go back with him to collect shells and plants for Twig's magic potions, whatever."

"I have some old friends visiting, Chris. I'm sorry. I can't just leave them."

I've learned not to react. "Three, four days, at most. Catch the noon balloon?" She doesn't respond. "What?"

Finally, I hear her sigh. "Chris, I don't know these guys Twig deals with. I have to be careful, babe. Just old friends, not new friends, okay?"

"Puka shells and wood orchids?"

"You go if you want. I'm working right now, and I have to think. Let me be predictable, okay? We both have to be more stable and serious if we're all going to be together. Wick doesn't need me along if you want to go. I'm sure he wants to be alone anyway."

"Look and listen. I'm going nowhere without you. It's whatever you want."

"I want what you want for yourself," she murmured. "My head's still spinning."

"Me too. This morning I saw a headless chicken running down Washington Street."

She started to laugh. "You're so crazy."

The poultry store butchers daily—a specialty only available in Chinatown—advertising chickens with feet for the discriminating shopper. The butcher lops heads, then pitches the struggling birds into a garbage can filled with convulsing carcasses and secures it with a piece of plywood. On occasion one will escape and dash across the street into the park, where the kung fu studio leads morning tai chi. Or it will collide with a delivery truck struggling up the steep hill and cover the shrubs with down and bloodied feathers. "It was being chased by a box turtle the size of a moving van. What a flash, huh?"

"I hope you're driving carefully today."

"I'm down, it's okay. I can drive and walk and work. I just don't know why I'm bothering to. I want to be with you. Did you get any sleep?"

"Yes, I slept after you left. But I'm still vibrating. Did we make love? Was it wonderful?"

"I think we were fucking each other."

"It felt like I was flying, like I was a witch on a broomstick."

"My broomstick."

"Give me a rest. Listen," she said, "can we spend the weekend across the Bay? I have this incredible urge to plant tomatoes, stick my hands in the dirt."

"Absolutely." Maybe we could look for a place for ourselves. Station wagon, dog, commute. Marry in a redwood grove. "Listen, I'm delivering Wick to the airport at midnight. Gotta run. Business at twelve o'clock high." It was a sepia-toned Gregory Peck, a creased officer's cap tight on his skull, wearing a leather flying jacket, with his hand at the door, struggling to pull himself up, to heave himself into the belly of the bomber, engines throbbing. He couldn't make it through the door, could not cross the threshold. "Can I see you tonight?"

"I have to go out early. I have a chance to sell something. Maybe later. Can you call?"

I thought I heard an invitation, but I was wrong. She makes me crazy. She will always have other men in our life. But I've agreed with myself to move slowly, ignore jealousy, give her time. I look up at the ceiling, trembling with the thunder of engines, squadrons of allied aircraft on a final mission, with the promise of victory. "Sure, sure. I've got to take care of Wick anyway."

I let the phone ring so long I imagine I can hear it from the telephone booth across the street from her apartment where I have stood before, watching, waiting for her to return. The twilight dust turns to night. Street traffic, headlights, the sidewalk parade make me conscious of the lurking spectacle I make of myself. I'm hearing voices. I imagine her lover is a pale specter with a workman-like tan outlining his arms, his neck and face. She now becomes a new temptation, efficient and anxious. She draws the fury and gloom with her hands rubbing his member between her oiled palms, then licks her fingers, a seductive dare, a challenge. He stiffens suddenly as she traces a line with her tongue. Who am I watching from the corner as she plays rocking chair to his steam engine, making the first long stroke clearing hesitation, oiling the barrel? Dust rises from the old double mattress on the floor and sets my nose to itching, but the sharp aroma of their bodies, fresh sweat quaking down his back, a sheen of wet across her face, then their soft talk as he laps at her breasts, catching an angry nipple with his tongue and teeth. She licks her hands and holds his spent penis between her palms, kneads it, rolls it, lays her tongue flicking at the head. She seems to wink at me, for me, and swallows his thick coil till I lose her face in his pubic bush, grazing.

Or I lean sweating beside the door left ajar. I can time their bumps and heavings and cries. He is a nursery rhyme. She lets him wiggle and wriggle inside her as if she'll die.

Or am I still sitting in the cool dark by the water heater listening to their tryst, my hands over my ears? She rides him, hugging the underside of a brown dolphin, receiving his thrusts and collisions, her hands locked at the small of his back, grunting and moaning as waves overwhelm all feeling save her pulsing, welling warmth, and the smell of a sea change, a tide.

These men of middle build, long slender fingers, prehensile toes, exhibit wonderful pectorals, and tall and lean ones uncoil to their knees. Erect, he can kiss his own member.

Her lover's stripping white duck pants and a navy blue chambray. And for a second, I catch sight of his genitals, a swollen magic wand, a delicate nest of dark hair. He turns his back to the door, his tight rump betraying no excess flesh. My mind's eye receives his sweet erection, warm salt streams I let slide around my tongue as I imagine them joined together.

Or she arrives late to prepare a supper, full of secrets and the aroma of her tryst. She leaves her underpants in her purse. She is still damp and ready. She is withdrawn this evening, given to sighs and downward glances at the shape of her figure. Her nipples are visible, rigid beneath the thin T-shirt she wears to the market. She revels in her body's sexual exposure, celebrates her freedom.

I overhear them making love.

"Are you working hard?" he teases. "Am I getting big?" He watches, seated at the edge of the bed, as she lies with her hands caught up between her legs. I am terrorized by our passionate complicity, our appetites.

These are the hours at sunset I spend waiting for her return. I see them prowl each quickened part, and the faint aroma of the sea hangs in the air. "I want you right now," she urges.

She straddles him, her heels riding comfortably on his shoulders, his erection secure in the grip of her sex. She's smoking a cigarette and sharing it with him. The waning light catches his profile, taut, oiled, his chest glistening in the shadows.

"Please," she says, "watch me come," she says, "watch me."

In the car, Wick is detached, objective. "Peter left me in jail."

"It was a weekend, Wick. Winnie said there wasn't a bond hearing till Monday morning."

Wick is sure that he has been abandoned by everyone. "I spent the first night in my clothes. I wasn't expecting to stay. The cell block had four cells with four beds each, a bench and table bolted to the floor in the common area. The gates at the far end showed open johns and showers. There were three others sharing the cell. I was given a clean blanket, no sheets, a stained pillow with no slipcase. Jail the first night smells like dirty feet, cigarettes, and, oh, this is interesting, burning toilet paper to heat the tin mugs of leftover coffee they bring from dinner."

On the freeway, Wick and I are stop and go.

"I entered the cell, and the beast, actually a sweet man, but a face only a mother could love, moves his stuff from the empty bunk, the lower he's been using for a shelf. Two other guys dressed in rumpled street clothes like me, and one fellow in jail garb. He said he was a short-timer, very pleasant, bad checks, I think. But the smell was overwhelming. I couldn't sleep, but I pretended. I didn't really need the blanket they gave me to keep warm. I used it to cover my head. I was afraid, Chris."

"Understandable." He looks vulnerable, tired.

"In the morning, the stink of Lysol. Nothing to read, nothing to look at. The rattle of metal, the smell of warm oatmeal. The drunks, the drug addicts, slept through breakfast, but not me. Meals came through a slit in the wall. Everyone was very polite. Once you have your tray, someone always helps you find a place to sit on the bench so you don't offend anyone. No sugar. You get a spoon. You eat breakfast, then you spend the hours: roll call, lawyers for OR, lockdown, court call, except weekends, lockdown for lunch. Lunch: canned stew, two slices of white bread, coffee, some salad. Dinner: spaghetti, thin-sliced overcooked roast beef, green peas, gravy, Jell-O, and cake for dessert. No rice. The candy truck brings cigarettes, magazines, juice. But I never felt hungry."

"If this traffic lets up, I can make eggs and bacon at the apartment, twenty minutes down the freeway?"

"Sounds wonderful, son. I thank you. Spent too much time in Hawaii. I've been dreaming about eggs and Spam on rice with a splash of soy sauce, myself, but I can wait till tomorrow. They can't seem to make rice in Atlanta. I had grits and sausage patties up to my ears. There's a mall they call Chinatown, ten Chinamen with Dixie accents who speak Chinese with the same question mark they use to say good-bye. Y'all come back, now, ya' heah?" When I picked him up at the airport, a group of Chinese tourists had stared curiously at the *lo fan* babbling in English, swearing in Cantonese with a southern accent.

"I can manage rice."

"Doubly obliged. I can't get my stomach to settle without it. A meal without rice, you know. Well, aloha Honolulu. I'm just a *Pake* Chinaman in disguise. My tropical exile exacerbated all my dietary sins."

"Just us Indians, Wick."

"When I'm so close to home, my language starts to slip and slide. Need to fatten up. Honolulu's a Chinaman's home on the range, or maybe just a feedlot. I keep moving west, and then I'm east. Are the gym and sauna at your place still working? I need to work these kinks out and have myself a good soak. How's your Melba?"

"I asked her to marry me. Did I tell you? And I'd like you to marry us."

"Of course I will. I have the moral right. Maybe not the legal one, maybe."

I have no answer for that one. I allow his fatigue to babble past me.

The freeway's still dense going north. The arterial's clogged. I need two exits before shunting around the malls. Wick dozes, his head against the window, his fitful snores rattling loud enough to keep him drowsy and talking. Even folded and bent, I see the resemblance to the vigorous athlete of my youth, his narrow face, his cheekbones, the shape of his mouth, the wiry frame still embedded in this old man. The last few years hiding under the tropical sun have not been kind. He could be his own mummy, draped in mottling mahogany skin, tight and dried like old bandages. I imagine this one will wind up beached, brittle bits of shell a new generation of children collect on that sun-drenched shore and string for anklets and bracelets.

The traffic's not moving. I need another exit.

So, how is Melba? Wick finally remembers me, who I am, who I was. But "how's Melba?" is complicated. I want to marry Melba, settle down together, be family. I could talk to her about all the problems I could barely explain to myself. And Wick's only one of them. I think now that Mary loved Peter more than she loved me. And Lincoln. I told Melba that Wick was the only father I'd ever really had. She understood when I described myself confessing to him at campfire, tears rolling down my face, that I was an imposter, that I had been baptized and received holy communion at St. Peter and Paul's, singing hymns and enumerating the Lord's Prayer with trade beads and the extra cadenzas that glory in my belief in Him, that forgives trespasses rather than debts, and the worst, that I might be induced to swallow flesh of the forked hoof at a Presbyterian Friday weenie roast. That Wick took me seriously and told me that I should only do what I thought I should do. And anything, *anything*, he underscored, that was wrong or I felt was prohibited by my own beliefs, I should not do. That he would never require me to do anything that I knew was not right.

Wick put a positive spin on the same message Lincoln left for me when he stopped cooking, when he quit the kitchen. Lincoln buried the cleaver in the chopping block. You know, like, we are not alone, like, he's coming back. Lincoln expected us to wait there for him, in the kitchen.

Wick led us out into the world, wearing his collection of baseball caps because he was always a little bald. I described him to Melba as the white man who could tell off-color jokes in Cantonese, and that made sense of who I was.

When I think back, it was all transparent, clear. Mary and Lincoln were family, but Wick didn't have anyone else, no adult peers. He was always in the company of kids, always the most imposing figure, the locus of attention paid by all the fatherless children in Chinatown. We lived in a bachelor society that regarded his behavior as only slightly suspicious. The missionaries, the lay teachers, China hands before the war, always alone, bachelors and old maids, more subdued, patronizing to the manners and mores of Chinatown—all of them watched over us. His was not a talent or skill that a parent usually cultivates. To be parental, an authority, demands obedience. To be a guide, counselor, spiritual advisor, requires respect paid to a young person that parents find difficult if not impossible to offer. That's Wick's strength. Or a least that was his strategy to command and, unfortunately, to seduce.

Among a generation that might inherit only our parents' exile and isolation, Wick gave and received acceptance. Wick reminds me of Uncle Lincoln, not physically of course, but the same kind of presumptuous arrogance. In a way, I have to envy the rogue in both of them, and it's catnip for the young and restless. They still exude that senseless independence that draws company for reasons I love to imagine in myself. No emotional clutter, no ties that bind, just a "howdy" with eyes fixed on the horizon, heading down that dusty trail. I'm thinking Lincoln was a loner like me. Wick had a posse. I'm thinking it's east versus west.

Traffic's stopped completely. There must be an accident. The driver of the diesel hauling a road grader two cars ahead has turned off his engine and opened his cab door, propped his boots on the window. He must be looking at the view. All around me, men in short-sleeve shirts are loosening their ties, women adjusting their makeup. Drivers are stepping out of their cars. I didn't bargain for this. I need to be gone. Who do I have to kill, what do I have to pay to be on my way?

Melba's soft whispers are still in my ear. Why does she still have other guys in her life? She doesn't trust me, thinks I'll turn away. I edge up on the shoulder, praying the CHP doesn't have the same idea, and slip between the semi and the cyclone fence, the car careening down the shoot, my right tires canted on the shoulder, pitching dust and gravel, shreds of waste paper and plastic bags woven into the fencing by my slipstream. I'm free, and that's a problem.

The sweet aroma of Thai jasmine white steaming fills the tiny kitchen. Wick's showered, wearing a bathrobe I keep for travelers. He's become a genuine prisoner of the Pacific Rim, addicted to the commissary and trade cuisine of the region. Liver spots dapple his face, neck, and arms with the pickling nitrates that bloom on his skin. With chopsticks, he scoots clouds of rice topped with two fried eggs into a large soup bowl, that and some of the canned sausage meat Auntie occasionally harvests in wholesale lots and divides among the several efficiencies, one- and two-bedroom condos near the airport, that fit our growing business needs. In the real estate market of the day, the condos were proving to be a better investment than renting. Although he'd never been here, Wick might guess that Winnie and I had shared this particular unit when we married. But he wouldn't know that we still did when she was in the mood for junk food.

"Eat like a beach bum, don't I?" Wick chortles. Bits of rice stick to his lips.

"Wouldn't it be a surprise if the world knew you guys like to eat from cans?" I pour three fingers of Hennessy next to his can of cola, which he eyes appreciatively as he paddles two more large bowls he'd blackened with soy sauce. "And wash it down with a generic cola."

Wick mimics Peter's opening monologue. "Vinegar and mayonnaise, catsup," the old man says as he levers rice after a bite of curling Spam dipped in the runny yolk of a fried egg splashed with oyster sauce, "a major food group."

When Peter and Wick first landed in Hawaii, the idea had been to merchandise the Chi Bar, with vague plans to open a health food store, an exclusive gymnasium, and a holiday camp for the fat and famous. But Chi Bars took Peter directly into the counterculture of food that had begun during the Vietnam War and really took hold as the entire country sat down to break bread together. Acts of revenge require reconciliation. Where else but in the backwater diasporas outside the traditional centers of culture and authority could people learn to survive on unmilled grains and soy products? Peter added a dash of soy and sea salt, a dollop of organic honey to the Chi Bar mix and sprinkled it on top of a drug culture that stretched from Humboldt County to Thailand. He also trademarked that cheesy smile, the herky-jerky sing-song he adapted for his iconic cartoon, the face of the Chinaman who had taken a bite of something slightly off but was willing to suspend judgment.

That attitude had been the secret of his success. Peter had scoffed at all of it. His *Wok Talk* formula adapted the Hawaiians' own sardonic contempt for their imported cuisine. When you say "aloha" over pig and poi, you embody "hello" and "goodbye." By heaping abuse and derision on the local cuisine, playing on local sensibilities, surfing the wave of the native revival movement, fueled by the paradox of the traditional reverence for American exports like cholesterol-clogging potted meats, he wove his organic, macrobiotic, vegetarian voodoo into a local TV talk and cooking show produced by the local Hawaiian public television station. In turn, public TV sold distribution and translation rights throughout the Pacific Rim, the Philippines, Japan, Hong Kong, New Zealand, Australia, and now to Washington, Oregon, and California.

But Wick's old baggage. We needed to send him back, put him away where his love wouldn't hurt anymore, wouldn't hurt me or anyone.

While Wick naps, I call Melba from the bedroom extension but she isn't home yet.

Wick's snoring can rattle the dead. Even asleep he wants a hearing, but no one actually wants to listen. Like Peter, who talks only about himself, no surprise. "No one bothered to ask me. Isn't there such a thing as seductive consent? I was a predatory minor." But they both love to posture.

Wick had been too ready to confess, to testify. Of course, no one wanted to listen, not to the complainants and certainly not to Wick. Never mind the statute of limitations—no trial judge, no jury, no one wanted to listen. Frankly, no one wanted to watch Wick strip, except Peter. I see now that he had always been a little too willing to bathe naked in the limelight, his mea culpas sounding more and more self-serving. Almost as an act of good taste, even the newspapers suppressed the detailed confessions he offered to the Synod. They were fantasies not unlike the possession narratives of demonic enslavement and incest that validate Christianity. If there were no heathens, there would be none to save: no God without the devil. Wick's tenure had been so much a part of the Haven's pastoral mission in Chinatown there was nothing to be done.

Leash him to a chain staked in the backyard, feed him scraps, call him Lucky and he would live a long time, like the turtles in the tubs, the gourami in the flower pots.

"Chris, I know I violate social norms and undermine the sincerity of my misguided but loyal service. But I fight to dispel the exotic and superstitious from the sensibilities of youngsters needing a guiding hand out of the ghetto, instill ideas of Christian love, forgiveness, redemption, and triumph over the barbarism of life as a constant war of revenge, of mindless retaliation." He ticks off his points as he weaves his fingers together. I imagine him dressed in Taoist mourning, white sackcloth, like the Ku Klux Klan.

"I know that I should not speak and would never testify on my own behalf. I can only allow myself abject regret. I sincerely apologize to all I have offended by my acts and by lying about them. In my genuine contrition, I accept all the charges that are brought now and in the future. I knew the moment would one day come when I would be required to look all of them in the eye." I think Wick, the martyr, loved himself more than he loved us. And no one wanted to look him in the eye, not this messiah who wanted to confess to everything, as if reticence signaled some conspiracy. "The tears from some, I do sympathize with and feel the need to reach out, to comfort. I understand the ambiguity, the confusion of their feelings towards me. But how many have stepped forward? Six? Seven? Only three, in the end, the three monkeys. Why aren't there more? We all need to look more deeply into our evolving sexual identities."

Then, speaking directly to the two of us, Peter and me, he said, "Look at the ones who loved me for that moment in their lives when they were looking for a man who encouraged them to expect more of themselves, more than their families could ever imagine, to reach out with imagination to the world outside of themselves, outside Chinatown. That's it, you know. Some of them loved me when they did not, could not, love themselves, their families, their own fathers."

Betrayal: victims always speak of it.

Mary offers her own untranslatable curse, catching it in her hand and wiping it against her sleeve. *"Kai dai yeh."* Poor Mary.

But what about Mary? I could never ask him. Peter might have.

"But I tell you, all in the name of love, I swear it." Wick's sincerity, his apologies, seemed strategically daring at the time. His confession forced everyone to imitate the monkeys, three stupid monkeys, the stooges, slapping at each other with deadly force. But the silent guard we have all had to post around him, his isolation, has had its intended effect on all of us, his Chinatown family.

Winnie sees us all of one piece: the family risen has fallen. She relies on the facts she can surmise from Uncle, from Peter, my own confusions, and from Auntie Mary's history, to rebuild. There can be no other way.

Peter bites each word. "Wick's survival comes from men who offer him unquestioning license to exist in Chinatown's milieu, who listen to his advice about affairs they have no interest in whatsoever. From women—he succumbs to their ministrations as big aunties, as mothers who feed him, who stuff him with all manner of victuals till he bloats and dies."

Peter calls from paradise after midnight, musing on. "Here is the pedophile, an animal denied in the village, on the farm, but tradition-ally recognized in the history of barbarian invaders. The Manchus sur-vived the longest, their dynasty in the silk-padded sty of the Forbidden Palace, massaged by eunuchs, fed and suckled, scrupulously examined to the degree where their turds were weighed and measured and their diets increased to make up for any loss. Their genes, tested by genera-tions of harsh regimens and ferocious exercise, made them difficult to kill. Four hundred years, nearly. But in the end, their wiry genome plied by decadent opulence fractured. So, too, Candlewick, Irish warrior stock, starved and toughened by the British Mandarins, takes a lifetime's worth of corruption, of mothering, of chastened acceptance, and plied with as many young boys as he could manage, will finally rest in his bier, death erasing all disguise, all artifice, all vanity."

So angry.

"If we all lived in the emperor's harem, Auntie would ask Winnie to poison Wick's food. Detect his weakness for Chinese herbal dialysis. Perhaps a Chinese doctor would feel his pulse and gossip about his weak kidneys. He'd be poisoned and die of a disease that would leave him with-out a tail. Turn him into a frog for his love of anus. Feed him till he dies."

Peter's the one who can look our Wick in the eye. Peter knows Wick's exile will always be internal, family. "He belongs to us and we'll keep him. This absorption is a Chinese invention. Make the enemy rich and successful, comfort them, then corrupt them by making them eat every-thing. That's the mandate of heaven. Revenge. If you aren't Chinese enough to seek balance, a center in your diet, you die of luxurious overindulgence, you die of acceptance. That's a Chinatown dilemma. Acceptance by one or the other means the death of you." Wasn't that Uncle's warning?

Peter's cuisine is a revenge on the world. Lincoln's cooking, eat everything including little boys, makes you dead. Aunties want to comfort, forgive, coddle, but they keep asking, "Have you had your rice today?" "Have you eaten?"

I know now that these white father figures in the confusing world of ambiguous expectations and oversimplifications are very important to me. And my fascination with them need not be dismissed so quickly, as Peter does when he spits "Pedophile!" "Rice queen!"

Wick once told me he couldn't remember anymore. "There were so many. Yes. You too, if that's what you want to believe. I hope that helps you. If it helps that I confess to you, apologize, then I do. Please believe me. That's all I want to do now. Help you to kill all the demons I raised in your life, robbed you of your childhood, robbed you of your ability to have a relationship with your own father. I am guilty."

What if he fucked a couple or ten thousand? What if it was an act of love more than rape? But we loved him, all of us. I did. Mary did.

"Chris, that's all I ever wanted for all the kids I touched. That they might have the capacity to know in their childhood that they were loved without demands, without that heavy load of expectation their immigrant parents pushed on them. I loved them. If they loved me back, all well and good."

Wick falls asleep on the couch before I can direct him to the bedroom. Just as well, since I see now I haven't changed the sheets in a while.

Instead of a father, I had Auntie Mary and Peter and Wick. Peter, my sassy older brother, a quick mouth ready to deal in two languages, already graduated from high school before I was out of elementary school, already living with Wick, the rebel who left large footprints that I could follow or admire and ignore, which I did, mostly. All the resentment against the absent, the distant, the unknown father belonged to him. He played the role of Lincoln's bastard son so I didn't have to think about it. His arrogance matched Uncle's, and he filled the silences, the absence between the three of us. But it's my turn now. There's Melba at the garden gate.

She's wearing an apron, waiting for me as I pull into the driveway beside our white stucco with a picket fence, ivy and roses, a barbecue pit.

Melba hasn't picked up. I cradle the phone. She's not coming home. I'm tempted to let it ring all night. Pathetic.

Wick took his toll. Peter would call me from anywhere, Peter and his nocturnal telephone talks, his midnight walks. Now he wants to lead tours, sex tours to Manila, Bangkok. Special blue tours to Taipei for the pedophile. Maybe like Club Med or Puerto Vallarta for men and women. Rent a motor scooter with Twig as his chauffeur.

"See Asia from his postilion, the nubile teenie," he says brightly. "I thought I might get lucky tonight. So I rubbed the scratch-and-sniff perfume circular from the Payright Drugs all over me. And, hey, I saw our father cruising Castro Street all night long. All those years. I never knew he was gay. In that melancholy way, hey?"

It's two A.M., but I have to laugh. When's the last time I heard Peter say "hey," his cure for the "ah" that signals the beginning of a Chinaman talking about anything and everything in the accent, the chink in his immigrant armor, from "ah' horse shit" to "ah' Gesu in ah' heaven wah." Ah' Christopher Columbus Wong, ah' Waikiki, ah' California, ah' mellicah, ah' universe, ah' Heyman, his first English name.

Winnie calls. Peter's in town. I ring his private number and count each pulse, meditating on a dry hole, a clot. "Hey, Peter, are you straight?"

"Most certainly. Straight and awake. What's the matter with your mouth?"

"Dentist."

"The lovely Leslie."

"Winnie says that Uncle wants lunch."

"No, thank you very much. Had one yesterday. Are you calling from heaven or hell? Wick's there?"

"Sleeping. I'll drive. Pick a place."

"Lincoln's out of the hospital?"

"For the moment. They're flying to Long Beach for a second try." I can't eat.

"Vegetarian okay?"

"Get real. Smoky oolong and ah' dim sum ah' fry wah. He likes it greasy, you know. I'll need to cleanse myself after that kind of abomination. There's an ablution I can perform for this. A strip of linen up the nose and out my mouth."

I taste the pad in my cheek, steel wool dissolving. "Tomorrow? About one?"

Peter comes at me in his midnight dark. "You have to slow down, Chris. You have to listen. You've grown up in the cuddle of your aunties for too long, you sweet soft thing. This is boy talk."

"Must we?"

"Hey, so I'm all lonely and bent, loving death, the anonymous loving. So I'm cruising the glory holes, looking for the quick masturbatory embrace by the video machines, see the tilt of a chin caught in the window gazing onto the street, that slowing, half-lidded appraisal, the exhibitionist en vogue: see me, watch me love myself. Are you afraid?"

Of course I'm afraid.

"I slip his tricots over his thickening pubic bulge. His cock springs forward at me, a slip of lubricant, clear spit I touch to my tongue tip, tasting his rheumy salt even as I pull his waistband under his scrotal sac so it all looms up at me, his rock solid cock, the pendulous swing of his rock as this scrotum stinks in the heat when I gently crush his nuts and heat his lovely muscle."

"Enough. Good-bye."

"Wait, wait," he pleads. "Listen, I have a secret for you."

"I don't want to hear your secrets."

"You don't love me anymore."

"Not like that."

"I know, I know. You're all gooey with Auntie's loving. And Auntie's gooey with no loving, no more. Bye-bye, Wickie. So many aunties. And how is Winnie, anyway?"

Winnie was never my problem.

I don't hear Peter on the line.

I have a headache. The Novocain is wearing off. The numb knot in my jaw is softening. I'm searching for aspirin. "Peter?"

Finally, he responds. "All right. Last supper."

"It's just lunch, Peter."

In my darkness, his midnight gambols, his insanities make me confront the craziness that I can't begin to explain, my need for Melba, my need for Winnie. We don't speak of it, but I know Peter knows. We don't have anyone, not even each other, to tell these secrets to. So he relies on the tried and true.

"Your Auntie Daisy's been dead damn near twenty-five years. But mine's still around. Did you hear how she slipped around and let the boys pull on her titties and suck hickeys, a little tongue, then run home all wet? If she lived, she would have taken up golf and ballroom dancing after marriage and you. Lincoln gets drunk and likes to talk about her, you know."

"Not to me."

"No, I know. Did he ever mention my mother? Ever even say her name? Not even in vain, no way, ever, never her name. Just one of the blossoms in the leather bouquet he whips out, flailing away, mostly at himself, I guess. And we're the chains that bind, ah' Chris, hey? It's a bitch. It's ah' bastard. Hey! But he loved yours, ah' Daisy, he did."

"He never says." It's the closest I've gotten to offering him consolation. And Lincoln—and Mary—never could.

"Well, the old shit. How about that. Damn his eyes and damn his lies." His voice breaks with genuine anger, suddenly, genuine grief, finally, for this moment only.

"Chris, you know how Uncle likes to mix 'em up in his stories. Keep 'em guessing. Who's the lady who poured whiskey with her blouse open that leaves her breasts hanging, her thick squash framed by a low décolletage, hey cowboy? That's all you'll ever know, Christopher, Uncle in his cups, staging his own mother's seduction. 'Boys, she sees me, my eyes drying the stain that makes her nipple visible, then hard like a raisin, wrinkled, sweet. She was a fishing village girl on the Pearl River Delta, smuggled to San Francisco to whore.'"

I've heard that story before.

"You get it, Chris? Do you understand? That's Uncle's auntie, right? That's his ma."

He tells the one about a woman whose first taste of ice cream, from a granite bowl submerged in a running stream, froze her vocal chords but filled her with such rich pleasure, so giving, that her next customer, a Chinaman gambler from Denver, bought her for himself, so soft to squeeze, tasting like milk and vanilla. The woman he called everyman's wife, the priest's housekeeper, the rich man's mistress he stole for one season for a gambling debt, are all stories that work a kind of revenge that let him teach us to love what we most despise.

Nightfall. Melba never went home. The histamines from the final dollop of Petit Sirah float at the bottom of my glass of consciousness. These dregs of insomnia stick like a Band-Aid, catching every stray thought, awake to every fleeting association Peter leaves with me, in the burgeoning darkness, in the stillness. His fury supplies me with the reconstruction of a memory I never lived, a history I never knew. Ah Lung Gung, Uncle, our father, Auntie's Lincoln, the Wilsons, Washingtons, a Hoover, Roosevelt and Grant, oddballs with no family names to call their own, named for greenbacks and steamships, or lost towns in the wilderness, these abandoned rogues of the bachelor society, orphan males who would marry into Chinatown Christian pioneer families with too many daughters, they would breed bastards like all of us and die or live past their useful lives, to be forgotten, ignored, sloughed from the family history. And that makes sense of us? All of us?

At lunch, Uncle slumps in his chair. His breathing is labored. Each bite of food—a bit of steamed bun, some long noodles, a tiny knuckle of pork—he washes down with small sips of four-star Hennessy the kitchen left at our table. The cigarette he bummed from the waiter smolders in a saucer by his untouched teacup. "Heyman, why you come back?"

"I thought this was your idea. Lunch?"

His eyes circle the empty chairs. "Smart guy. Watcha guys doing these days? Where's everybody today?"

Peter shrugs. "Off to Hong Kong, tomorrow. Big business. We're going to shuffle industrial gourmet, microwave ready, east-meets-west low-fat, no MSG. I call 'em 'wraps.' They're your pizzas, your spring rolls, eggrolls, hell, burritos reinvented. I've got them in the chains and upscale markets. I tell you, it's the latest, it'll be the wave of the eighties. Tomorrow the Pic-N'-Pac, Safeway."

"Wrap what?" I ask.

"Imagine rice flour tortillas, sheets of filo, potsticker dough, think calzone, a roll of pizza, the burrito. The entire civilized world wants to eat like a caveman, Christopher. It's all those buffet-stained dresses, the à la king on your gabardines, canapés that ooze from both ends, sandwiches that leak dressing on the rug. I can freeze-wrap a rice flour tortilla around any combination of filling and spice, give it a shelf life of a year, and make a fortune. Hell, the vegetarians have been doing it for years. A wrap and a cup of curried dal makes you want to assume the lotus position."

"How come Mary never wants to eat anymore? Where is she?" Lincoln's chin drops slowly and his chin nestles softly in the large cloth napkin tied around his neck. He's fallen asleep.

Something in Lincoln's plea, almost like pity, makes Peter rouse himself. "That makes three of us. We miss Mary. We all love her."

Uncle allows a painful chuckle at the familiar ribbing that comes when we're together, alone, the three of us. It starts in his throat and leaves him wheezing, a wet cough he spits into a fresh cloth napkin. "Me too, when I'm not so goddamn old now. I could catch 'em all and leave you guys in my dust." He nods in his chair, avoiding Peter's challenging stare. "Maybe not your funny stuff, I guess."

Winnie has dressed him in a suit and tie, suspenders and vest, hoping his fastidious outfit would somehow dampen his appetites.

"I know we're all the same." He looks at me. "I know American girls too. All kinds." His tongue works the dry chapping along the corner of his mouth. The brandy must make his lips sting, and he dampens his mouth with the tea-soaked corner of his napkin.

It's a familiar saw. He's feeling okay now, or he's feeling very bad. I can't tell anymore. I can't eat anything. I have to wait for the tea to cool, but the waiter keeps refilling it. I can't explain why I want cold tea. I don't have enough words. Why do they always talk at me? They want to talk to each other. They have the words. And I don't want to explain myself to Peter or Uncle. My predicaments always make the meals longer. I'm distracted by a high-pitched ringing in my ears. I visualize amputated nerve endings trying to complete their circuits, like the fuzzy roots of freshly washed scallions drying on an unfinished plank warming in the sun. Dry hole, ripped from a dry hole.

"She was a social worker for you, boy, Mary's old man sicced on me. She drove all the way from San Francisco. She was born in New York.

This was her first time working in Chinatown, a whitey that's not from the YMCA or some dago nun with a mustache from St. Jackoff. She's all hot from the long drive and I make her something to eat in the kitchen, no trouble, no, no, pour some tea, and I send you, Chris, out back to play with Lucky. She's unbuttoned a little bit, big tits pushing against her brassiere, a white blouse, hot and sweaty. I tell her the hot tea will make her cool even in the kitchen. 'Let the sweat cool you,' I tell her. I hand her a clean towel to mop with, smells like jasmine tea. All hot and steamy. She undoes a few more buttons and starts to blot the sweat down her chest like maybe I'm a blind man. Then, afterwards, maybe we wipe down with jasmine tea and do it all over again. She was fat. I didn't have a bed in the kitchen so we did it against the wall, on the table, against the chopping block, sitting, standing."

"A big girl."

Why does Peter encourage him?

He's panting, his face bruised with drinking. "Bigger than me, even. But I always did kung fu when I was young. My horse was strong. You can't push me down, never."

"Legs of iron, thighs of steel," Peter singsongs, "superstud."

"She always came visiting, even after your aunties took you back to San Francisco."

"They all thought I was infected. By you, by Wick."

"It's not me. You weren't born like that."

"Born queer? Is that what you want to say?"

"No, no, okay, okay. My fault, I know."

"Lincoln?" Peter looks up. It's that cheesy smile he uses, the Chinaboy chewing on something slightly off but willing to suspend judgment.

"Hey, I say so, right? What else is there to say?"

Peter sips tea, then with a catch in his throat, he says, "Goddamn, Lincoln, do I call you dad now?"

"Naah. But don't you worry. I don't care. It doesn't really matter."

"Thanks."

"Anyway, your mama's family, they gave you to the church, both of you. But I loved them all."

Peter urges him forward. "And do you remember her name?"

"Yep." The sound of him cuts off abruptly, his breath like a sleeve catching on a nail. He waits, listening to his heart beat. He fingers the knot in his tie, loosens it to dig at the collar button in the folds of his throat. "Yeah, sure. I remember." It's his favorite line. "I call 'em 'Baby.' Every time. How can I forget that, right?"

"Not Violet, ah' Rose, no Hyacinth, no Lilies of the valley, ah' Petunia, Iris, Tulip?"

"No, no. I remember them too, but not Tulip. Never a Tulip," his laughter rumbling dangerously from his chest. "Daisy, your mama," he says, looking at me, stabbing the air with his glass. "They took you away, boy, but that's okay. They always got what they wanted from me. And I'm always glad to oblige."

The flower names that smell so sweet in my family garden, all my aunties ranged against him, are like blossom petals at his feet. A contagious bad boy, put him in a dry hole, let him rot, let the flowers grow.

"Thank you, Chris. I hope Wick wasn't too much of a problem? Is there anything I should tell Mary?" It's after midnight. Having lived in too many time zones, Winnie never bothers to check. If she's awake and a telephone is near at hand, she calls.

"No problem, Winnie." It was just Wick passing through. "He looked like another tourist ready to spend six glorious days basking under a pineapple."

"Lincoln's having a bad evening. Did he eat anything at lunch or just drink?" Mary keeps her distance from all of us and leaves me to Winnie. I always wonder what bargains Lincoln struck with Auntie to keep us all together and apart at the same time. His coarse stories persuade me now to think that he had all my aunties for a while, each in their turn, wives to produce sons that were late in coming. Four daughters before the first of three sons was produced, and no sons from their sons until I arrived. Auntie's family must have been worried. And the one I don't remember, my own Auntie Daisy, which one was she?

"When did Wick leave?"

"He left late, after eleven. There was a flight cancellation."

"Did he eat?"

"Yes. I made rice and eggs and opened a can of that sausage. And there's all that Spam, Winnie. Keeps forever."

"Don't save that stuff for my sake. Not healthy."

She's been talking to Melba. Odd that it's what Wick craves. It's either the nourishment that keeps Wick predictable or I've poisoned him on Auntie's behalf. I'm loyal, I am. That's the only measure worth taking of me, that I'm loyal and undemanding. Auntie chooses Winnie and Winnie chooses me. Lincoln, uncle, father—he never said—never chose me. So it's done. Wick's gone for the time being, Auntie. I've killed him for you. Are there others? But no, there's no one left. You say let your enemies live close, and you feed them, and that's fine because they're nothing to me. I'd as soon cut their throats if I were angry enough, provoked, or if Auntie asks. What else are families for? To feed, to nurture, to seduce.

I had Peter's apartment whenever he was out of town, so one night Melba and I took the chance to experiment in his kitchen.

"Have you eaten? Can I make you something?" Melba arrived late. I'd just restacked Peter's turntable for the third time and was humming the guitar lead in to a Bud Shank jazz bossa rendition of "Fly Me to the Moon" when I heard the bell. I buzzed the door, then stepped back into the kitchen.

"There's some consommé I can warm."

"Oh, yes, please. That would be so groovy." She let her coat drop at the top of the stairs and hurried to me. She held my face tightly in both hands to kiss me, as if I might flinch or turn away. "There wasn't any bus, so I had to walk from the studio. I'm running on empty."

I had perched myself on a barstool at the long island in the studio kitchen where Peter held his cooking demonstrations for our gourmet tours package. I'd left most of the lights off, dimming her climb up the hall stairs. A single bank of halogens dappled the maplewood counter top with hot, bright circles that dramatized the industrial look of Peter's operating theater.

She kissed me, a playful brush of her lips across mine. "You waited for me."

I felt the tip of her tongue darting, spearing, as she leaned her body awkwardly against mine, felt the heat rising to warm her cold cheeks. When I opened my eyes, I was met by her steady gaze, examining me for any sign of irritation, impatience, accusation.

I pulled her close. "Why are your eyes open?"

"I'm afraid of the dark. I feel like I'm in Macy's housewares? Like shopping in the dark?"

I hadn't thought of it before, but she was right. The major appliances, refrigerators, ovens, stove top, food mixer, and Peter's latest high-tech gadget, a microwave oven, were matched in stainless steel. Pots and pans hung above the counter in orderly rows by size, and knives were sheathed in wood, save for two Chinese cleavers with rolled steel handles Peter kept on their own chopping block. A two-burner butane hot box for the woks sat in an asbestos enclosure to trap the explosive inferno he demanded for the stir-fry I was warned to avoid. I scooped the aspic Peter had left in the cold locker into a measuring bowl and set it spinning. Scallions for garnish, for the raw green, for the aroma to cover the gamey stock. Noodles. "How about some Japanese spaghetti?"

"Soba. How thoughtful, Chris. How did you know I was dreaming about buckwheat noodles?" She prowled through the apartment, exploring in the dark, until she found the light switch in the back bedroom and small bath. I heard the water running.

I poured the broth into lacquer bowls. There was a separate dipping sauce for the noodles. I remembered to garnish them with stiff parsley curls, which I coiled into a woven basket, and I centered my presentation in a pad of light as she returned, smelling like soap.

"Is that for me? Namaste." With an unstudied bow, Melba met the rising steam with her palms pressed together. She tucked the stray curls of hair behind her ears, inhaling the steamy cloud she let wash over her face.

"What are you doing?"

"Saying grace." Her hands cupped steam and her fingers drew invisible nourishment down her cheeks, catching herself around her neck. "I once met a very sensitive medicine man who taught me to scrub with the smoke from burning Scotch broom, eucalyptus leaves, even tobacco. To begin a fast, to end one, I stimulate all my senses to honor the food, its nourishment, and to honor you. You offer me food, Chris. It's a sacred act."

"Didn't I tell you that I'm an Indian too?"

"He wasn't an Indian. He was a healer, a very sensitive person. I think he saved my life."

I was fixed by her every movement, every gesture. The hot lights colored her green eyes a translucent jade, caught the splash of pale freckles that dapple the right side of her neck, sprinkle down her shoulder.

"What? You're counting my spots again." She caught herself instinctively, and raised her chin to meet my steady gaze.

"I'm connecting the dots, looking for a secret message, a genetic tattoo."

"I was a leopard in another life." She circled the counter, sniffing across the row of condiments and spices. "Saffron threads, sassafras, sesame paste. Alphabetical order?"

"I don't know. This is Peter's classroom. He might have it all alphabetized, I guess. I don't really cook, a few things."

"Me too. I stopped cooking in Bolivia in self-defense against everything, my ex, the heat, the daily surprise meat that landed at our door: mangled peahen, speared piranha, guinea pig. Even the thought of food made me nauseous. I had to cure myself of meals."

"But you have to eat."

"Oh, God, I eat, I'm always eating something. I like to graze. But no fixed mealtime. I gave up breakfast, lunch, and dinner." She rinsed a single strand of soba in sauce, wound it twice around her chopsticks, then, leaning forward into the light, she caught the curl of it between her tongue and upper lip and inhaled it, a droplet landing on the tip of her nose. "This is perfect, Chris."

I couldn't pull my eyes away from her. "It's a noodle. Have another. There's broth."

"When my savior first saw me, he could tell I was really sick, that I was dying, starving to death. And I was. The thought of preparing food blocked my appetite. I thought it was a mental disorder? Like I was really crazy? I'd make something, and when I sat down to eat it, I'd taste each ingredient, each spice, separately, the salt, the onion, each one overwhelming the other. The smell of it all together made me crazy. So we started fasting together, eating one thing at a time, bread or pasta, a potato."

"I can't imagine what that's like. I've grown up in kitchens."

"You've never fasted? You should try it."

"Stop eating? Never."

"It's not not eating. I restrict my diet. After we'd eaten a month's worth of brown rice, I thought my appetite had died. I wasn't hungry anymore, but I was weak, listless. Then we went on a water fast, and I'd never felt such energy come into my body. Fasting made me so sensitive, so cleansed. I was like a plant, a cornstalk in the middle of a sunny field, making human chlorophyll, nourished by sunlight. It made me a perfect receptacle for aromatherapy. Smells could nourish me. It was as if the esters, the molecules of aroma, could stimulate my body to feed itself. He could see my auras changing colors."

I nodded slowly, staring into her beautiful face as if I was staring into a mirror, examining the most ordinary, the most familiar nose, the shape of her eyes, her pale brows, hoping to disguise my abject, my wanton surrender.

"Our bodies radiate bands of energy some see as a spectrum of color."

I was blinded by her ideas. I searched frantically for some coincident idea that might connect us. "Is it like an herbalist taking your pulse?"

"I never thought of that," she said approvingly. "I suppose so. He'd never met anyone with such a receptive sensory personality—at least not someone who wasn't also allergic to the modern world entirely—that he could treat indoors. He knew I'd spent two years in the Amazon. He helped me reorganize myself."

"He wanted you to live with him in a tent."

"In a house without corners."

"A cozy wigwam." That slipped out before I could stop. But she didn't seem to mind. "This was in New Mexico, near Taos?" I'd seen the travel posters.

"There was this tepee he'd set up next to an Airstream trailer he shared with his grandfather, a retired mining engineer with Alzheimer's disease."

"What's that?"

"Like selective amnesia, permanent and progressive. I couldn't stay. But he saved my life."

"Are you feeling better now?" That made her smile.

"Yes." She returned my gaze then lowered her eyes to sip another strand, and looked up to find me still staring at her. "This is really wonderful. Are you really going to watch me eat it all? I feel a little naked."

"Every bite. I didn't know food had such an effect on you."

"My confessions?"

"Yes, I want to know everything about you." I knew I was being too earnest, too much the innocent. But for the first time in my life, I was with someone who would let me inside. She wasn't edgy. She wasn't impatient. I didn't have to pretend to understand. I could ask and she would tell me without any reservations.

"Feed me food like this and you can ask me anything."

I was overwhelmed. Melba let me see her in her every guise. She held nothing back. "Ask me anything." She repeated this invitation whenever I was with her, by her touching, by her physical ease, the physical attentions she gave me without a thought, her spontaneous embrace, her hands reaching for mine. She'd catch my sleeve to make a point, touch me, brush my face, my arm, lean suddenly into me, nuzzling her face in my chest. She would trap my hands, grip both my thumbs to secure my attention. It was as if I had never been touched before, never so casually, never from anyone so lacking in physical inhibitions. When she was with me, when we walked down the street, she stayed close enough for me to feel her presence, awash in all of her smells. I could hear the air she was breathing. I was always aware of the rhythm of her breath. She leaped across any physical space that stood between us without ever measuring the distance, without ever looking down.

Bent over a small basket of soba, Melba uncoiled each strand attentively. She peered from behind the curling bangs cascading to her brow, a moue at my fixed, my rapt attention.

"I'm staring, again. Taking notes. Sorry."

"What do you know now you didn't know before?"

"I've discovered how to make you talk: feed you with a little dried tangerine peel and sake in the dipping sauce."

"I'm not so complicated."

"I want to know you completely. Tell me something else."

"You should know I always want what I don't have, what I can't have."

"Like what?"

"Families with kids, big ones, even, that can talk and walk by themselves. That might be fun for a while."

"I guess Auntie Mary knows best. She told me that you had talked about us, about moving in together."

Tears began streaming down her face. She brushed at them irritably, smiling.

"What? What's wrong?" She came to me, burying her head in my chest, listening to my heart beat. "The matchmaker?"

"No, Chris, it's not that. These are the people who adopted Twig. These are kids from the war. Auntie asked if I could help. These are the kids that look like the world, a world that came apart. Oh, God, Chris," she said, laughing at the absurdity, "I hate my white flour complexion."

"You want to be Chinese. Everyone does. That's why we're so many."

"I've always wanted to look that way. Like your Auntie Mary, like Winnie."

Melba lifted a shoulder, a dishcloth across her mouth. "I want to have Asian eyes. Because men are such fools." She was laughing. "I'm falling in love with a guy who wants to feed me, domesticate me, oh damn."

"I want a woman who never eats. How does that happen?"

"Chris, you're born to it. The family connection."

"It must be racial."

"I'm flattered, Chris, that you want me." She took my hands in hers. "I feel nourished by your attention. You remind me how wonderful the ritual of food-making can be. You're making love to me." She brushed the back of her hand across my forehead. "I feel you inside me."

Of course, Melba never actually speaks this way. I seem to hear the words when she returns my gaze, a strand of pasta twisting on her fork proffered to me. How does she keep that gamin gaze lit in her eyes? I want to take her, protect her, roll the shades in the morning to let the first light play luminescent on her face, to be the first thing she sees, my tender regard the last. There are times when I want to kill her, I am so jealous of the lives she lives without me. We can never be apart. If I feed her well, she can be mine forever.

"I don't know if I can be the kind of person that stays forever, Chris. Are you?"

"I'm forever."

"How can you know the future? I might someday have to leave." She drops her face, staring at the counter. "It's always me. I'm the one."

"I love you. I promise that nothing like that will happen to us. I'll want you forever."

"I'd like a glass of wine, please."

Peter prefers stemware for the wine, the manipulation of the fingers to manage the specific gravity of the rolling liquid, the metaphor of a flower, a tulip at the end of its wood, a glass dollop rising there against her lips. I could see with Peter's eyes the tilt of the glass bud spilling wine she sips like first kisses. Her lips are pursed against the rim, her nostrils flared, her eyes shut, eyebrows close, tiny furrows on her forehead, all speak to her concentration, her entire attention devoted to the act of drinking. She opens her eyes and smiles, knowing I watch her. She lets me stare. My intense scrutiny never bothers her. She understands. She gives me permission to observe the sacrament, this transubstantiating miracle I first experienced at the altar's rail, at the nave, at the altar, between God's knees.

It was soon after that evening that Melba and I moved to Santa Lucca to join the expanding family enterprises. With money Auntie invested for Uncle Lincoln, the family had optioned several properties in the county. Most had houses built after World War I as summer cottages for the city's fog-bound and remodeled over the decades by necessity, encrusted with enclosed porches, with parking decks strapped to redwood trees, crumbling foundations, blackened shake siding with panoramic views of the suburban sprawl all the way to the Bay.

As well as being home base and a major intersection for dealers in high-quality marijuana flowing from Thailand, Honolulu, and the verdant Humboldt triangle, the county had the reputation for harboring artists, writers, and film-makers and as a haven for the cutting-edge acid rock of a decade past that was still popular throughout the Pacific Rim, ideal for the band, ideal for all of us.

We were given a small place with a small yard that stepped down a steep embankment below the big house where Peter had installed Twig. Melba now had her garden, and we made plans to build up into the attic for her studio.

Rather than leave him to his own devices, Winnie persuaded Wick to set up house with Twig, one more refugee among the dozens converging on Santa Lucca, Wick's little joke on the immigration authorities. It seemed as if Wick and Peter might find some accommodation with one another. Wick could rediscover his calling among the Yuon. Peter came out when he was in town, wafting across the bridge in a cloud of smoke, a tight-chested exhalation he'd acquired along with a fey stammer to accommodate a growing clientele for his cooking classes.

Lincoln, failing quickly, was never far from our minds. Auntie Mary had always kept house and family together and now there was Winnie to inherit the next generation of us. I was sure we could all stumble along forever. I have always cherished my role as the youngest in my family, surrendering happily to the inevitable example of those who came before me and simply dared anyone else to follow. I felt prepared to accept the responsibility of my role in our ersatz communion we called family. But how to understand what was happening to all of us became increasingly difficult.

Of course, the social chemistry of the times included a sharp increase in the amount of tetrahydrocannabinol in the marijuana that flooded the recreational drug market, or so we were told as justification for the sudden price increase. Twig distributed regular shipments of the Hawaiian red dirt pakalolo the native agriculturalist movement harvested as the principal cash crop in a back-to-the-land movement to resist capital development fueled by Japanese tourism. And, as Wick prophesied, the recently defeated armies of the West spawned a vast trade network for the clandestine packaging and movement of vast quantities of cannabis and heroin. With the Central Intelligence Agency promoting cocaine manufacture and distribution to finance counterrevolutionary movements in the Latin Americas, at the same time pacifying all vestiges of domestic civil disturbances, the antiwar antiapartheid movements, with a vast pharmacopia of narcotic palliatives, America—everybody's diaspora—succumbed to disco. We all began to experiment with discrete amounts of psychoactive drugs, less than 200 milligrams a dose, in blue dots pasted on wax paper that fell from the Tree of Heaven, a harvest of forbidden fruit.

But there we all were, pioneers in suburbia, Melba and I a little pale, blinking in the dappled sunlight with a clear view of the freeway and the Bay beyond and soon to be joined by our very own tribe of Yuon refugees passing for Vietnamese Khmer, family all surnamed Huynh in Vietnamese, and Wong in American, a not unpleasing spectacle to mine own eye, to parade through the final quarter century. It felt like a time of accommodation and acceptance and so we all of us, every one of us, took up the challenge, declaring, "Accept this."

6

The morning, like every morning in Santa Lucca that centennial summer, prickles with buzz saws renovating the neighborhood, the sound of second mortgages being reinvested. Living alone, I am constantly tested by familiar sounds, the smell of the seasons, a new day's heat, to resist the nostalgic apathy Melba's absence leaves me with. The steady hiss of commuting traffic rises on a breath of hot wind from the single arterial that bisects the valley to billow tattered curtains of bay trees and molting plum. The hillside, terraced with two-story redwood-shingled homes with carports topped with corrugated fiberglass, electric yellows and greens, oscillates to the whine of a ripsaw dividing dawn from dust through the hybrid groves of silver spruce, Chinese willows, native oak, curtains of eucalyptus, and ailanthus where journeymen prop and bolster the sagging winter-blasted facades facing wet southwest.

The air is filled with the smell of rotting fruit. I hike past retaining walls wired with blackberry briar as my footsteps raise a moiré of dust and heat shimmering under a canopy of suburban garden, planted, and then abandoned. My Eden overgrown. A neighbor's dog nuzzles the dead lilac bush looking like an abandoned bedspring at the gate, finds a splash of morning sunlight, and holds the spot for warming that's good for perhaps an hour before the high shade of midday envelops my unpruned homestead. From the deck I spy vistas of the unimproved and improving lotscapes, a neighbor's collapsing carport, someone's abandoned rustbucket convertible at odd angles to a buckling wall where water leaches from the hillside pools, a steady rivulet leaving the curbside dank, a rime of chlorine to mark high water, where small insects sip at the vapor rising in the heat. Oak bolls hit the fiberglass roofing over the carports with an explosive crack. Plum trees loaded with fruit are doubled over.

Abandoned, I've remained in this house too long. It's well past the time to leave.

I would stay for the sound of the shower, the tattoo of pipe and tub rattling at dawn, the light framing the bathroom door, the air steamy, fragrant with soap, a cloud condensing around the aura of my dreaming, a chill mask settling over my face. My somnambulant attention would be drawn by the sound of Melba's bare feet crossing the hardwood floor. Half awake, I still imagine her dressing, hurrying. It's only a dream, not unpleasant, her humiliating but erotic habits always arousing. I can never lose the sight of her, and I always feel the empty space she leaves behind. I'm even nourished by the possibilities of Melba and her latest muscular companion—he would be thirty-something, an Italian, an American in Rome? Poor, the baker's boy, a vegan, gaunt, all lean muscle mass, obvious bones, the constant invitation, the wide stare, inviting possibilities, shy, available. I imagine myself an animal grazing between her legs as he penetrates me, in a field, a pasture where deodorants and menthol cigarettes are cultivated. Endless coupling becomes a sweet numbing to lull me to my sleep, a story I hear in my ear as I wake in the morning. "Fuck me," she implores, she invites, "take me, be inside me, I want you." And her bed companion, the new lover to her endless desire, young, gleaming with encouragement.

I boil water for tea. I'll have lunch with Auntie Mary, a long afternoon at a dim sum restaurant in the Sunset, where she will sit patiently, feeding me and waiting for my fumbling explanations of what it was that happened to us all. The images of that season rehydrate like tea leaves, chrysanthemum-petals-become-flesh, knotted buds swollen with the balm of warm water, floating lees in a sky glazed turquoise.

Following Mary's instructions, Melba and I moved into a cottage tucked into a tight curve off a narrow street below Uncle's haven in a grove of second-growth redwood trees, one room that had been variously divided over the years, finally becoming three rooms with a kitchen and a bath, a total of about 800 square feet, with buckling floors of layered linoleum peeling from the baseboard that were poorly providing the illusion of symmetry. A deeply rutted driveway led past the house, past a long-overgrown patch of garden on the south side, to a small garage filled with rusted hardware, an ancient claw-foot bathtub, old doors and window frames from successive remodeling projects. Water-stained redwood paneling with shelves and cabinets covered with a lighter grade of the same wood hung throughout the dark interior, a shade to match the shadow cast by the trees and kept that way with one electrical outlet per room, save for the one bathroom, where a four-way outlet hung from the ceiling light fixture, a final safety feature to keep fools like myself in harm's way.

I stepped back from the bathroom entry, overwhelmed by the smell of damp and mildew. The thick trunk of a redwood tree sent lacy tendrils to peer through the window someone had thoughtfully left open. I suspected Peter's hand, but it was probably Auntie, come to think of it, asking Winnie to let some air in. More than slightly humiliated, I was about to suggest that we buy a tent when I heard Melba cry from the front room.

"Chris, it's perfect!"

"It's a dump," I responded in kind. It was the stuff of movies.

Melba had thrown open all the windows and discovered that our front entry was framed by a Dutch door. "Look, honey, we have a fireplace. Watch." She knelt beside the metal hearth (which I was soon to discover was the only source of heat in the entire house) scrubbing at the rust with her finger.

"That's it?"

"You're such a city kid. Watch this." She opened the damper on the chimney pipe rising to the ceiling and lit a match. "Are you watching?"

"You want to burn the place down and collect the insurance?"

She blew the match out. "See the smoke rise?"

"Smoke signals, send help."

"The firebox draws perfectly and so does the chimney. We can have a fire tonight."

We first settled in the front room with a mattress laid on the floor in front of the fireplace, where we could tend the fire late through the night, reinventing ourselves, listening for creatures prowling in the garden. The street was unlit, and when the sun went down, I remember the darkness as unsettling at first. Then, with the porch light off, I looked up and saw the night sky ablaze with stars and felt struck by images from my earliest childhood, from no conscious recollection, the primordial night sky reflected in our deepest subconscious, genetic memory.

I told her about my summers with Uncle in his trailer in the desert, of temporary shelter, when I imagined we were nomads living beside an endless road.

"When I stayed with Uncle I thought we were Indians, a lost tribe. I grew up with the idea that I was an orphan."

"But you always knew you were from somewhere, China, China men," she said, tentatively, testing our new vocabulary.

"American-born, orphans, possibly illegitimate. Chinatown. It was home base. Internment. The reservation."

"You're lucky, Chris. I never had that. Our family never stayed in one place for long, always moving. Dad was an hydraulic engineer." Sometimes, she recalled a native East Texan, retired military, who finished his career at Scofield Barracks in Hawaii, where he'd been inspired by the industry of the migrant. "'The slants, they got the right angle, especially when it comes to business.'" She watched me for a reaction.

"His neck was red."

"Now don't get huffy. He wasn't a racist." Melba deepened her voice. "'You know I'm not meaning anything personal. Just an old-boy affectation, gets me around the plantation quicker. My own people, my trash, now, they worked for nothin'.'" She fires the stem of wheat straw–wrapped homegrown marijuana I learned to recognize among the potted garden plants she kept on the sunporch of her studio—palms, coleus, spider plants, a large corn stalk, sunflowers—to disguise the dusty gray hemp.

She wistfully imagined her past, inventing, reinventing. "He loved to travel, so we were always packed and ready to move. We spent the longest time in Egypt. That's where my mother died. I watched the priests pour oil on her body. They wrapped her in linen bandages and put her in a coffin the shape of a boat painted with blue sails hung by a gilded mast." Melba pointed to her enameled scarab whose antennae served as our roach clip, steadying the glowing coal of cannabis resting on a brick between us as we sipped smoke. "That's the last time I ever saw him. We shared some hash he'd scored from the priests inside a pyramid, and when I woke up, I was living in Cartagena or maybe it was Samarkan, or a beach in Goa."

"Your mother died."

"Yes." She looked up from her pillow. Her tears welled up, glistening, pooling, then spilling past her ears.

"And you smoked dope with your father? Your mother too?"

"Yes. Not every day; I mean, they weren't drug addicts or anything like that. But they used it to create a kind of bubble that kept us together wherever we went. So who turned you on?"

"You do." We were so easy together, almost frictionless as I slipped inside her.

"I know. Go ahead. Yes," she urged me on, "Don't, don't wait for me."

Physically, it felt as though there could never be an impatient moment between us. We simply made ourselves available to each other, inventing intimacy wherever and whenever we felt the other's heat. I would begin and Melba would leap past. She taught me patience, the erotic possibilities my jealousies sparked as we recounted her former lovers, my marriage to Winnie, my earliest confusions regarding Peter and Wick. We devoted days and nights to living without clothes, days of fasting or one meal at the end of the day, by the light of the setting sun, picking with chopsticks at a cold dish of eggplant and tofu smothered in vinaigrette, sipping green tea, always in an anesthetizing cloud of marijuana.

"When Peter moved to Honolulu for his TV show then met Twig, there was mowie wowie, red dirt pakalolo, Thai sticks from military bases, the music scene. I was just old enough to be attracted and he was my older brother, so I tried it all."

"I've always wanted family, an older brother. It takes me a long time to feel that I belong anywhere. I'm so used to being a one, never a two or three. Milo said that's why I'm so fixed on textiles in my art work. All the loose ends, spinning, weaving fabric, the symmetry in the patterns I tie."

"You can have mine. I've always had one—actually two, if you count Wick. Peter and Wick were always a pair when I was growing up. I was always the youngest. Lincoln and Mary were always inventing a family, tying up loose ends. Peter's the loosest, of course, the most exotic knot."

"But I love Peter, Chris." She moves restlessly in my arms, gazing directly into my eyes. "Don't be jealous."

"Everybody loves Peter. I'm used to it. In my whole life, everyone wants me to tell them how, where, what about Peter." I trap both wrists above her head and we stretch as far as we both can reach. "Or why."

"Whys and whats?"

"He likes men. I wait, a breath, a heartbeat. My desire for her so naked, we lay together, arms and legs entwined, the tortured confession I hope would bind me to her forever.

"Me too."

And she makes me laugh, an overwhelming laughter that is quicker than thought. It blooms across my consciousness and rises as coincident waves that steal across my reflexes, sweeping past inhibitions, bursting over the walls of fear, the years of constraint and distance I've kept to secure myself.

"You do. I know you do." I cannot keep silent. I want to howl like Lincoln's dogs. Am I weeping? How can we say these things, distinguish our appetites, the hungers that want feeding. I cannot staunch the laughter, even as we crush and grind against each other, both of us caught in my blind fury. I'm laughing and crying as she laughs and cries, begging me finally to climax, which I cannot accomplish, which I cannot complete. What is this place, where am I when I hang suspended by desire above her calm appraisal of my frenzy? "I can't."

"I can't either."

"It's never happened before."

"It's okay. It's probably the stuff, Twig's grass, that Peter left for a housewarming present."

"How thoughtful." There can never be a time without him, without all of them.

"That makes you mad. I'm sorry. I touched your anger. There's so much."

"I'm not mad. Really. He's always there. They're always right there. I can't make them up, can't imagine them any differently than they are. I sometimes wish they would just go away."

"And Wick too."

"Yes." And you too, in the end. But then I would end up losing myself, all the impatient anger, the smoldering anger and jealousies that hold me to myself.

"And white people." She strokes my face, tastes my tears, consumes me entirely. "What did the rest of your family think about you all?"

"About homosexuals? Peter was always gay, before I knew what that meant. And when I was old enough to understand, they didn't need us anymore."

"Not that. Of course Peter's gay. Gay people are always gay. I was thinking more about Wick. What he did is different, but people think it's all the same. It makes some gay people afraid of themselves."

"When I was growing up, we didn't talk about it. He was Uncle Lincoln's friend; then he belonged with Mary. Crazy. I always thought it was because

Wick wasn't Chinese, that he was a white man living in a Chinese family, that he was the orphan." I hold her as close to me as possible.

"Is that so important? How do I fit in? I like young men. I'm white."

Only the slip of confession, now the erotic emollient, binds me to her forever. I had in mind to keep our distance from all of them, from Lincoln, from Peter and Wick, from Peter's lover, Twig, and our new tribe of cousins.

"Yes, you are—but nobody cares." I feel her legs pressing round me. "You're only a girl." I had in mind to secure us, to build a wall to screen us from all my family's permutations. But Melba made the screen transparent by stepping back and forth, erasing the distinction, attracted to the illusion of belonging to a family, a communal tribe. And I slowly began to love this evolving apparition of family Melba helped me to contrive.

That summer the family began to multiply beyond recognition, beyond the boundaries of our imagination and our ability to organize a coherent identity. It was Peter who knew or should have known what was happening. I now think he was watching, observing, fascinated by Twig's rediscovered adopted family and his growing obsession for Wick's grandiloquence—or he was jealous. It's a family trait, a habit we share, that watching, that envy. Twig wanted more from the music he created; that was obvious, and his downfall. Why is it that artists always want their work to be more than it is? We'd watched this moral infection in ourselves, and Twig gave himself, gave us all over to it, that moral certainty that there is more than the facade we decorate with what we weave or scribble or paint, the song, the dance. Lincoln and Winnie were traveling. Mary had sent me with Melba to Santa Lucca to watch over Wick and, I'm sure, to spy on Peter and Twig in the old mansion she bought and had begun refurbishing. All of us had been magically made whole again, all in the name of family as we became a commune that took its name from Twig's band and its organization from the summer camps Wick once organized for the Haven, with all the familiar activities: camp crafts, recreational dances, outdoor cooking, and campfire chats. Wick, especially, had rediscovered himself in the care and organization of our tribal cousins, a few of whom by an illusory coincidence were members of Twig's long-lost "family," the group with which he had first immigrated before escaping to Honolulu.

If Wick played the father, Twig was the son. The younger cousins would follow Wick's instructions to pursue apprenticeships in construction work, gardening, recycling, the way their tribal elders did. But in the evenings, on the weekends, they became Twig's roadies, loyal, if a little edgy on crystal and ice.

Melba, with children of the Yuon as well as the neighborhood in tow, children who seemed to miraculously appear then disappear, gave herself over to the local tai chi assemblies organized at Wick's suggestion in Santa Lucca's town square. She even experimented with segregating herself, sitting at meals with the women and especially the children, because only the children spoke English. She taught them macramé, helped prepare the evening meals. Melba and the kids together burned our vegetables and tofu over charcoal braziers, patronized but otherwise ignored by the wives of the older Yuon. The children attached themselves to Melba even as they fell easily into their routine of collecting paper, bottles, and cans, crushing aluminum soda cans and packing them neatly in paper cartons. Their playground was half builder's emporium and half recycling center.

With so much time spent outdoors, we immediately lost our city pallor, and, to my eye, we seemed vaguely but fashionably anorexic and native. I can still smell the aroma of rice cooking outdoors, Thai polished white, perfuming the air rising from two restaurant-sized rice cookers. A hose gurgled in a washtub where we rinsed our fingers as we ate. Other children from the neighborhood joined with ours to run between the shrubs and trees covered with dyed fabric. Pendant bells and whirligigs sounded and windsocks in the shapes of fish and insects hung limply from lines strung from the eaves of the house through the trees. Candle lamps flickered on stonework and the polished granite altars Wick's crews wholesaled to their landscape customers. All summer while Wick, sometimes Twig, and the tribal cousins worked on the house, there were children everywhere, dousing themselves in pool water, dashing through untended sprinklers, their hair damp and slick against their dark tans, all of them wrapped in tie-dye.

During the day, when Twig's cousins were out and about the county, the women were working in a business mall converted from an elementary school Santa Lucca had decommissioned because of the decline in school-age children among the generation who could afford to buy real estate in the county. Wick had made the suggestion to Peter, who nego-tiated the lease. At first, the women manufactured earrings, soldering and wiring bits of glass and metal parts imported from Africa, exploiting loop-holes in import restrictions for raw materials for costume jewelry. The shop allowed them space to cook, a place for their children to wander, and with Melba's encouragement, to weave an imitation of the Hmong *Pandau* that they were taught at the training skills center in Oakland where their group had first landed. The younger girls had been taught by Urban Corps volunteers to do fish prints and linoleum print blocks employing traditional designs copied from photographs the crafts instructor at the center had collected. Melba suggested they string found objects and attach them as decorative ties for the prints and weaving. These items were less labor intensive and brought a better profit at the flea markets.

There were one or two suspicious neighbors who routinely kept watch by quizzing the children, snapping photographs of the remodeling Twig's roadies were performing to the property, listening to Wick's fab-rications, or hiking the trails above the property with their binoculars while birding or collecting wild orchids. But Santa Lucca soon became more or less accustomed to seeing Wick's tribal women squatting at School Plaza, waiting for the flatbed to pick them up, our oldest a toothless grand-mother sunning herself by the low three-faucet fountain between Room One and the library-turned-hot-tub-emporium, hunkered on a spread of newspapers, scraping a small hill of ginger root with the back of a chopstick, the occasional flash of fire and white ash from incinerating garlic skins rising harmlessly over the basketball court.

After tai chi in the Plaza we would trudge up the hill, the sunlight failing in the dense foliage, Melba leading a band of us chanting from her English lessons, "Lions, tigers, and bears, oh my," still flushed after following Twig's elaborate "clamoring monkey" set. At the commune, hummingbirds darted through the trees, hovered by the feeders of red sugar water, sipping their fill, while bees gathered, dancing in the sweet spill. Ants trudged in steady columns from the drip to small mounds that dotted the dirt hill our tribal cousins were excavating for a retain-ing wall to run the length of the property.

Melba said that in the dark all of us seemed to belong to the same tribe of summer. We all began speaking in metaphor. It was a silly sea-son. Maybe it was the dope. But we thought we had a plan.

Over that summer, our tribe was joined by numerous others, cousins and family friends, to help with all of our enterprises. Only the kids spoke fluent English, already having spent time in Nebraska, Texas, Florida before escaping to the West Coast, or a year or two on the streets of Oakland with other mostly Vietnamese strays, like Twig, who arrived at their point of embarkation in Thailand, the Philippines, Hong Kong disguised as the men of families to which they were haphazardly assigned.

Wick spent much of his day recording and transcribing their oral histories, tying bits and pieces to his sermons in the evenings. In the DP camps the refugees would agree to form large family groupings in order to invite sympathy and beat the quota the immigration services had established to restrict entry by unattached individuals. If they were bright and winsome, willing to pretend in order to survive, they could find their way to America, an eighteen-hour flight.

Imagine: in the span of a day, they could leave the squalor of the razor-wire compounds, draped in wet laundry, the smell of latrines, smoke rising from kerosene stoves, a view of their future staring back at them, the watchful eyes of a thousand and more, just beyond their sleeping mats, and find themselves in Oakland. Once settled in temporary housing in America, the stray males would be invited to leave their adopted families and find shelter with others like themselves. Some headmen who had enlarged their families in the relocation camps by adopting young men like Twig quickly learned that in this new land girls were more important, more able income-producers, more amenable, more loyal. There was an abundance of orphaned boys who had to find more efficient ways to survive. Some prospered on the streets, preying on immigrant businesses, petty extortions and drug dealing. Still, they were boys, lost sons. Twig was lucky. He had escaped before he could be abandoned.

According to Wick, Twig's ersatz family worshipped a scrappy young warrior they called Baba Lan, speaking GI lingo, with a quick smile and a tender regard for his baby sisters. He grows tall in camp, and leads a group of older boys through the fence to barter and scavenge. In California, in Santa Lucca, a reunited Baba Lan, who now called himself Twig, looking younger by a few years than his thirty, is rail thin, muscled, but always thin, with a little potbelly. His navel sticks out a bit and he is tattooed, a multicolored dragon over his left breast. That summer he had a fringe of scarlet hair drawn like a wooly string around his jawline, a pale mustache, and bracelets: wooden beads, a black wire bracelet made from the pubic hair of a water buffalo his cousins salvaged from their jewelry-making, and a thick gold chain that he bragged was a gift from a Vietnamese fan living in San Jose, a college student, the youngest daughter of an officer in the ARVN in exile. In the sunlight, one could see that a burnished red gleam shimmered among the fine black strands and that his hair was thinning. He rediscovered a private language among his crew, who called him Baba Lan.

"Baba Lan is a Chinese name?" Melba was endlessly fascinated by the family that suddenly surrounded us.

"'Baba's' like 'papa,' and Lan is the Vietnamese name he took at the Hong Kong DP center," Wick answered, his head bouncing up and down to punctuate his reply. "His nom de guerre."

Melba fell into the style of the kids, especially the designer fingernail polishes and pedicures she got free from the nail salon the commune financed. We were both in awe of the cousins' other enterprises—barbershop, sauna, hot tub, and later, massage parlor.

Melba offered her hands over the breakfast table. Her nails were dark blue with a different figure on each one.

"Honey, does it wash off?"

"Of course not. Aren't they so cool?"

"You don't want any of it falling in the food."

"Chris, everybody thinks it's cool. Twig said so. Winnie did hers. Even Peter liked them." She stood and glared at me from over her shoulder. "'Hey, girl. That's bad.' And you know what else?" She pranced around the kitchen.

"What else?"

"Twig, I mean, Baba Lan does tattoos. He's a pussycat. He gave me a gold chain. See?" She dangled the short necklace with a traditional carved white elephant, its trunk raised.

"That's very pretty. It's ivory. Very nice work."

"Rat bone," she sang.

"Rat bone?"

"Twig's cousins, they all do them. Very extreme."

"Don't tell anybody."

"Chris," she said impatiently. "Everybody knows and everybody wants one. He's got tigers, monkeys, turtles, frogs, pigs—the entire zodiac.

They're kind of expensive. But I got a family discount. Winnie bought the whole calendar for a charm bracelet. There's earrings, and lots of other things."

"Like what?"

"Dog tags."

"Real dogs?"

"Sure, the ones the neighbors think we eat. No, silly. They're like ID bracelets for soldiers. This one's in Vietnamese, but you can get them in Laotian and Hmong and even French. So cool."

"Very. Maybe I should put in an order."

"Too late, Christopher Columbus. You'll have to be nice to Baba. Me, too. Take me dancing."

"Well, maybe something for Mary?"

"Been there. Done that. Baba gave her a wonderful tiger. Didn't you see?"

It's true. I hadn't. Like Wick, like Peter, I was watching Twig's alter ego, this Baba Lan.

Peter would have noticed Twig's changes quicker than I did. And he would have blamed Wick, as he did for everything else that happened. After all, Twig was the rock 'n' roller we all wanted to be, in constant need to reinvent himself. With Wick supplying the details as fast as he could invent them, Twig was creating Baba Lan's history in song, creating urban legends about the street gangs that roamed the California interstate, moving from hamlet to hamlet where "the lost and forgotten men roam": West Oakland, San Jose, Fresno, all the way to LA. He was testing the persona of the abandoned guerrilla tribesman—dressed by the CIA, right down to the black raincoat and cowboy boots—living in the heart of Little Saigon, who just happened to play rock 'n' roll with a guitar he swung like a chainsaw.

The band had opened for the Sopwith Camel at the county fairgrounds, making their entrance on the flatbed and closing by pitching weighted baggies and twisted bits of fabric fashioned as bracelets in the colors of the *Pandau* fabric the cousins sold. At his performances Twig wore a gold coin bracelet around his wrist, a thick gold chain dangling from his neck, and *Pandau* belts like bandoliers fit for a modern Malay pirate. His tie-dyed shirts, sleeveless skivvies, let his tattooed arms darken, obscuring the lurid

portraits of Chinese dragons and Vietnam-era military slogans that deco-
rated his body. The tigers and eagles on both shoulders faded into the pattern of fighting white elephants at his neckline. And in the black light that
bathed the band at their club venues where everyone smiles neon blue, his
tattoos turned paisley, a wild cosmetic design that attracted the ladies.

As Melba and I played house, Peter began supervising the remodeling
jobs he contracted throughout the county, including the bungalow Melba
and I shared. Wick was too busy inventing his ministry, describing his
world vision for the millennium to come. What he wrote became lyrics
for the Tree of Heaven. With Twig's eccentric improvisations and Wick's
New Age psychobabble for ammunition, they were creating fusion, Twig
and Baba Lan becoming one.

It was a busy time for all of us. Mary, along with Uncle's still-sharp
eyes and Winnie's legs, had invested the family's money into a complex
mix of second mortgages and FHA-approved reconstruction projects,
remodeling homes with the tribal immigrants Wick collected off the side-
walks of Oakland as they peered from the windows of public housing at
the hostile poverty, the infectious lassitude beckoning just beyond their
stucco compounds. While our erstwhile tribal cousins supported themselves scavenging cardboard and recyclables, the government provided
basic training in carpentry, electrical work, and plumbing. Then, with
the savings and loan industry pouring money into housing, employing
cheap labor, Uncle Lincoln said, "Now you tell me how anyone can work
that kind of magic outside a whorehouse."

Our enterprise was endless. We were constructing Santa Lucca's first
Asian Tenderloin in a single mall. Lincoln experimented by hanging out
at the Cafe au Lait with Winnie, where he had the cousins making iced
coffees and café d'amour, a glass coated with milk syrup and the drip
from a cafe presse over ice. He watched the summer pass there, at the
foot of Mt. Tamalpais, as bicyclists, trekkers, tourists of all sorts landed,
as Santa Lucca began to resemble a way station in Nepal.

One Sunday afternoon, Lincoln, Winnie, and Mary arrived in Heaven,
climbing slowly up from the street below, where Winnie could safely install
Uncle's Continental away from the construction debris that narrowed
the already narrow road, tourists visiting some exotic excavation. Auntie

and Winnie were wrapped loosely in tropical linens, both wearing large sunbonnets with sheer nets that wrapped around their necks. Uncle sported a baseball cap with the insignia of the USS *Ticonderoga* and baggy white shorts. He looked amiably ridiculous, sweat socks and flapping sandals raising dust in his wake. He was wearing one of the Travel and Tour aloha shirts, the one from the *Luraline,* on which he claims to have once done duty as a steward, in fifty-two, the year the Chinatown lotteries were forever abandoned by the tongs when hundreds of butchers, bakers, fishmongers, waiters, and cooks descended on the unemployment office, not for the meager stipend but for the identification papers to document their legitimacy. Was it the confession programs the McCarthy hearings spawned to deport illegal, possibly Communist, subversives that had broken the grip of the staunchly conservative tongs, throwing the ticket writers out of work, or the sudden influx of new immigrants forcing the creation of new employment opportunities outside of Chinatown that sparked change?

"Never just one side," Uncle barks impatiently. "Not this or that. All one thing." Or he might laugh and make a joke in Cantonese, repeating the formulary of the know-nothing, no-use, nothing generation to follow. The innocuous old man, alert, fragile, reaches out his hand, which is always met. I discover we have a garment factory in Bangkok that not only manufactures our shirts, but also forges immigration papers. I'm never really told directly about the network of business interests in which Uncle engages. It's simply assumed that I know or I will ask if I need to know. Or is it assumed that I'm not ready to know until I learn to ask? Whom to ask is an issue of face, of my perception of myself and my status. Indirection, inference, intelligently employed, is perceived as a sign of my maturity, at least from Uncle's point of view, as is my loyalty to Auntie and my conciliations with Winnie.

On Winnie's arm, Uncle moves fearlessly up the broad gravel path in the sweltering summer heat. Having so recently negotiated the tropics with his new bride, he can cross confidently into the dappled shade of the yard, home the hunter, the sailor, the candlestick maker. His face is as dark as the children's, but it is probably his poor circulation that creates that mottled flush. His coronary arteries are failing.

Auntie and Winnie nod, smile. Winnie offers a powdered cheek for me to brush with my lips, then is pulled quickly away by Auntie who wants to watch Twig leading tai chi on the patio. Auntie and Winnie are both wearing bracelets with dangling ivory figurines.

Later it's Twig who's first to greet Uncle as the food is being served, appearing almost magically from the smoke billowing around the cooking fires. He leads Uncle by the elbow and draws him aside. He bows slightly, as if to bring his forehead to Uncle's hand, but Uncle prevents the gesture firmly. The two are quickly joined by the other male cousins as they chat in a mix of Cantonese dialects, watching the women preparing the skewers. I can see that these formulary customs make meetings easy, a familiar vocabulary of food, health, children. Uncle walks slowly among the cooks, reviewing the dinner preparations as if tallying the day's accounts on the barbecue the Yuon have made into an elaborate abacus.

Finally, almost reluctantly, he excuses himself and joins us at the table we've set aside for ourselves, his reluctant kin, as Twig becomes a silhouette on the other side of the curtain.

"Welcome to your house, Uncle," Peter says, extending a gratuitous hand, surrendering his chair, drawing a joint from his shirt and setting it ablaze. He inhales deeply and offers it to Uncle, who declines. "I'm old fashion," he laughs. "I want a San Miguel."

I stiffen at Peter's bravado, but Uncle is easy, even genial with him. "Peter, I hear everybody's doin' the tai chi hula, huh? In Hong Kong, I saw everyone doing the same stuff real early in the morning before it got too hot. Old folks on the balconies of the shopping malls, in the parks, on the street. Really works, I should take it up. Like jogging, right?" He stoops down, picking foxtails from his socks.

"Nice hat, Uncle," I uncap a bottle and offer him a glass.

"No glass. This hat, boy, was a gift from American military surplus, a grateful quartermaster I met in Subic Bay." He pulls the brim down low. "So how y'all? Everybody keepin' outta trouble, hard at work, I see, at Fort Wong." He gazes dubiously past the debris that overlooks the front entrance at the scaffolding outlining the wall.

Wick joins us. He's bright-eyed, sipping mineral water from a paper cup, and looks ready to tell a story, a new revelation. "Lincoln, you're back. Welcome, welcome. You should see the work the boys are doing to the place."

Lincoln nods. "Indians, thick as flies, in mufti, disguised as Orientals." He shakes his head, adjusts his cap again, looks up past the trees. "There's nothing like America. How's that?" He drinks deeply. "Cold beer and barbecue. Yep, been gone a week too long, stranger in a strange land and all that. I don't mind telling you. Now, no offense, but it sure is good to talk to a white man again." He explodes with laughter. "That's how they talk to me. Yeah, yeah. How're ya'll, Wick?"

Our grove darkens as the light fails. A florescent buglight snaps at gnats. The figures of children dancing around the garden catch light flickering from a candle flame in the windows of the house. The laundry hangs luminously. Teeth glow in the darkness. On the lawn, the trees cast long, twisted shadows against the smooth facade of the rising wall.

We hear the women's laughter, Winnie undoubtedly reciting stories from their most recent trip to Asia. Uncle looks ill, sits awkwardly in the aluminum garden chair. "Can't keep up these days," he says. "Five, ten years ago, I'd fly from Olongapo to Bangkok to Hong Kong tourist cheap. These days, money's so good there's a labor shortage throughout the Pacific Rim. In Honolulu the locals refuse work only the immigrants take. The Guandong farmer's son buys Hong Kong dollars at the Canton zoo from the tourists watching the monkeys. You got the call girls making the market for dehydrated papaya juice at the White Swan Bar in Canton City. Taiwan exports U.S. dollars to Switzerland in bags of cement; I heard there's a chain of fast-food restaurants with foundations poured over American dollars wrapped in fiberglass packing to avoid the Greengang's tariff. With the war done, things move fast."

(Uncle's predictions were always on the money. At the end of the Western millennium, I watch Star cable, CNN, MTV from an air-conditioned Holiday Inn within view of the peaked roofline of the Forbidden City. I walk the streets early, before the heat bears down, humid but not too hot. The street temples are packed. My local house of hocus pocus looks like a floating restaurant, tricked up to imitate a Bangkok call girl, every inch enameled and paved with lacquer and gilt.)

"Lincoln, you always worry when things look too good." Wick wants to moralize.

Peter tries to stop him. "Wick has made a career out of analyzing all that Chinaman worry."

Wick patiently objects. "Peter, Peter. You remember Hong Kong, the temple walls that come neurotically alive in the Taoist imagery writhing on the walls? The facades resemble my own earliest nightmares. Everybody exhorts the deities to protect, defend, or save them from birth, death, life, money, security, power, revenge, all human passions, all obsessions. Nineteen ninety-seven: one thousand, nine hundred and ninety-seven metaphors, all such illusions masking the transparency of life."

Peter blows smoke over Lincoln and Wick. "Facades," he repeats. "I like that. Lunch at Jumbo's in Aberdeen, floating dim sum, the best dim sum, floating in the middle of the harbor. What a lily pad. What a facade, hey?" Peter lobs a stone. "Building bigger facades, yes." He ignores Wick. "So you're reduced to carrying Winnie's shopping bags, Uncle?"

"Yeah, bag boy. Little bit of business for you, though. New hotel deal in Bangkok, landed some condo space in Hong Kong, you hear me? These guys keep me busy."

"What about China?" Forgetting, Peter again offers Lincoln a hit.

"Dicey right now." Uncle ignores Peter's outstretched hand. "Might buy farmland. The locals want to build an airport. But no money, honey. They're still pretending, serve the people, all that crap. They're killing the next generation. Can't last much longer. Nobody's eating right. No food. The very idea makes me hungry. Let's eat."

The women serve on platters directly from the cooking fires, the night sky as deep as the ocean. Winnie has taken Auntie and Melba indoors.

"Everybody needs food. Food first, renewal later, at least for the Indians, right, Wickman?"

"I'm an Indian too. We're all Indians, Lincoln. It's the facades, all the masks."

"Hey," he laughs. "That's what I said. The whole world's us," he mutters. Uncle folds an arm around me, leaning on me. "You know what I mean, Columbus." He nods at Wick, closing the circle, and Wick nods back.

"Now, Christopher, speaking of the Indians, what in the hell are these guys building there?" he asks in a stage whisper. "Damn it, they're a clean foot inside the surveyor's stake but that ten-foot corner is clearly illegal. And that's a gook flag in the corner. Pardon my French, boy, but you know what I mean. From the Indians' point of view, the war ain't over yet."

Reinforcing rods woven through the patterns of concrete stitch an intricate foundation for the ongoing construction. When the kids brush against the sides of the freshly poured concrete, their bodies and clothes turn chalky. They clap the dust on each other or slip up to an unsuspecting adult to leave their palm prints. The foundation had already been plumbed with lead pipe that would eventually irrigate the hill.

I have no idea. "The flag says 'Valley Lumber' on it, Uncle."

"What the hell we advertising Valley Lumber for?"

Peter laughs. "Come on, Uncle. They tie it on when the flatbed's loaded beyond the bumper. Tells everybody we're coming with a load."

"That's what you say. I say it looks like Cong, just like they look like Cong. Makes us all look suspicious. Be a little careful. Winnie's right, you know. We all have money tied up in this piece of property. Let's fly an American flag."

Peter pinches the burning butt end of the joint between his fingers with a little saliva, then eats the roach, listening to Lincoln talk past him, watching Wick.

"The country lost people in that shithole war and I don't like us throwing up a goddamn pagoda looking right over everybody's front yard. 'Sides, it's bad for business."

With the slightest edge in his voice, Wick tries to dismiss the words, raising his hands to catch them. "It's not a pagoda, Lincoln. Look at it. It's a wall. It's a memorial."

"A memorial to what?"

"Us. The Indians."

"How about you guys give me a clue. Just tell me in American so I know where the money's going."

Wick stands and begins to pace. "You were there shopping in Olongapo, Bangkok, Saigon. Making business. Canton, Shanghai, Taipei, Singapore. We were all of us there, we're all from there at one time or another. Now we're here, right?"

"Right, right."

"It's a memorial to us."

"To us?"

"Like the Statue of Liberty, Uncle. We want one for us. For immigrants."

"Christopher, can you tell me what the hell he's talkin' about?"

Of course, I can't. I never could.

"Uncle," Wick adds, "think about it. It's a Trojan horse, a Trojan pig, if you like. We've got this business, it's always been our business, okay, your business. Now you're putting all these people to work, employing all these people, they're running in and out of the neighborhood and the county's beginning to wonder why."

"Well, shoot, now there goes the neighborhood. It sure as hell gets me wondering why. You know, like 'They're moving in?'"

"They're here. They go to church. They come visit this temple, this memorial to remember their dead, their MIAs, the people they left behind, a facade upon which they can inscribe their loss, their victory, their history. It's perfect." Wick looks at us, satisfied.

"You're sure it's not a Commie thing?"

"Of course not. It's church," Peter laughs. "Maybe even tax deductible. I was thinking maybe a parking lot, if we could buy the parcel below. I mentioned that?"

"All right. I know that part," Lincoln concedes. "I'm wondering if we can be sure that they can tell us all apart, cowboys and Indians. Why does it have to be so big?"

"So we can see it from the moon, or at least from the freeway. Uncle, what good is a memorial if you can't see it?" Peter mockingly argues.

"Best kind," Uncle snaps.

Wick says, "Again, what difference would that make? So, yes, we raise the Stars and Stripes, we promote private enterprise, a little old-time religion, we're off the welfare rolls. It's a promise kept. No matter how far we travel to survive, we are the same people. Lincoln, you know that," as if Twig were grinding out a clanky, bluesy national anthem, a slack key jangle, prodding the air with his guitar, gel lights melting red, white, and blue across the stage.

"Yeah. Okay. Maybe. But will everybody?"

Wick shakes his head slowly. "Why worry now? I mean, if they don't know now, when are they ever going to learn?"

That was the first time I realized what they had in mind. The wall was a memorial to the Asian dead.

Uncle really didn't know what the next step might be, only that we were all out of control. After all, it was Uncle who had agreed to this late reunion of tribes. He wanted to leave something of himself for Peter. Maybe he thought he was saving Winnie for me. But for Peter, there had always been Wick. So when Peter found Twig all by himself, Uncle saw an opportunity. Twig was probably a hood some merchant wanted off the streets. It didn't matter. For Peter's sake, Uncle had done a favor for some old friend and found Twig's family.

"And I'm not dead yet," Uncle insists, but he soon would be, leaving Mary and Winnie to watch over me.

A hot night in the city inevitably signals a cool Bay crossing. The dividing wall of fog that spumes between Land's End and Fort Point always puddles at the feet of the Golden Gate Bridge. I drive between bands of summer heat and the chill wet, a bank of fog. Shivering in the humid blanket of July, I park by the yacht harbor and walk Northpoint Beach to the Marina, to the bottom spit of sand that slides into the Pacific, lit by the reflecting jewel boxes tucked into the dark hill behind me, the carbon arc's brilliant silver stare across an opaque ocean. Here at Land's End, where the roiling water begins, the vaporous, clammy mist sits for an evening with no wind to blow the ocean's smoke away. In this cloud, I can follow the logic of our family chimeras, our demise. It begins and ends with Lincoln, sitting in his counting house, dividing then redividing all his money, Mary and Winnie always by his side, pouring tea and honey, and by the door stand Peter and I guarding the entry, while Wick rails at the stars, lit up like a Roman candle.

That summer Wick began each day by ingesting small amounts of LSD, experimenting with what we then carelessly, ludicrously assumed were measured doses of this psychoactive stimulant laced on sheets of blotter paper tattooed with various cultural icons: Mickey Mouse, Abraham Lincoln, Jesus Christ, an atomic mushroom cloud. He would wander or sit speechless for several hours at a time, examining the details of a flower, a bent nail, any object that might bring some order to the rush of connotations and associations the drug compelled.

My own vague recollections of the experience—impressions, really, because the drug seems to induce a self-protective amnesia—came as an assault on my sense of social inhibitions. I imagined painful, wrenching confessions, babbling for hours to Melba, and sex with various body parts of my familiars, even Lincoln's dog behind the trailer in the desert. Melba assured me that I would sit quite still for almost the entire day without uttering a word, refusing food, and weeping as we coupled with our private hallucinatory demons past thresholds of language, deliberation, and inhibition, leaving us with only our most fetal instincts to meet. The aftereffects of the drug itself seemed innocuous enough, although there were and are enough clinical anecdotes to warrant extreme caution. Still, in my limited experience, it seemed only to exacerbate a closer scrutiny of myself that might remain for a day, for a week, even a month before all my vainglory was forgotten. It was amnesia that became my anecdote for introspection. Or so I thought.

In Wick's case, as he was wont to rationalize his addictions, the obsessive energy the drug unleashed was brain food. He was voracious. The years he spent pursuing his ministry returned in full force, and since he was more than forthright about his past indiscretions, letting us, our community, anyone who cared to listen make their own judgment, his public contrition was more than enough, more than we actually cared to hear. We were, after all, co-conspiring.

He was immediately popular. Young people had always found him engaging enough, but with the band, with Twig, Wick was mesmerizing. The events of the day became his text. He would spend hours poring over a single page of *Time, Newsweek,* the dailies, the underground press, weaving the news into an endless soliloquy that he could perform. He became Twig's opening act at the Café au Lait in Santa Lucca.

The audiences for their messianic rock and roll were never large, and loyal fans, disciples, fewer still. Drawn first by the Tree of Heaven's languid mix of slack guitar and pentatonic progressions, the bells and gongs, the young vets, black and white, who'd first crossed the blue Pacific with pictures in their heads of palm trees and rice paddies, and returned with the stink of napalm and night soil, cordite and rotting fish in their memories, heard a sound they thought familiar. There were Asians born in America with a faulty grip on the language of their ancestors, uncomfortable in their skins, trying to stay a step ahead of the new immigrants, the newly arrived, who must confront their own assimilation. I recognized them too easily, saw my own needs being met by the same coincidence, a chance encounter at a café with some messiah like Wick who could alchemize race, culture, politics, sex, and rock 'n' roll.

Wick loved to practice his calligraphy in public on a small table crowded with his ink sticks, block, and brushes. The merely curious might settle for the phonetic representation of their names in Chinese. But here and there young Asian Americans wandering uneasily between the white counterculture and yet another wave of Asian refugees might risk their hands with a few strokes they recalled from their childhood. Soon Wick had a following.

Wick points to the band, at Twig, then at himself. "Let me introduce myself." He dons the rough hemp shroud of a Taoist necromancer in mourning, fly whisks dangling from his wrists, red string necklaces strung with tiny *Pandau* patches, an unfinished piece of bone carving. "Dr. Theodore Candlewick, herbal shrink, marriage/family counselor, advisor on adoption for Chinese girl babies, I consult on homosexual and lesbian issues, issues of sexual abuse, of refugees, illegal immigration, survivor guilt. I have come to know victims as only one who victimizes, one who has been victimized, can know. I've performed crosscultural mediation between the Red Cross, the Buddhist clergy, and the police in attendance to the surviving families of the Hmong children machine-gunned by a survivalist at recess. I was called in by the UAW to counsel two auto workers, a father and son who beat to death a Chinese American they thought was a Japanese import with—what else—an unemployed baseball bat." He pauses.

"I told them I couldn't tell the difference either. Could you?"

The audience is equally divided into those who laugh and those who are repulsed, still uneasy about sharing the anxieties surrounding their racial identities with others like themselves.

"Good news. There is no difference. The Filipinos, Hawaiians, Chinamen, Japs, the spick and spam, the ones the color of gooks are history's MIA's: missing-in-America. But you're not missing; you were never missing. You're here. Didn't it all begin as the scum on the molten edge of a vast cauldron, the DNA forming in the grease of a cooling universe?"

Today such talk hardly seems at all risky. But back then, the issues of our race, our place in this society as the Vietnam War remained mired in scandal and recrimination, were important. We survived. Were we the enemy or the victims? Wick, always the shepherd, leading by example, suddenly found himself in danger of being trampled by the chaotic demands of the next generation, as if my own weren't enough to compel him forward. We of a certain age, American-born, a certain disposition, commuters wandering back and forth across the bridge Wick once helped to design, joined hands and jumped.

"Now you cookin' bra'!" Twig rifts from the bandstand.

Peter rolls his eyes. He's not enjoying Twig's evolution. "Late-night TV. What a bore."

Peter's cooking for me again. We've come home, back to Peter's kitchen, his classroom, because we know we've bitten off more than we can chew. "You want squab?" He's prepared two small birds, lacquered rosewood, the curling detail, fried lace nesting against orange slices, tender sprigs of coriander, a smear of bean sauce. "You'll like this. Egg noodles in a garlic fish broth, scallion and more garlic bits with the sour breath of lemon grass. The cultural detritus sweeps through the Mekong Delta and into the soup bowl, a rich, fertile loess to plant your tongue in."

"Nice, Peter. Home cooking."

"Like the pasta?"

"It's good. Egg noodles?"

"No eggs. I got the recipe from a kimchi palace in Koanamoku. They're hand pulled. A little ropey, heavy winter fare."

When can we talk, when can we talk about me, I want to say, but he sees me. When he needs me, he sees me, feeds me.

"But you look good, lost a few, yeah? Melba starves you? Don't bore me with all the details, but I can listen and shudder at all the right moments. I love you. We're brothers. How's the quail?"

"It's good."

"I tell you, Winnie and I, we went to hear Twig at the Neon Moon the other night? Uncle's crappy, don't ask. I thought she needed a break. We played name games. Remember, they were The Persuasions in an earlier incarnation."

"Born again."

"Yes. That's good. We sat around inventing new names. How about 'Buddha's Demons'? How about 'Ginseng?' For the copy artist, 'Spam'? Very Waikiki. God, my boy Twig has the most beautiful skull, not round, but the long Indo-Malayan fruit warped by tickets, by famine, by languor and melancholia." Peter fans a deck of flour skins and folds a dozen potstickers. "He's taken to shaving his skull so that it gleams under the hot spots. He's paper and glue, the rice potbelly, thin bones, sunken eyes. Rickets keep the hollow look. Tree of Heaven, a little vulnerable, just this side of pathos. He loves it. Fits with the family Uncle found for him."

"All the cousins?"

"Right. He's Baba Lan again. He makes a better orphan." Peter drums his fingers on the sideboard. He's very thin and the cosmetic sunscreen is slick and obvious on his forehead and around his throat. "How about 'Children of the Dust'? Give it the refugee twist. Winnie translates that from Vietnamese into Chinese, into English. Twig doesn't know, doesn't have enough history to care. He always says the music comes first." Peter begins laughing to himself. "That's so sweet, no? Island naïf. Now I think he's banging the ladies."

"Girls?"

"Sorry, Chris. Lover's tiff." Was that a tear he brushed aside? "God, he was hot last night." Peter has an ear for music, the radio, the movies. His ears have always been the way to his heart—so eclectic, even for the clash of Japanese techno-pop and slack key bluegrass the Tree of Heaven creates, the loose and limp, the goosey hemp reggae languor. Twig, the Tree of Heaven, could do it all, of course. The Pacific Rim has a vast ear for the cacophonies of cultures exponentially expanding in the ether. "'White Christmas' in July, that makes the expat cry," Peter sighs.

"I know. Now he's got Melba wanting to dance a number with kids and tambourines, glossy tank tops."

"Me too," Peter twists around the counter, "I look good in glitter." He swings his powdered fists, punching the dark.

When I asked her, even Winnie conceded, "Twig has fast hands. He could be Hong Sau. The band should be called the 'Taipeng Rebellion.' He's such a bad boy," she teased. "I can tell when Peter's overheated, Chris. Smells like his shaving lotion is burning."

And Melba, of course. "I love him, Chris, they're all too crazy, Peter, Twig, and Wick. They're a bust." Melba could keep up, but she kept herself apart—for my sake, I thought. She had a steady source of weaving materials from Twig, enough hemp fiber for her artwork and more than enough by-product to market discretely. Of course, Twig and the boys were a bust—drugs, paraphernalia, the aroma of good smoke, of incense, of scented oils. It was only a matter of time. But for that short moment, we all seemed to be touched by something magical. And, in truth, perched on his branch, Twig could make rubber bands sound good.

"So Winnie and I, the crowd, we couldn't peel away from the sight of this bad boy. We finally got down between sets and stayed glittered till dawn. I haven't slept much since. It's an ice crowd—really tough on my metabolism."

Peter gnashes small bones and lets them spill on his plate. "Some gift from God lets a few poor mortals create music to translate the human experience, beyond language, without words, and artists like Twig are thus twice-blessed to wrap up their physical presence in the invisible clothes only emperors suffer to wear. And as long as they play, they are naked, and no one cares, no one sees, until the music stops. Then, suddenly, he slouches, his diffidence hangs like old clothes, but something, something, what was it he created, stacks and stacks of chords, a grand clef like a ladder climbing to heaven."

Twig had arrived on the mainland as a sun-blasted beach boy, with a hint of paint to show that he belonged to Peter. That summer, under Wick's tutelage, reunited with his paper family, he found himself, found a cause, something to which he could attach his music. Twig and the band covered themselves in surplus GI camouflage and became jungle warriors in flack jackets and bandoliers, dog tags, and the pins from spent grenades. They became a mirror of the vanquished army, the loyal remainder, the abandoned, as one of Twig's graphic choreographies dramatized. Over an endless loop recording helicopters evacuating across a sea of voices shouting in Vietnamese and English, we were left with the image of Twig looking skyward in stuttering strobe light as, variously, taps, the "Star-Spangled Banner" in homage to Hendrix or a drum-and-fife version of "Yankee Doodle" completed his soundscape. Wick would weep after every performance. "Twig's posse, all those Vietnam refugees, have become Cambodian undesirables the Khmer call Yuon. It's astounding to me. They're probably more Chinese, as in more Wongs, Chris. How history does repeat."

Peter could only stand and watch like the rest of us.

To anyone who will listen, Wick confesses. "I no longer have any talent to lead prayer, but Twig does. All this music about death and abandonment makes me blue and I don't know what the hell to do. Does that scan?"

"We learned to perch on our knees, bang our foreheads on the floor, and beg from missionaries like Wick," Peter mutters. "Oh, save me. Prey no more."

"This is genuine prayer, Peter. The way Twig climbs skyward, he can talk to God," Wick insists.

Wick's born-again inspiration came from what he thought were the circumstances in which our new cousins found themselves fleeing peace and resettlement in Southeast Asia and surrender in Honolulu, in Chinatown, the familiar exile. Twig was his validation. But Wick's influence on most of the recent immigrants like our tribal cousins was negligible. They ignored him for the most part. They'd seen missionaries in the DP camps, the useful meal ticket, the sponsored escape. They had third and fourth languages to hold their families together and a contemporary history of migration which sharpened their instincts for survival against the forces of dispersal, of assimilation. Wick didn't see, didn't understand. He was reconstructing an old ministry. He wanted to save them. Wick did not come from a generation whose spirituality had been supercharged by the chemical hosts that were then so abundant and attractive, in such variety. With the advent of hallucinogens, Wick never knew what hit him. But who did? There had already been cases: a wandering Irish priest from California who was found dead in the Sinai, the Charismatic suicide cults, Buddhist terrorists in Japan, Tibetan lamas undergoing guerrilla training in the Colorado Rockies. We were Wick's audience, students, young women filled with all the unexpressed aggressions of their mothers, the shell-shocked veterans who envisioned themselves surrounded by the immigrant backwash of the enemy, and a small but growing diasporatic minority, wondering if we'd crossed some bridge or were standing at its center, preparing to jump in the pursuit of our identities.

Wick let his hair grow into a lank, white queue. He cribbed from the worst global nightmares. He lectured from his own drug-driven hallucinations to define a role for us, to describe a retreat, club ecstasy, Shangri-la, where we would be enveloped in communion, nirvana. As Twig's concerts at the local colleges and cafés became popular, Wick became a fixture on the sidewalk, his diatribes underscoring the anxieties of a new age forming, the need for safe haven, a joining together, a new gene pool.

For a season, Wick had the opportunity to revisit the prophet in himself, another headless John the Baptist.

"Would you believe Wick told the crowd that Twig is the messiah who would alter the gene pool?"

"The genetically disturbed. I can dig that." For Melba, this was familiar territory. Here, there were old friends. She led me to the Ali Achmed College of Music and Dance on the mountain up an unpaved county road that met the fire trails, a cluster of summer cabins that had been converted into living quarters, offices, and studios linked by a series of covered wooden bridges set in a redwood grove. I was suspicious, but they were on Melba's list of reliable clientele, from North Beach, from New Mexico, from Goa, who had continued their trek into the counterculture with their children. It was a familiar, transposable vision, the smell of sandalwood, men and women dressed in tunics, in gowns, the faintly bony profiles of children raised as vegetarians. Even Twig joined us once, to attend a recital of the cognoscenti, sitting patiently for hours of theatrical performances of faux Hindu epics that taught the children a lengthy vocabulary of Sanskrit words for sexual parts in a monotony of drumming and a paralyzing hashish that left even Twig smiling and quite still.

For the while, I was persuaded, even enthusiastic. Wick and his familiar mission, the discipline of tai chi in the plaza, that Melba wanted me with her, and the endless drumming made our world seem meaningful and somehow uplifting. But the object of everyone's attention, Twig himself, was quite different.

One evening when Melba was in the city, I found Twig staring at Wick's wall and asked what I could do. The trenching had been completed, but they were still preparing the foundation. He pointed at the concrete mixing sled.

In the early evenings, Twig and his crew would labor on the wall, working shifts, learning to wire the reinforcing armatures, pouring concrete for the first posts. We hadn't talked much. I found him, just as I found Uncle, confusing and intimidating. On Peter's arm, on stage, he seemed aristocratic, almost ethereal. But standing there in his shorts and zoris, white with lime and cement dust, he seemed more approachable, even friendly. It was the tone he struck with me. I'd heard it on the streets of the new Chinatown, a little too aggressive, curious, unevenly spaced, impatient for a response, waiting to imitate whatever I said, using my words, my voice, guessing my opinions as if he couldn't trust his own. I was Peter's little brother, after all. We were the family he was only now beginning to know.

"Wick a punk too, Chris?"

"Gay? I don't know. I mean, not like Peter." I hesitate.

"I'm asking you." He catches his tone and lets the mild spray from the hose splash us both, as if to apologize. "Hey, I just wanna know 'cause I admire the dude. He's like an older brother, right? I like what he says, all that survivor shit. He's right. I can feel it all in the music. But all this family, chain of command, is hard to keep track of, who's the star for who."

"Twig, you're Baba Lan, you're the man, you're the whole show."

"Music my life, brudda, all show biz."

He's joking, the island moke, to make it all seem casual. His head bowed, the light catches the blue gleam of his shaved scalp. I want him to like me. "Not all for show. I love the antiwar songs. You give Wick a chance to strut his stuff too."

"I love him. He makes my music more big than lock 'n' load for the grunts. Same music in my head." Twig takes the mixing hoe away from me before I spill more of the slurry on the ground. "But Wick, I hear stuff too. Is it true?"

"About the boys?"

"Bad stuff."

"Yes."

"Whatever." His voice shifts, a slightly ominous sigh. "Shit. I seen that before. That's the trouble you get into with the missionaries, man. But I never heard one tell everyone I'm Jesus H. Christ." He suddenly relaxes and confides, "This place is a bust." He passes me a towel. "I smell food. Let's chow down before the hippies arrive and scarf it up."

We walk down the hill together in the fading light. A basket of rice noodles sits under the oak tree, and a Wong woman has a pot of beef stew we ladle on top, a savory mix of beef and tendon, ginger and bean sauce. A small group of familiar faces appear, kids I recognize from the café who follow Wick's communion lectures and the offer of a free meal. They bring vegetables the cooks have learned to nonchalantly dump in the stew, and, of course, homegrown marijuana they willingly share.

I tell him, "Food makes the moment count," as I think Peter might say. Twig's a little wired, too, anxious. He wolfs down his food.

"Draws flies, too. In jail, man, food's really important," he begins. "You know I did time?"

"No, nobody said. But I'm always the last one to know."

"Uncle didn't tell you? Oh yeah, you're the kid. That's okay. It was a scam. I did fourteen months of a two-year sentence for criminal conspiracy in Honolulu. People wanted a fall guy and I volunteered. I let them hang me for another guy, a head man with lots of responsibilities. Took his name, turned myself into Huynh Ba Lan for the cops. Like I was my evil twin. I already knew how to be in jail. I even know what it's like to be born in jail. So what if I'm twenty-seven instead of seventeen, a FOB, illegal, no ID. So now I've got ID, if I want it. Played lotta guitar in jail."

"I don't understand. Mistaken identity?" Whose scam? Uncle's scam?

"Yeah, you can say that. I make them think I'm this gambler instead of me. They was going to get me for something anyway. I owed some money, anyway." He smiles. "Lotta money. Bad debts always get spread around, so I owed lots and lots to lots of people. So suddenly I'm Huynh Ba."

"You're not really?"

"Baba Lan, for those guys. That's what they hung me with. Twig's good enough. Damn, I grew four inches, gained twenty pounds. In jail, I'm healthy. Eat Jell-O, drink milk. Saw a dentist for the first time in my whole life."

"A new man."

"A bad man, shit, yes."

I feel kinship and a certain dread beneath this silliness, another orphan's story the family can share, the absurdity of my hunkering in the bushes with Twig, Baba Lan, smoking dope and whispering in choked voices. It isn't the time to ask about rat-bone carvings or the paint on Melba's nails creeping past her cuticles to cover her hands like the tattoos that coil up Twig's arms. All I could do was wonder if they hurt—not their actual rendering, but their presence writhing on his skin. Painted nails and flesh, worked bone, the infectious languor, the food, all dress me, prepare me. But for what I don't know—to eat or be eaten? The garden is a jungle. Cannibal stew. I'm giggling.

"Yeah, so listen."

"Listening." I'm not aware that I am listening until he asks. Voices from below disappear. The night is upon us and I feel its silence, a dark drape closing across a stage, the hush. Listening.

"This Wick stuff I asked about? I seen guys like that in the joint. They're not punks, and nobody wants nothin' with their stink. Even guys with stuff, you know, guys with guys they've punked, they think they're straight, but they're punks too. That's me. We live in between. If he's the jock, the pitcher, then he owns the punk who owns the stigma. If they're doing flip-flops, then they're both stuff, both wearing pony tails. This is jail stuff, and maybe outside I can be anything I want. That's Wick's whole thing to me. But you know the reason I ask about Wick. He's like the pitcher, the jock, who doesn't want to know. And when he flips, bad things happen. You get it?"

"Sure." I understand his intensity but not the words.

"Usually, he keeps up a good front, very macho. Lots of status having a punk. He gets to satisfy his needs, right? And he can even make money off stuff. Doesn't bother me. Punks—you'd be surprised how easy they go along. There were regulars, fags, yeah, but regulars, you know. No stigma attached."

I'm nodding to the rhythm of his words. "Right, okay."

"Then, suddenly, the same motherfucker you see for a year, every day like, asks if I want to make his bed. I pass, right? Stable dude, old con from Folsum, still telling time by the bells."

"Stable dude, right." I'm staring at his arms. I want a tattoo of my own, a tiger like Twig's.

He stares at me expectantly. "We're the same. Brothers."

"I'm wasted," I confess.

"Brothers, man. Peter, me, you. But what's Wick?"

I can't explain it. I realize I have never even tried. "Wick's an old friend of the family, Lincoln and Auntie Mary's. They rescue Chinese babies. You've heard him. He wants to create paradise in the back yard with rescued Chinese babies."

It was just like Uncle to dote on Winnie and worry about Melba. He hated the ersatz tattoos and shuddered at the mention of body-piercing jewelry. "She wears clothes, ah?"

"Melba's real cute, Uncle," Mary assured him. "She wears scarves from her head to her toes. And she waves her hands and arms like little snakes."

"You tell her Chinese people eat snakes," his face squeezing like a lemon, his eyes shut tightly, tearing at the outside corners.

Winnie expertly mopped his face with tissue. "Ah Lung Gung, I never ate snake before."

"No?" He looked at her, amused. "I can cook it for you."

"How?"

"Not hard. Ginger, garlic, onion, wine." He recited a litany of herbs and spices, their medicinal properties, depending on the snake, depending on the season. "Better not for young girls," he added, falling softly into a restless sleep.

In the evening shade of the garden, the dancing glow of the burning joint between Twig and me illumines the dark. I feel our knees bump.

"Like, in a way, we're Wick's rescued babies, right?"

"Right. You can see it that way." I want to agree.

"But he was doing 'em?"

"Not babies. Boys." Like Peter, talk to Peter, ask Peter, I want to say.

"That's fucked up." He pinches the glowing ember between his callused thumb and forefinger, then swallows it.

"Yeah."

Like family. Like Melba, I can say now, Melba defended Wick, like kindred spirits branching from the same tree, Wick insisting they shared a respect for spirituality often lacking in the younger generation. He saw how it was revealed in the vocabulary of her dancing. He and Melba regarded the adoption of a language that erases the obscene from the words describing sexual parts as salutary, for example, where Uncle Lincoln saw snakes. And Melba, whenever she sensed my confusion of loyalties to Wick, would insist, "Wick's right. Everything that goes into the melting pot pops out a shiny new thing."

In what I imagined to be one of our more lucid moments together, I even described the hypnotic monotony of our meditation practice to Peter, but he simply scoffed. "I thought you were all doo-wopping for Twig. Melba wants belly dancing? With bells on her fingers and rings in her nose? Seven veils?" And in a leap, I'd lose him. "Hedy Lamar, she wants to be Hedy Lamar?"

"I don't understand," Melba said. "What makes Peter so cynical?"

"Maybe it's this race thing Wick is preaching. It makes him jealous that Twig's so close to him."

"Poor Peter. That's what Wick's talking about. We need to go past the race thing. That's why we're all together, no?"

I didn't know. But there were warnings. Uncle had known Twig's family before there ever was a Baba Lan, before there ever was a Twig, before Peter had ever met him. And Melba was hearing the same rumors Twig had cited. We were a bust. Back in Honolulu, Twig and the band, the whole Island scene, had been carefully observed and cultivated by the narco establishment, the dealers and the law, even as the band found refuge on the mainland and began slowly to dissolve in a bright cloud of amphetamine, cocaine, and ice from paradise. The cops loved them because everybody, the bad guys as well as the dupes, congealed around the band and would come floating to the top in the cold light of day.

But just being part of it—the partying, the commune, the long afternoons with Melba—seemed like an endless rite of passage where every day and every night we could tumble over the momentous, the miraculous, all in a grain of sand.

"Twig makes me afraid." Melba had recognized his attraction the first time she saw him back at the Neon Moon.

"Did he hit on you?" Did I want her to say yes?

"He hits on everybody. He doesn't even have to say the words. Twig fucks for survival. He told me he wants us all to have his children, and his children to have his children."

Melba had made it a rule that we could talk about anything when we were in bed together. I love making love to Melba in the afternoons. We watch each other closely.

She senses hesitation. "Yes, but?"

"Please, please, lie down. Can we?"

She laughs. So easy. "Would I sleep with Twig?" I love to watch her reach behind her back as she peels her blouse over her head. She lets me catch her, hands above her head, pressing against me, sweet surrender. "Yes."

"Say anything."

"I wouldn't be surprised if that's what's meant to be. Survivors find each other, Christopher," she murmurs as I nuzzle her neck, my fingers twisting aimlessly in her hair.

"I'm an Indian brave."

"And I'm Fanny Brice, you idiot. Pocahontas? Me?"

"What's to compare?"

"Twig and me?"

"Yes." I tongue both nipples in turn.

"Oh, yes. We're twins, don't you see? We come from somewhere that will never exist again. It could be just a time and place."

"Twig told me he felt like we were all brothers, me and Peter." I'm nibbling her ear lobes.

"That's very good. We can share, if you're not afraid."

"I'm not afraid with you." My need for her is always urgent. I slip between her thighs and meet her, damp and ready.

"Don't stop, please. Go on, babe, you can't wait." She lies back with a pillow under her head. When I look down, I can watch her hands on her breasts. "I love it that you're watching me, being watched. Twig and Wick are always watching."

"Wick's a bust, baby." Have I lost her? Have I lost myself?

"Keep going, baby. It's okay."

But I couldn't keep up. I wasn't sure. "Wick's stoned all the time." Wick's voice and words are with us constantly: We're all refugees from the Fall, some enormous collapse of something that makes our need for each other larger than what or wherever we come from, larger than family. It's the gene pool. We all learned to survive the Fall, the death of the past. We don't rise. We lie down together. We settle, and in that settling we become equal.

"Don't stop, babe, please."

"It's all right." I can't release. It's the dope. "Later. I can wait." But it's not true. I can't wait. Especially when I am not sure what it is I'm waiting for, or that when it comes, it will be what I want. Left hanging, suspended in midair, I'm constantly aroused.

We kept Wick because he was family. We were responsible, loving what I would rather despise. I don't know how else to explain it. He couldn't be trusted to wander freely, speaking without the constraint of belonging to us. He was both prodigal son and father. He was always there in Lincoln's place, by Mary's side, sheltering Peter, and ready to lead me, knowing from where I had come. You don't choose family. They are there before you and after, and each one of mine is accountable to me as I am to them. But there he was again, on his knees for Twig.

I smell food, a hallucination for sure because the front deck is littered with strips of burnt aluminum foil marbled with amphetamine residue. Candle fire illumines the living room, where a small group gathers to smoke and listen to Twig play and Wick ramble. The doors are left open in the warm summer evenings. There are children wandering about, scuttling below us in the yard, their chatter a counterpoint to the scales floating above the guitar Twig plucks with hypnotic attention, the same notes, the same arpeggios, repeating over and again. His drug-induced trance opens doors to all longing, all feeling, the itch that wants scratching, rubbing.

Twig smiles and whispers something to a cousin who hunkers over yesterday's newspaper splitting seeds then spitting the shells between his knees. I'm envious. Twig is remarkably limber and can just about touch the floor with his butt with both feet flat on the floor.

Wick's message of salvation to our attentively stoned audiences in the evenings at the café and at the commune, his pronouncements, become more exaggerated and absurd.

"Asian immigrants carry a mandate from heaven, a mandate that requires you to construct and divide, exploit and return the profits to the family, the village, the homeland. But that's an illusion, economic determinism disguised as something holy, something spiritual. Look how that illusion loses its potency over successive generations. Some argue that our ability to make distinctions about who we are here and who we are in Asia is essentially whimsical because we carry a foreign mandate, a sensibility forged in a very different universe—yellow people. The same problem has been noted in the West. Attempts to clone cells beyond the second generation have resulted in ineffective or transparent duplicates that are not viable. We all understand the initial need to organize, the need for association, but the seeds of corruption are also evident. That is the method and madness Chinese historical science has always predicated.

Kingdoms rise and fall." He pauses for effect. "It's time to rise again. Celebrate who we are. Love each other."

Wick announces our wedding date on such an evening. "I'm going to marry Columbus and Melba on the day we commemorate the wall. It's perfect, don't you see? Theirs can be a marriage of all of us."

Melba and me, Adam, Eve between God and the devil. Or were we led by Monkey ravaging the garden of fruit and flowers? We couldn't know. Everyone had their own answer. Maybe Winnie had a bigger picture. She understood that her green card days were numbered when she married Uncle. And there was Auntie for counsel.

"From their union, a new people, a new kingdom. We need to spread our seed, cast it as widely and as far as possible. Create new traditions, new ways of forming families, communities."

Wick affects a slight stutter for his sermons. "You s-s-see," propped on a pillow with his back resting against the wall, his legs stretched out, looking decidedly uncomfortable, scattering his notes in his fervor, but tape-recording himself while he speaks, "there are no more victims, no more martyrs. Generations have been sacrificed in order that we may live, prosper, and with a new consciousness create the next generation. All of us together represent a fresh infusion into the gene pool. We've arrived with the rising tide. Here, and now, under the Tree of Heaven, we have a simple mandate: to make ourselves new, to become like one, to see in each other what we want for ourselves, to want for ourselves what we want in each other."

I understand now that Wick was deeply disturbed, too many hours with *Time* and *Newsweek* guiding his psychedelic reentry, gesturing for us to join him at the middle of the bridge spanning the unknown, begging us all to join hands, to jump.

"In this American century, the world all over has seen so much, has participated in so much death, we are afraid to love each other. Don't you feel it when you hear the reports of natural disasters in the world? Ten thousand feared dead in a Mexico City earthquake. One hundred thousand missing in Kerkistan. A generation lost at Chernobyl. Don't you feel the universe heave a sigh—a sharp intake of breath? Feel it? We are the survivors who have escaped from the holocausts. The soul of the world can no longer afford this karmic weight. We see the world's soul turning even as we approach the millennium. The perpetual circle of historical horrors moves centripetally towards oblivion. Think of it. China uses Tibet as a nuclear dump site while the Buddhist monks the CIA trained conduct guerrilla war from bases in Colorado. How far back must the Dalai Lama regress to discover the reasons for Tibet's karmic destiny? What catastrophe dooms Tibetans to seek balance, to escape the karmic wheel in Lhasa? Tibet is the final hallucination. We are that faint wisp of snow and dust blowing from the final peak."

In the evenings, Wick is theater to a racially mixed crowd looking for salvation in a contemporary Shangri-la.

"We have evolved in the diaspora: Eva, Monterey Park, Daly City, Chinatown, the ID, Stockton, Lime House. In the meanwhile, all around us, all about us, America spins images of us. We become the Vietnam the world watches on television news, we are R&R in Honolulu, in Tokyo, Shanghai, Singapore. One more time we see our lives in the movies, on TV, and one more time we see the enemy is our father, and we are the innocents, the victims. Loving what we are taught to hate, despising images that we cherish.

"How do we learn to love ourselves? We ask because we must. It's a fragile paradise, people. We have to hate ourselves for wanting what we are. It's crazy, but the movies, the culture—Suzi Wong and William Holden, Brando, *Sayonara*—we suckle them like mother's milk. They explain us."

Then Wick would smile that enigmatic smile. It was his smile that I should have suspected immediately. I pretended to listen, to understand. It was a way to stay with Melba. But he was mad as a hatter, a messiah on hallucinogenics, a stoned lunatic.

"Mother's milk," Peter counters, "is a passing wind, old man."

But where Uncle was an anonymous donor, Wick gave Twig legitimacy. Twig even threatened to abandon music.

"Twig, I feel your rage. All that hooting at your 'Tiny Bubbles' must remind you of playing for the Schofield Barracks short-timers or the Presidio military clubs. The artist's dilemma—you're castrated by the crowd." It's almost morning. Wick rolls over, then rises to his hands and knees. Hands from the crowd reach out to massage his shoulders and neck while he slowly regains feeling in his legs. "You experience a confused sexual identity. You become a Wanchai prostitute. Chinese history celebrates Madame Goldenflower sleeping with the Germans during the

Boxer Rebellion. The Frenchman who sleeps with the female imper-
sonator. I want to be a bridge, I want to be used."

Peter's in the bedroom counting to three. Melba spins like a bottle in a
circle of choices. I'm trying to keep up, but only Twig is left standing,
perfect pitch, in tempo.

Peter looks in at the crowd. "It's the transvestite chorus singing 'Honey
Buns' from *South Pacific*."

"Peter, the musical?" I am actually thinking of the movie.

But it's Twig in Peter's voice who replies. "Hey, Chris. I saw that movie
one hundred times." Twig hears me. I'm not dreaming. "'Den' after dat,
I sleep on the beach at Hanalei Bay for a week one time, singing all the
songs with a *haoli* girl named Nellie. Or was it a nelly boy named *Haoli?*"
He giggles. "I forget, man. They know all the words, and I play guitar.
Fasting, don't eat nothing. Just smoke weed."

I catch Melba's eye as she whirls by.

Peter's head appears mounted on the wall, moving in time with the
music. "Can you wonder why Twig's got this gift, this genius, this mélange
of country-western Honolulu swing, why he's so tempting, so seductive?"

I am repelled by a vision of Peter and Melba licking their way across
Twig's naked torso.

Twig is caught in a bright circle of light, murmuring to an invisible
crowd. "They love my body. I sing and they want me to take off my shirt,
hey people?"

Wick's voice is raspy, hoarse. "Twig is in the right place at the right
time, the right person. He carries the right DNA, right at the edge, a
new millennium beckons, all hyphenated and truncated, newspeak, plastic, homogenized." I catch Wick staring past Twig into the crowd, searching. "The world soul turns in on itself. It needs a new body to regain
paradise. Look how we live now. We rely on homeopathic practice, the
Asian diet. You remember the old practice, Peter and I, how ecstatic we
were with the endorphins of exercise. Look at us, how beautiful we are.
Look at what we can become." He looks from Melba to me, to all of us.
"Look at what we have become."

"What? Slack-jaw dope fiends playing rock 'n' roll, hey bra'!" Twig
collapses against Peter, giggling uncontrollably. "Sorry, sorry."

Wick joins the laughter. "That's good, that's right. Laugh. I started by laughing at you. We are the new people. We are the new gene ocean. The East, the West, we are *tsunami*. The rich aroma of hashish glowing in the hookah, the smell of DMT, acrid, a burning rubber band, like ether."

Twig bumps heads with Peter. "Hey, brudda fadda, don't give me no Spam shit or all that victim stuff with your children in the dust. I'm a panda. Dig it? I'm a loner too. I hate people pulling at me, telling me how my music makes them feel. I don't give a shit how they feel."

"You young people don't know what it is to grow old." This was Wick trying to go one more round with the young contenders, basking in their admiration, hopelessly addicted to his own message. "As I grow older, bits of me, at my witless ends, chip and break off, like pottery, stunned pottery, lint and thread catch and hang from my toenails and dust balls ride my cuffs. Sharks wear amphora. Trees wear moss. I catch lint. Each disservice I meet with tolerance, forbearance withal. I want all struggle to end. I want all turmoil to cease. There is no revenge in me. I say this because I—we—have all been raised in anger. Taught to struggle against all tides, all currents, to beat upwind. No more. Not for me. The world I inhabit suits me. I'm shaped in its fabric of experience. Here, I live, I am. Will you join me?"

He buries his face in his sleeves or whispers for water. "But attend me. Be patient." He softens his voice. "I have always felt that I looked at myself through another's eyes," he says, sweeping the room with his gaze, "like a voyeur, this self-conscious ego revolving in the warm bath of my own regard."

At our evening meditations, we complete breathing exercises that leave us gasping, force us to pant in a cadence Wick directs, leading us to exhaustion, a carbon dioxide depletion to leave us faint but attentive.

"From what you see of me, I see myself more wholly, more completely. And I learn to trust you, trust myself in you. I wanted to share this with you. It's all becoming a part of my new practice I need you all to understand." He brightens suddenly, fixing us with his shining eyes, something revealed. "If you can't explain this back to me, I won't be able to explain it to myself," he shudders deliciously as waves of something invisible, perhaps a smell, a quick hallucination, a neuron fire fed by the cocaine and synthetic mescalines he has lately added to the mix wash over him. "I know I use you, all of you, so shamelessly. Have I abused you?" Wick shapes our recollections with invented rituals, the history of our tortured

China past, the disconnected fragments of our culture become exotic in exile, the foot-binding, misogynist nightmare whose demons our distant families employ to hold us close. It is familiar and affecting, the anguished cry of us all, how to love what we hate, how to love the other in us, the child we abuse, our own.

Melba indulges me these weeks, sitting, knotting her macramé from her basket, accepting quick tokes from the joints I hold to her lips. Between us, with our new consciousness, there grows a revealing intimacy as fragments of my life are reshaped in Wick's vision of us, like a clear path, a new bridge built from our senses, an eroticism that swells and subsides with our very breathing. I even dare to share images with Melba of Winnie and me. I recall our snug premarital couplings, the infinite regression of sex with her, our sexual initiation, so infantile. "Don't hurt me," she would plead. She would offer each part of her anatomy separately, every part of her a sacrifice to be abused, like a child: this is my foot, my knee, my pubis. Undressing her was like changing a baby's diaper, revealing a hairless infant who smelled lightly of witch hazel.

"Love the other in yourself," Wick intones, "Make love to your other. Only then can you have the love of others. You all are the beginning and the end." Licking his fingertips, he reaches for a candle flame among the several burning in bright paper bags filled with sand. "See the smoke rising." He directs his gaze at the single incandescence. "Ignore the fire." His fingers dance above the flame. He wets them once again, then catches the flame above the melting wax to extinguish it without wincing. On those endless evenings, warm and still, the smoke rises as we courageously pluck at our own candle flames. "The airy nothing that rises from the fire feeds all who have come before us. Our ancestors can be only what we provide them in this sacrifice we call our lives. Walking shadows, we give them substance. They can be only what we become."

The days after the nights before, it became my routine to walk up to the big house, clutching my beach towel, swim goggles, skin lotion, and a retort box of a nonfat dairy beverage made from brown rice and spring water. Up early or late, cultivating insomnia, Wick would plant himself poolside, a deep copper tan and a thick mat of white hair on his chest and back, fisting a mug of coffee, studying *Newsweek* as he examined the text of each catastrophe for clues that might help him predict our fate. Around ten, Peter would appear, aroused and irritable, prickling with that amphetamine nettle under his skin.

Sitting uncomfortably nude, we all argue. It's the season.

Peter, back from Honolulu, has the *Santa Lucca Journal* and is holding up the front page of Section Two featuring a photo and article about the family enterprises. There is a picture of Wick and Twig with the band's poster in the background. With only the briefest mention of Twig's concert dates in the county, the *Journal* had instead focused on the Reverend Dr. Candlewick's "church," on Twig as Baba Lan, and on their immigrant enterprises, a reunion of refugees to color Twig's legend as the foundling, the war orphan. Wick's in his guru uniform, all white, loose blouse and floppy pants. The photograph insinuates that an old man, a father of one of Twig's roadies, is the tribal patriarch. In the background he leans heavily against a high post supporting the construction, as if to favor a bad knee, an old wound, an enormous fatigue. A shadow falls across all their faces and makes their lips black, a portrait of trial and endless suffering, defiant, prototypically ancient. The old man imitates Twig's uniform, the same black denim pants, black poplin raincoat down past the knees, cowboy boots, and a campaign hat with a tightly curled triangular brim and a cord securing it around the chin.

Peter laughs wickedly. "I couldn't resist. He followed me home from Cafe au Lait. I thought he wanted to do a story on Twig and the band. I fell asleep on the terrace and when I woke up, voilà."

"You made the news, Wick." I ease my way into the pool, past the surface of dead leaves, groping past the pool sweep to the layer of thermal cold, a kick-start for my idling heart.

"No, I, newsboy," Peter yawns.

Wick's not laughing, but he seldom does. "It's a good story. People here are curious and they deserve to know," Peter continues. "The newsboy, the reporter. Dr. Candlewick's latest pastoral conquest. Poor young what's-his-name had his sights set on *Rolling Stone*."

The water is tepid, heavily chlorinated, halfway between a hot tub and a toilet. I manage two lengths submerged, deafened by the pressure of water in my ears save for the primordial echo of air bubbles I slowly release, skimming the blackened lees at the bottom, then twenty laps at an eight-count. I do another two under the water, finally breaking the surface at the shallow end, shaking my head from side to side to clear the water from my ears, and continue pacing myself back and forth, feeling the water slip past, the sun on my backside, ignoring their squabble.

The newspaper story describes our commune as a religious retreat and multiservice employment center for refugees. The memorial wall is mentioned as well as a description of the cousins' work as tree cutters and gardeners. Their logo, which juxtaposes a Stihl chain saw and a power mower with a figure wearing a safety helmet and goggles circumscribed by a Tao mandala, is recognizable in the poster that advertises the Tree of Heaven.

I would stay forever in the water, but the two of them feel it necessary to include me.

"Advertising, Christopher, image-making. Very self-actualizing. It's the essence of creating something from nothing." There is always a cynical, jilted edge now in Peter's voice that he uses to cut away at Wick. "Don't change the believable, change the believer, right Wick? Not so hard?"

"To create something you first have to be able to create nothing," Wick says patiently. "You know I've taken a vow."

Peter laughs, "Wick thinks I'm the one who is lacking conviction."

I didn't want to understand what they were arguing about, only wished they would stop. But I was bound to listen, for Winnie, who always asked, as well as for Auntie Mary, who never did.

"Good morning, Chris." Wick never looks up. "Don't mind your brother. When you cross too many time zones, people forget who you are. It becomes harder to catch up with yourself, jet lag."

"Aren't we all sick of this?" Peter sneers. "It's a story we've heard too many times. A different slant, if you pardon the expression, on the left-overs. Baba Lan, orphan of our faithful Indian companions, settles gratefully in the land of the free, smoke rising from the top of his tepee, dreaming of buffalo."

Twig has been pissing in the bushes. He emerges from the hillside, sweeping past the timber bamboo bursting with tendrils in the redwood planters. He climbs onto the diving board, testing its stability, then settles into his "horse," heels flat, knees under his hips, elbows akimbo, wrists swiveling in a slowly executed kung fu set. He gleams in the sunlight, bouncing on the suspended board, moving easily through "the tiger." "Nasty, Peter. Bad night, bra'?"

"Good night, bad day, man," Peter says carefully. "Love at first sight, love at first light."

"Be cool, baby." Twig balances on his toes, his spine coiled back, breastbone pointed to the sky, palms flat against the invisible wall, arms stretched, a slow windmill, climbing cliffs. To me he seems to reach too far, well past the point of balance, from where he will surely fall. But my angle in the water, wading in the shallows, some trick of the sun, leaves him perched, stretched full length from his fingers to the tip of the tiger's tail.

I smell coffee brewing. Melba doesn't drink it, but the boys keep a pot going behind the bar. I drip naked to the bar, add a shot of dark rum, and toast the hosts. "That's a cup of coffee."

"That's a 'mug' in American." Uncle Lincoln crunches up the gravel path, alone. Winnie has dropped him off and gone to town to check the café receipts.

He surveys the yard. "How can you swim in this? The pool's a toilet. Why don't you have one of the cousins clean it? Damn shame. This place is nice." He carefully balances on one foot and kicks at the rotting flotilla lapping the side of the pool.

"Careful, Uncle. They're already making five an hour. Chris, maybe you can ask Melba to get the kids to do it?" Peter offers.

Uncle slaps a rolled newspaper against his leg. "What's this thing in the paper? How come I don't know I own a church now? What church?"

Wick nods. "We talked about this. The time's right. Baba Lan and his people are Americans too. It's the red, white, and blue. It's centennial fever."

"The neighbors complain. Parking, too many people, too much noise, stuff like that. And Twig looks dangerous in that picture. Why did you let them take a picture of the wall? Who's that guy, anyway?"

At first, Lincoln hadn't discouraged Wick from using our cousins. Lincoln and Winnie said it was good business. Wick thought it was good for the victims of war. And Wick helped Twig market the look. These native cousins were exotic roadies in their camouflage. But then Uncle began to worry when Wick started preaching in public. "It puts them in everybody's face—here are the folks you left behind."

"Good business," Peter says, imitating Uncle.

"Not in this neighborhood, Peter. Too many, too soon." Uncle turns, looking for a place to settle himself as I move a chair into the shade. "Chris, you know what I'm talking about. We're the neighbors now."

"Uncle, have a little faith in our fellow Americans. We're tenting tonight on the old campground. This land is your land, this land is my land. Right, Wick?"

Uncle tires easily, but his patience, especially with Peter, remains unflagging. "Peter, this land belongs to the bank and the officers who serve double duty on the planning commissions that issue building permits, business licenses. And that monstrosity, what are we doing with that retaining wall going right through the middle of the property? That's a waste." Uncle looks at me for some sign, some hint, then turns back to Peter, shaking his head. "Why don't you stop for a while, Peter? Take a nap. Put some clothes on." He steps around the pool and settles in the shade. To me he says, "Peter's flying too much."

"The wall—damn thing's huge, of course," Wick conceded with satisfaction. "Twig scaled it so that it slopes with the hill. Everyone who's seen it wants to decorate it with different facings—wood, paint, whatever. Have people contribute memorabilia for a small fee. The building inspector objected when he saw the plumbing until I told him it was for the sprinklers."

As I later learned, the town council had taken up the question of ordinances and building codes, compelled by inflammatory whispers of an invasion from the resettlement community the federal government had established for refugees at the north end of the county. Peter argued before the planning commission that providing work for one extended family represents the city's shared responsibility. Most of the refugees had settled in the traditional inner-city ghettos, but the commune had found a niche in a suburban enclave, residing at the edge of development, propelled by the flight from the cities, a traditional motive in this county. While Peter was on one of his trips to Hawaii, the building inspector visited and became alarmed. The city wanted to know how many people were living there and demanded that Uncle apply for a use permit detailing the building projects.

The division between the adjacent lots the commune held in common followed a gully eroded by winter runoff, water coursing from the street above that the city let drain over an uncurbed road, crumbling macadam that dead-ended in a copse of bay and eucalyptus. The wall was narrow, barely visible at the top of the hill, ten feet wide at most at the bottom of the property. The crew had positioned large black rocks as a catch basin disguised as a rockery, and behind this facade of mountain and streambed had built a small pavilion from which to observe the fall of water. The rocks, which the cousins had scavenged from the coast, small boulders traced with bleached mussel shell and covered in black petroleum pitch from passing tankers' bilges, sat fixed in a channel of concrete and river gravel that were heaped at the base, all quite grotesque. Even in full sun, with the glare rising from the gravel, the twisting black surfaces absorbed light like large hunks of soft coal. The pavilion was surrounded by large planters of banana and taro, their broad leaves shading the ground, and pots of timber bamboo to catch the sound of the wind, the falling rain, to keep the stillness in the summer heat, to cast shadows, a moiré repeated in the tracery filling the pavillion's two window spaces.

After Peter returned from Hawaii, he had responded in a cocky letter to the city—an error in judgment, or perhaps on purpose—that the construction was not a fence enclosing the property, since it had only two extensions, one of which cut across the backyard on the diagonal. He also pointed out the obvious angle of the wall, sloping from the ten-foot flag at the apex and running to ground level over the length of each leg. It wasn't a fence he wrote, it was art. He had Twig sign the letter as Baba Lan.

Uncle takes me by the arm and walks me up the hill. He's breathing heavily. He looks over the wall, trying to see past the screen of trees to the neighbors. "Chris, Winnie said Peter has some funny business with a charter to Thailand for sex stuff. What's the matter with that guy? And how come Wick's picture's in the paper with Twig?" He waves vaguely at the wall. "Let's stop everything for a while. Make everything peaceful."

Lincoln shades his eyes, squinting at the bright reflection from the pool, a demi-smile of forbearance, suddenly out of touch. "I give you guys family to take care of each other. Even Baba Lan has one." His voice trails off.

At Lincoln's funeral, I try to explain that summer to Auntie. "We were in search of our ancestors."

"What ancestor?" Auntie smiles.

"Our fathers."

And here she begins to laugh, an exclamation interrupted by laughter, helpless laughter, floating in the delicate lily-blossomed air of the human bower we create at Uncle's grave. "Ancestor?" Auntie tries to hold her composure, and, failing, turns to catch the eye of her grandnieces who are making funny faces. "He was an orphan."

There's Peter pinch-hitting for Wick, the divine, lecturing past the uncomprehending crowd gathered for Lincoln's interment. Wick sits graveside on a folding chair, lecturing to himself. "To be a survivor from Asia in this land, to have fled some mad war, some colonial satrapy, some holocaustal slaughter, simply to pursue childish vices and to assure the locals that nothing serious is threatened by our presence, that nothing serious can happen here, to be trivial is the price we pay to live, oh yes, and the price of dying."

Mary and I stand apart. "Was I? Am I?"

"What orphan?" Auntie says. "I'm not dead, not yet. Winnie's not dead. Eat something, lucky dog."

Wick mutters continuously. His face is still alive with tics, his hands still fumble and tug. Not at all like the waxen mask Lincoln wears on his empty skull. The living cannot help but wiggle and sweat, the turmoil of life writ large in every moving wrinkle. But the dead, their deepest creases lie unmoving, still. The coins the undertaker propped between Uncle's lips are fixed firmly, and the fingers laced across his chest are quite still, quite still. I almost expect to see his rouged lips pucker then spit silver dimes in the air. Heads or tails, kid, call it before it lands.

I hear Peter speaking softly. "Are you listening?" Peter the divine addresses the open coffin. "I want to tell you something about everything."

Dead is dead. Let the past be the past. In life, I defend myself, my family, my friends. Pursue every small loyalty, and eat everything. Do not awaken me. When I left my home, I went anticipating my return, the welcome of friends, the relief of family, wealthy, wiser, to pursue my ease among the familiar comforts and simple ambitions and, once again, to disguise the amazing in me, the vain loving vanity I could inspire in myself if I were left to my own resources, not held to account by the relief and welcome that still awaits me, or so I imagine in my exile.

Was there ever a mother, a father, or just a cockerel hung at the neck by the village matchmaker chortling the marriage curse for the delight of family and neighbors? Some poor young girl finds an empty bed beside Uncle's mother, letters from a scrivener's collection smudged with a stranger's thumb.

Auntie taught Winnie well. The girls could also have died of plague in Havana, revolution in Mexico, a race riot in Kandy, Darwin, Malawi, Abu Dhabi, Cheyenne, LA, or in a rice paddy at home. In the villages, mothers traded daughters for daughters-in-law to keep the memory of their husbands and sons in all their familiar places. The obsequious were nursemaids. The obstreperous—not a few—could be sold for prostitutes simply by offering them the enticement of emigration. Regardless, none were ever welcomed home. Like all daughters, Winnie never needed a father. But she did need a husband. And a green card. And Lincoln, as a last act, saved her, adopted her by marrying her. Auntie thought that she would feel more secure with a real estate broker's license. Winnie worked part-time for a title company, even toyed with a marriage brokerage— a post office box that promised to arrange cross-cultural marriages— and advertised it from Manila to Miami, from Palm Desert to Scottsdale. Winnie married Uncle on his deathbed as it were, and it was Winnie who finally sent all of us packing, to create new places where everyone could be safe, if not together, because together, we were certainly not safe.

While Twig is still performing in Santa Lucca, we spend a crowded evening milling with the local audience, who finds the Tree exotic. We've gathered behind the bandstand. Twig has told Melba she can dance. She taunts him nervously. Her stage fright makes her aggressive.

"Sexy mama," Twig murmurs. He offers a joint to our huddle.

"They're not here to see me," Melba giggles. "It's you."

Peter joins us. "You light them up, cowboy. Isn't this fun, all the boys and girls?"

Twig offers a cellophane envelope. "Me, me," Melba whimpers. She's sandwiched between Twig and me, sniffing from the ivory spoon around Twig's neck, doing her little bumps and grinds. We're all oblivious to the stares of the crowd lingering between sets.

"I want to be a rock 'n' roll star like Twig." She puts her hands on his hips and dances him from his corner towards the light, their spectral smiles glowing.

The drummer has made his way through the clutter of wire and microphones to his traps and begins slowly rolling across the edges of the cymbals with his mallets, occasionally striking the gong and gamalong bells initialing the Tree's unique percussive identity.

"Come up there with me tonight, Peter," Melba invites. "We can all dance together. You want to dance with Chris all by yourself?"

Twig punches me lightly in the chest. "Hey, bra'. You can do it, too. I seen your style, man. You do the cranes and the crickets, the birds and bees. I seen you train like a natural, dude. It's like the wisdom was already poured inside you, at birth."

"Twig, my brother. No disrespect, man. You're the man with the music."

"That's right. That's right. So now you all have to kiss me, lick my butt for luck," he laughs excitedly. "You know, when I hear something, some music, some instrument, some moke beating his beer-can hat on the table, I can take it in and make it part of my songs. It's like the band thing. I hear all the parts, all the voicings, and everybody's doing this thing I hear. But one day I'm going to distill it all into just me. Cut all the extraneous stuff and just have the songs filter through me. I'm always training myself; practice comes first. With a synthesizer and computer I can run a hundred tracks from the keyboard and the guitar. Every voicing is an ancestor. Can you dig that? It's all inside me. Everybody, really. You just have to hear them talking. You have to have a good ear, right? That's what they say about musicians. Good ears to hear the tune, the spaces in between, the intervals, perfect pitch, all that bullshit. A good ear hears what's already there, what's already been heard a million times."

He moves in closer to Melba again. They stand chest to chest as Twig loads the spoon. "Man, when I was on the beach playing guitar for getting pakalolo and brew from the mokes, I could hear the stars burning in the sky when the surf sizzled across the sand. That night sky was a gigantic speaker talking to me, playing all the sounds, all the music that has ever been played. All I had to do was choose which ones to sing first, where each set should lie, make my voice like an octopus against a coral shelf and fill all the spaces in between. I could never figure how anybody could fall asleep on the beach. Wherever I see the night sky I hear music. The music comes to me like a jet plane taking off, leaping for heaven.

In airplanes I'm watching through the little glass window, so I only see the silver skin tremble, smoke flying. Then it's like the stew pops a hatch and I'm buried in the blast. Man, I can hear the sound of stars burning."

Melba dances a tight circle round around us, with her hands on Twig's butt. "I have to watch myself around you Chinamen. You all have got these moves."

"I know." Twig has Melba by her hips as she wiggles closer. "I'm a quick study, learning how to be a righteous Chinaman, right? Girl, we had all the restaurants in a lock, you know."

"That's not what I meant." Melba brushes Twig's chest with her lips. "That's Chinatown, and you were a kid."

"We gave them protection and they gave us free food, apartment in Oakland, San Jose, a nice place in Fresno with a swimming pool. Better us than the blacks or the Latins, right? If you're gonna get robbed, might as well be by your own, ah?" Twig lights another joint. He holds the smoke in his lungs, bobbing and weaving with the effort not to cough, not to expel it too quickly. "Right, right. You say hands up, you want them to speak your language." The smoke is discharged in two explosive bursts that send him reeling into some pony-tailed guy looking for the toilet.

"Then Uncle's Lincoln creeps up to us in Oakland."

"That's funny, too. He didn't run you over."

"Man, I walk faster than he drives, you know. Hey, bra', now, no disrespect."

We all softly trade slaps, moving to the rhythm of the crowd.

"Music, man. It's electric hash frying in the sky, static pulsing, it's the shortwave I use to sleep with. I imagined I had the war in my ears, listening to air traffic over Honolulu, especially when I got the Marine pilots singing when they scare themselves all over the sky, take a piss, think they're gonna die. When I started playing in the clubs, I wrote some songs about what I heard over my headset. That one was 'Sky Fighter,' did real good. We had to do the country-western covers to survive, but I could play for warriors. I felt like radar spreading out and finding them wherever they were, you know, like the song, '. . . land, air and sea,'" he sings.

"That's tight, man." Peter raises his voice as the noise level in the club begins to peak with impatience.

"So suddenly, I understand this old guy is offering an all-expenses-paid vacation in a Honolulu jail, and I'm the winner. Payback for my cousins from camp Hong Kong in hell, all the names and dates, and I'm officially Huynh Ba Lan, two-o-three-o-dash-eight-eight-eight, super lucky. Do a favor and it'll come back."

Melba's surprised. "Babe, you knew Uncle before?"

Peter says, "Arranged marriage."

"Naah." Melba sways back and forth as Twig looks down at the tops of her bare breasts. I have nowhere to put my eyes. "He didn't know who went to jail. I was just a favor to keep peace between the old and new guys. Just business. Keep it in the family."

"He knows now? How come you guys never tell me anything?"

"Of course." Melba catches his hand as he drums his fingers across her body. "You're just a girl." He lets out a howl. "Oh, wow, luau. I just started stackin' the chords like in choir practice."

Peter is tripping. "I heard you singing inside little music boxes tucked in the big green valleys. Hawaii has natural cathedrals, so God songs just float from the lowest dingle to the highest peak. I heard it from the sidewalk, guys singing in their garage in Ewa on the weekends come floating over the houses on barbecue smoke. They like to pitch everything high, in falsetto. Then I heard you."

Twig, caught by the pedal notes from the bass player, adds, "Then I tell 'em to get that nasty hiss with the cymbals, slack-slapping rhythm and the gamelan bells. And I think then I have everybody's attention, eh bra'?"

Peter nods feverishly. "Shouldn't we be smoking opium, bra'? If we are really righteous, we should score some. I never had that before."

Melba bumps up against me and winks. "How am I doing, babe?" We're all aroused.

"That's perfect, yes. Where can we buy opium?" These are my brothers.

Twig straightens himself. "Show time, cousins. You gonna stick around?"

Peter snaps his teeth at Twig. "Yeah, man, I mingle real good."

Maybe it was the crowd that night, Sunday, late, last set. What passes for bikers in the county line the back walls. Twig and the band are wired, snorting minuscule clouds of amphetamines from the Islands he hails in a nasty number he titles "Tropical Ice." They gleam in the flashing strobe that pulses to match their slow grinding as they touch and rub each other. Twig's down to his Day-Glo surfer shorts, hanging low on his hips, as

Melba kneels between his legs, her shoulders banging against his knees, her loincloth wrap caught on the string of her thong, hips pumping orgasmically. Twig slides his hand up and down the neck of his guitar, feigning masturbation, and feeds her riffs that pulse then wash across her face.

"Do it, man, yeah! Bitchin' slants." The hoarse obscenities punctuate the music, and the band is caught in an endless loop, searching for the bridge, lost in the tangles of their choreography, watching for the climax that doesn't come. The drummer finally begins the accelerando on the gong: one strike, then a roll to catch their attention. But Twig and Melba ignore the cue.

"Bust her bubble butt, man, do it." Their gyrations continue. "Gook her, Chink, play 'Tiny Bubbles.'" Suddenly it's ugly. A drunk in a field jacket and sandals charges the stage, but he slips, knocking tables over, spilling bottles. "White bitch! I'll fuck her, I can fuck her!" he screams from the floor as others begin their own charge or perhaps retreat from the threatening melee. It was late and hard to tell.

Melba stops suddenly and the band breaks off in disarray, with only the gong beats holding to some foregone finale. Twig takes her hand for a quick bow to bring the set to a close and as he raises her arm her bra snaps open, spilling sequins and talcum that float in the spotlights.

"Yeah, yeah, tiny bubbles. Baby, gimme some of that titty."

Melba slips behind the cover of the amps bank. Twig has moved between the stage and the tables now to close the ground between himself and the fallen drunk still trying to clamor through the overturned tables and broken glass, still shouting. "I fuck up gooks for a living, dude, my turn, my turn," he snarls helplessly, coughing and spitting, his hands and knees laced with tiny cuts, bleeding in a puddle of beer.

Twig, now only a dark shadow at the edge of the stage lights, dappled with splashes of concrete and resin, stands with his hands to his sides. Only his legs locked in the classic horse stance betrays his preparation. The drunk looks up and laughs at the slight figure. "You want me to fuck you, Chink? Fuckin gook, motherfucker." He wobbles to his feet as the crowd backs away. "Hey, piss-face monkey, you know about 'incoming,' you Chink shit?"

Peter is on the bandstand with the mike in his hand, whispering urgently. His sibilant plea comes over the sound system sotto voce, like a snake hissing, "Security, security."

The drunk straightens himself, brushing his legs, then begins a long, arcing roundhouse swing with his right fist, still clutching a broken beer bottle. And without seeming to move, Twig closes the distance, dancing inside the taller man's reach, and catches a wrist with his left hand, at the same time twisting around as if to face the stage, as if to make an exit. Instead, Twig straightens his right leg, slamming his heel low to the groin. As the drunk bows suddenly, acknowledging the effectiveness of the heel strike—as does the watching crowd—with a low moan, Twig's concealed right elbow catches him on the bridge of his nose, which blooms in a dark scarlet smear past his mouth, spilling across his jacket. He falls forward with his entire weight and would crash to the floor save for the wrist lock Twig keeps, the lever that breaks the left wrist, releasing the bottle and leaving the upper half of his torso suspended over his knees, head bowed, bloody drool flowing in a long string.

"Enough, Twig, he's down," Peter barks across the room as Twig launches then aborts a palm strike to the elbow joint. He releases the wrist lock and his hands drop to his sides as he dances away from the unconscious body, scanning the crowd, listening, watching for the next attack. But this time there are no others. Just a stupid cowboy, no gang, no trailing phalanx, no army this time.

"Oh, man, fuck that dude up." Murmurs from the crowd. There's a cynical applause as the club empties, like a crackling of gunfire that follows the crowd pushing through the exits into the bright, moonlit evening.

There were rumors of sexual scandal, pederasty behind the pew, rape in the rectory, the perfect body of St. Stephen wrapped in a bloody drape—or was it white tissue—impaled by the martyr's arrow, deliciously, in the right thigh. The wound is like a snake bite, the venom foams and drips; Father Wick will kiss the hurt up to God in heaven where all souls become the body and blood of Christ our Savior. Ahhh men, warriors, ten Indian braves, ten, and two were Chinamen.

Rise, now, Lincoln, hallowed be thine name. Thy kingdom come, thy will is done on earth as it is in heaven. Give us this day our daily rice and we forgive you all your trespasses, save those we own ourselves, from the womb.

I have forgotten more than you two will ever know, spilled it, left it uneaten, and so much undone. You were nothing.

But I remember we lived together for a while. We camped beside the highway. You cooked and sold good eats to travelers and we threw baking flour on each other and we looked like Casper the Ghost.

I don't remember. Ghosts? I don't remember. I remember demons. I remember Indians. I am a ghost now. Did I look like this? Is this what you remember? I've forgotten it all. Who are you, anyway?

Shades, Lincoln, Uncle, Father, now dead, unexplained.

I dread the ringing phone. It's Wick calling from some asylum for wayward Presbyterians, in a reunion with the Catholic priests who have fallen between the thighs of their charges. Ah, requiem. Purgatory on earth, if not in heaven's hell.

"You see, Chris, they actually loved my loving them. I know how hard that is to admit, but after the first time, when they were finally sure that it was they I loved, all of them—not their behavior, their intelligence, their willingness to serve, to do anything I wanted them to do. It was each one of them, singly, wholly, their lovely bodies, their warm flesh pressed to mine, that gave us both happiness."

Over the phone he would shout, "Bully!" with gusto. He was a charismatic figure, robust, camp songs before the bonfire, homilies, not the syncopated rote coils of the Irish priests and nuns, who sounded like British war movies I watched on Sunday afternoons when Peter and Wick would leave me sitting alone with my TV tray, fried chicken, and lemon wedges.

Wick confesses for the assembled at the clubs, at the commune, whenever he's asked. "I loved those boys. Even when my behavior was inappropriate, beyond the bounds, you know I still loved them. And they know it too, as men today; they know that the love I gave them, spiritual and carnal, was sincere. And they know that they will never feel that, receive that from anyone else ever in their lives. That's why they are so angry. They confuse my love with the love of God that touched them everywhere. They fail to make the distinction, but their confusion is understandable. But I never spoke of God, never. God is unknowable, a vast mystery. I'm just a man who loved them. And they don't know how to accept it. Their anger at me is that shame of their own. They know now as they knew then that what we shared was love. And they can't find it anywhere else, can't allow themselves to even look.

"What was terrible about being loved? I know I must not say so publicly. I keep my mantle of shame—what's that wooden wheel felons were forced to wear, some Manchu torture device stripped from a chariot? Should I wear a tattoo on my face? But that shame is woven from a thousand threads of sexual anxiety, a uniform of humiliation I would gladly wear in exchange for one just man to overturn the hideously oppressive strictures governing filial piety, the worship of dead ancestors, and all the exotic savagery and barbarism that results. I say 'exotic' and 'peculiar' and 'perverse.' Ironically, maybe not. Its most abject victims are its most zealous defenders.

"It wasn't sinful, Christopher Columbus Wong. It may be terrifying, larger than you can imagine right now. But it was always in the name of love."

He's right. Wick was always right. He taught us how to stand before a urinal, how to straddle the throne, to wash under the foreskin. "No one ever taught you before me, not the words, not the acts. Not your mothers, and certainly not your fathers."

Don't remind me of childhood again, Wick. You make me equate my entire Chinese identity with the acts of childhood, infantilizing the culture of Chinatown, equating all things Chinese with the act of growing up. It is as if growing up Chinese in America is child abuse.

Melba and I make love by the wall, her wicked smile leading me past the sounds of others at their separate passions. "Melba, we should have brought a sleeping bag or something. These rocks are digging into my back."

She's slipped her shirt off and moonlight cascades over her sweet breasts. "Be a man, lover."

"Christ, the world can see you."

She rocks back and forth in her straddle, the sky brilliant with stars, a shimmering dark ocean.

"Let 'em look. I love it," she says, her voice carrying well past my hearing.

"Jesus, Melba," I hiss. She groans aloud now, a hungry grunt she punctuates with her hips and the familiar clenching of her sex.

"Just hold still, baby. Let me do the work."

I remember the feel of her nipples caught in my waxed finger tips and the press of river gravel under my butt. I see the wanton grin broadening as she works each separate trembling, and for this time, I remember I could hold back my own, something sharp working under my shoulder blades as her shudders became convulsive waves, a hot tidal flood, her clamoring filling the silent night.

Later, before, the morning chill roused us, we could hear the muffled squeaks and cries all around us. I was ready to leave. But she held me down, her wet whisper in my ear, "Amateurs, baby."

7

Wick rants until he can no longer rouse himself. His chest moves up and down, a thin line of drool glistens at the corner of his mouth. His scalp and forehead blush in the heat from the light falling from the window. I want to move him into the dark or close the blinds entirely, but I'm forever paralyzed, frozen in time and space. There's something I want to raise when he awakens. I can't remember what it is. I know I'll remember as soon as he's conscious. What was it? Something about Mary. Something Melba said about Twig and Peter, how they share something we never had, or lost, or left somewhere, meaning to return for it, and simply forgot that it was ever there, that it ever existed.

In my wanton longing, I read the love letters Melba wrote to me when Twig was still in jail, something the three of us share that he will never see.

4 MARCH, *Oakland*

Dear Chris,

Twig's a genuinely talented musician, with all his many shortcomings. He thinks I don't respect him, that all I want is sex. But it's not true. People like myself with the rudiments of the keyboard, who whistle in empty hallways, can love such talent and loathe with envy the artist, especially as a beautiful young man. I was seduced by his affectations, oblivious to his genius, I patronized his untutored theories and relieve the irritation his arrogance engenders by completely sublimating myself. My diet of humble pie leaves me quaking and expectant. I never have to plan. I wait for direction, for the wind to blow. He's an orchid, dumbfoundedly rooted, flourishing in a rare space, requiring warm, moist air and tropical light.

I had a dream that he's ikebana—you know ikebana? The

slow appraisal of bloom and branch, a rare arrangement of physical beauty, good genes, a digestion of drugs that cut and rip, that burn fat for fuel, his pupils tight on the night sky, listening to the sizzle of stars. He has the ocean in his eyes, Chris. I can watch the breakers coiling in mile-long white strings illuminated by moonlight, dark tracks marking the outline of the shore that from the sky might seem to guide like landing lights, the glide path to some exotic home base, the wake we would follow anywhere, that circles the beach, the reef.

Melba will never see my own correspondence. The voyeur's journal is privately arranged and always unrecognizable to the object of his desire. They've all made their escape. Twig no longer sulks in jail while the rest of us wait impatiently, our temptations locked in that same cell. It's much easier to love them from some impossible distance. Twig was always better when he was on stage, better when there was a crowd to haul at his strings, our wanton souvenir.

Wick figures here. Did he persuade us to follow him? Were we seduced? Or was he, finally, like Twig, the shape the crowd wants watching, some glittering figure of heat and light, incandescent in the night, shaped by hammering strikes of our attention, our desire, blows against the anvil that bent him to our shape?

Auntie would have had me believe that it was Wick and Twig who had inspired all of our cousins' cottage enterprises, wanting to make good by imitating Peter's globetrotting distribution of the Chi Bar, not to mention her mentorship of Winnie. All of them tried, even Melba, to match Uncle's ambitious nature as I never have. That's why Winnie and Uncle married. When Peter first arrived with Twig, it was in Uncle's nature to find Baba Lan's family, create family, even the fiction of family. Winnie would stay married, Auntie said—if not to me, then to Uncle. He was very old and needed someone to guard his door, and other such comments that I think were lip service for some future reconciliation, which, of course, is moot.

In the fall of that summer, Wick forged a check for forty loads of concrete to be poured on successive days, and by the following Sunday, Baba had the workers dismantling the forms, spraying the gray behemoth to reveal the rough shape of the concrete wall, its rise and fall across the landscape, its oblique conjunction now a coincidental reminder of Maya Lin's Vietnam Veterans Memorial and of my marriage to Melba. Wick's wall bore no names. In his testimony to come and Wick would claim that the wall was for Asia's millions, dead or missing, that our fathers had been responsible for killing. But that was for TV.

It's winter, or at least the feel of it in my empty house. Rain rattles on the panes. I press along the window seat, kneading the old wood against the pane, and feel the moisture. Beads of water pool in the impressions my fingers make, color the weathering stains each wet season to come on the redwood frames the gypsy builders installed after the cousins respectfully abandoned us after Twig's arrest. The new construction remains unfurnished, empty.

When the living room was reconstructed, new light exposed the original linoleum, which we covered with parquet tiles that rose in the winter along the interior wall, then settled in summer, leaving a clear fault line on the floor now covered by an ancient Oriental rug and shaded by a fern that flourishes in the gray light and first rain that seeps through the spongy window frames. The rain falls softly, the first storm of the season, hesitant, a cold vapor, a drifting fog too heavy to float. With no wind to push it past, it becomes a wet that darkens the shake roofs, inks the hillsides green, a suburban batik where winter washes away the summer wax and scribbles the landscape in crayon, a willful child who smudges the borders that pre-figured a page in a too familiar book. The edges are obscured, the cracks and fissures sealed by the swollen damp. There is a silence beyond the occasional hiss of tires on wet streets, the flurry of rain in the trees, a quiet that burgeons in a room behind a closed door.

The bedroom door gives with a sharp, impatient crack.

"We'd better have somebody sand this door down again," she says.

I play the game. "They're not coming this afternoon." I watch as she staunches the seeping damp with rags the crew left by the stairs. "Not in this weather. Besides, I think they said Winnie had them this afternoon to finish her paneling. And the roof of the big house is still covered with plastic. They'll come Saturday if it clears."

The cousins had labored Tuesdays and Thursdays through that summer, remodeling our attic. Shirtless, sporting bright native bandannas, hand-carved wooden beads which they traded with the neighborhood kids, camouflage cutoffs, and Nikes, they flew from the scaffolding like human flags, turning their renovations into war memorials.

What can we say? What can we safely recall? Twig languishes in prison.

"Poor babies. They're all lost without their Baba Lan. I saw them hanging clothes over the lilac bushes in the front of the yard, doing a communal laundry with the garden hose. Wick wants them to stay here. They're putting all their energies into finishing the wall." Wick had moved them all to the house. "Have you seen what they've done upstairs?"

"I was waiting for you." Oh, gallant gesture.

She beams. "Thank you, dear. I want to paint when the weather clears. Wick said we should do that before the floor's done."

Melba goes up the attic stairwell, running her hands along the new wood, clapping the dust with her shoes. At the landing she swings the knobless door open. "It's beautiful, the aroma of new wood."

Wet wood, I mutter to myself. "Shall I come up?"

"In a minute," her muffled echo sounds triumphantly, "in a minute, dear."

I hear her pace the new addition at the odd angle above my head. Her footfalls trace across the ceiling. What has always been the familiar texture of white expanse above our bed becomes an underside that, unexpectedly, fills me with a sense of caution. I have the feeling of being old and fussy, the same awkward emotional posture I felt when Melba later insisted tearfully that her studio remain unchanged.

"What? I can't hear you." A squeaking joist sounding from an interior wall bears the weight of her exploring the new construction. The attic had become a maze of spaces leading to hidden alcoves behind the outside wall. Exposed, a subfloor behind the hall closet, linked to a crawlspace that leads to the first floor, was transformed into a whimsical storage space in the new addition.

"I told them to stuff it with something, old newspapers, baby shoes."

She appears at the top of the narrow stairwell. "Come see," she beckons. "It's huge."

A gust of wind sends showers dripping loudly through the labyrinth. Water flows past the roof gutters, streaming down the hillside, a steady sigh filling the empty room.

"Listen to the rain. It's a baptism." The plasterboard walls are smeared with caulking. Wiring protrudes from the unconnected conduits partially concealed by the painters' drop cloth spread across the floor. The demi-construction seems like an unmade bed.

"Any leaks?"

She taps the floor impatiently with her toe. "Knock on wood before you say anything like that. I mention baptism and your imagination leaps to leaks, but not in my room. I won't have you in here if you're going to go all soggy on me." She shakes out and smoothes a drop cloth over an expanse of new floor. "Only dry blankets here."

"Now that it's here, what will you do with it?"

The air is heavy, the room bright with new paint. The intoxicating aroma of varnish and glue makes fucking frenetic, aerobic exercise. The friction, heavy breathing, the liquid slippery numbness as she reaches and retreats, pulling at me, then slips away. Our sweat pools in the hollows of our bellies, our legs and feet slipping, twisted and knotted, my hands locked beneath her buttocks, we rock and heave. I am distracted, my toes looking for purchase on the drop cloth, my breathing, the obscene clap of skin slapping skin resonating against new wood, the space filling the sound of the occasional passing car.

"Can you come?" She idles as I lick at her ears, draw circles with my tongue around her nipples.

"I can go on for hours." My elbows suggest not.

"Hmmm."

"Am I taking too long?"

"No, no. But I have to pee," she confesses.

She returns with a towel and dries us both. We lay apart, sharing the towel, her hand curled around my penis. "Sometimes I can only come when it's quick and dirty. When I leave my shoes on." She begins to touch herself, her fingers plucking at her nipples, slipping her hand between her legs. "You get hard watching me touch myself."

"Do tell."

"Do you?"

"A solid turn on, absolutely. Talk to me."

"I love it."

"I know. Tell me, no secrets."

"I'm coming."

And she does as I watch, an involuntary shudder that traps his hand between her legs, slapping flesh, a lubricous sighing, human voices murmuring, tempting agony, his fluting encouragement, the two of them rubbing against each other. She steps out of her clothes. In a modest subterfuge, she hides from me and unbuckles him from behind, slips her hands into his shorts, molding his thickening erection, hand over hand, as she hugs his legs, catching his pants, and riding them to the floor. She catches the warm spill in the palm of her hands and rubs it across her chest. As he kneels to her, taking the fingers of one hand in his mouth, she guides his thickness into her sex, and she turns her head to look me in the eye, helpless, bidding.

She whispers fiercely in my ear that she wants him inside her, to bury himself inside her sex, that she wants me to watch as she comes rhythmically to his reach and pitch, his length and heat, and I say yes. He hunches between her legs, his taut cheeks jumping left and right, legs and back chiseled, and he plunges his thick rod into her middle as he lifts with his arm beneath her. She grips with her legs and arms, her embrace pressing all of him. She wrestles his hands and fingers, his feet, knees, legs. She slides over his hips and chest, legs wide, wiping their spent juices all over him until she finds his mouth, his tongue.

Or she undresses in the alcove where a bank of sinks, a small bar, and a mirrored wall provide a small stage. She strips quickly, but, suddenly shy, scurries furtively to the shower, her entrance met by a cloud of steam. When she returns, her hair lies wet, plastered against her skull, and she seems vaguely alien, extraterrestrial. She turns.

Where to put my eyes? I see too much. I want to hold her in my arms, support her trembling until I'm sure she's stilled. In time, I finally learn to read her body, feel the tides of her desire ebb and flow. Too late.

She kneels beside him, determined to lick the length of his body. She begins at his feet, lingers at his kneecaps. Her lips purse tightly around his stalk, catching him on the underside with the tip of her tongue. He groans as she gathers his penis in her hand, brushes the flaccid shaft across her forehead. I watch it swell and rise horribly. She cocks her head, slyly pricing the dramatic profile of his towering erection, and her fingers grasp his shaft, working its tip against her cheek, her lips, encouraging a cruel smile of lubricant with her tongue. Her face shines with sweat as she mimes a lipstick with the head of his penis at her pursed lips. She spreads his legs and caresses the insides of his thighs, licking the pale soft tissue, catching his silky pubic hair with her tongue.

Her voice caressing me, warming me, she grips my penis loosely, rocks me in the cradle between her legs, one hand at her sex, the other on mine, whispering with some stranger, a lover she fucks.

But Twig was no stranger. He was family.

I smell him between us, a coolness when first I taste between her legs, something left over, something he spilt. "You want him too," she urges. "Let's all be together."

She steps across the room and playfully hides behind an angled beam that conceals a storage alcove. "Keep it empty for now. I can fill it with my echo." And her echo was all she left, resonating everywhere.

"I don't know what to say. I can't explain. If you want me to leave, I will."

One of the children, running a slight fever, has missed school this morning and Melba holds her for comfort, perhaps as a shield. She sleeps fitfully, her legs tucked in Melba's lap. One stained sweat sock gathered at her ankle, Melba has covered her bare foot with her shirt, snug against her stomach, to keep each other warm. The child's tongue works against a tiny piece of jewelry piercing her lower lip, the hematite pearl, its blue gleam floating in the delicate pink wash of her mouth, half-open, snoring softly.

"Are you sleeping together?"

"Yes." She heaves a sigh, "Yes, yes." Melba lifts her legs and stretches against the child's dead weight, her toes curling, eyes shut tight, sunlight flooding past the dense jungle of the window boxes into Twig's second-floor bedroom.

My eyes are dry. I want to make tea, eggs, and toast for her, for both of them, something to slake the arid calm, the emptiness inside. If we walk home, just a few steps, really, if we take the path through the garden, stumble down the hillside steps that aren't quite finished, the refrigerator is stocked with fresh juice. Snaps of rosemary and thyme, a scoop of butter in a slow frying pan, softly beaten eggs—I would work them with a wooden paddle as they gathered into a drift of tender folds. The aroma of herbs and warm butter would rise in the steam to envelop us, to nourish us, to entice an appetite we could share.

But we can't leave, not yet. The child's sleeping. She's found her own refuge for the instant. I have questions. I must practice patience here. I listen to her heavy breathing, her little snores.

What would we be if I could mail us to China like a postcard? We might venture like pilgrims to wander the antipodes. Two strangers, but invisible, we would move anonymously past the pedestrian cattle guards that surround the Forbidden City, the two of us stepping mute through the din of a village marketplace.

A summer rain fills the cups of lily pads skimming the placid lake at the Summer Palace. They tip and their perfumed brimming empties into the water. Linking arms in the Chinese fashion, we walk cautiously along the crumbling path, the low earthen dikes that separate the rice paddies from the river, three indistinguishable shoots of grass in that muddy water roiling with bottom feeders, turtles, frogs, carp, and catfish. We climb a sacred mountain as the sun rises and find ourselves shivering in a cold wind on some temple-topped crag, beating the dust from our jeans, our tennis shoes slipping on the rime of moss and damp that never dries in the shadow of the Great Wall.

"Did he do something to you? You're all right?"

"Yes. No. He'd never hurt me. I've hurt him, Chris. You, too. He wouldn't. He's innocent." She twists around and wipes her eyes with a free hand. "No, it wasn't Twig, never him. It was me. I chose to be with him."

"You chose him." Did she ever choose me, even once? Wasn't it I, always in pursuit?

"I wanted him. Seduced him. Fucked him. Yes." Her voice finds the dark in me. "You know, he needed me. Like you needed me. I like to be needed, Chris, not wanted."

How would we be in that exotic refuge? Tongue-tied. Oddments in old clothes that hang over our hands and shoes, laundry dried from a rope, not fluffed and shrunk by the dryer, no highways lit with carbon arcs, no electrical zap to provide the appearance of movement. We are specters wandering among China's empty monoliths, drawn by magnets, by cultural gravity, with only the moon and stars to count the days. That and a propensity to follow in the infected footsteps of our past, a mild habituation to cannabis and other hallucinogenic plants we employ to stretch our adolescence, we would hold each other for this brief respite before the smothering embrace that would kill us.

"I don't understand. You were stoned, a roll in the hay. I'm sorry. I want to know. I want to know if I've lost you." I have never understood, but I have learned that I can love what I hate.

"No. Yes. I don't know either. All I know is Twig's in jail. That's probably my fault. No. I don't know." She's pressed herself tightly against the child's legs, perched on the side of Twig's unmade bed.

Although the room itself is quite large, the furnishings are simple: a single shelf of bricks and board along the wall, no books, an expensive short-wave radio, a collection of records and cassettes, Japanese and American magazines that feature martial arts and high-fashion pornography on the covers. A weight bench and barbells sit next to a full-length mirror—for posing, perhaps—and a black *yi* hangs from a hook along its side. There's a shoebox filled with cellophane envelopes and a beam scale next to a rather ornate teak jewelry box with brass frog fittings. Bad habits dying, I run my finger across the scale's pan to test for residue, but it's spotless. No desk, no other chairs in the room. I can only stand or pace.

"You were together here?" I'm by the window, a safe distance. We had made love in a bower I could have seen clearly from a balcony, if there were a balcony just beyond.

"Here, yes. There, yes. Twig has a place in Oakland too. That's where we were yesterday."

"So this wasn't on the spur of the moment. You've been together for a while."

"Yes. Yes, you need to know. We've been meeting here as often as I could get away whenever I knew he would want me next to him."

"You mean right here in this room?"

"Damn it, yes. Listen. Yes. I fucked him right here. This is the bed, this is the room, in this house, usually in the afternoons. The first time, at night. Once in the morning. Yes." She raised her chin as she spoke, to send the words across the room to me directly, without interfering with the child's sleep. "Do we have to talk this minute? Can't you wait?"

I want to sit, not stand like this, interrogating.

"I had to take care of him. Everyone wants him. No one asks what he wants. He doesn't know how to explain, and neither do I, not right now at least."

Moaning suddenly, the child in her arms turns fitfully in her sleep and works her sock off, rubbing one foot against the other.

I see the ragged dream of China in the denim aprons hanging from a laundry line tied across the windowsill in the yard behind Lincoln's trailer. I smell the steeping crust of burnt rice, Auntie's remedy for bellyaches, flatulence, a meal that has gone uneaten, rice left in the pot. It comes to me in the vaguely acrid burn on toast or instant coffee, the aroma grains rendered from fire and water, from burning, then drowning the ash in cold water. It's a final recipe before what's left becomes the slop for Lucky's dog bowl. Savory at the instant of its creation, what remains is a cold paste.

I fumble with a window in my imaginings and it slips open too easily. There is nothing to deny. No surprise.

I began a more than casual observation of male parts. I marveled at the variety of shapes and colors exhibited by men Melba might find attractive. My tastes were governed by an especially titillating phrase she once used—"big hands and loose hips"—but nothing more decisive, no specific criteria for judging this torso in conjunction with those tight cheeks, the tight ass all women envy, not the even disposition of pubic nesting, a symmetrical scrotal sac. So unaware is he of my observation, my judging the heft and dimension of the phallus, how even the tissue of circumcision, what ratio of thighs and sweet embrace? Men in constant eye of one another, carefully avoiding comparisons, secretly evaluating the strengths of this temptation or that inevitable liaison that determines the inevitability of the next.

Winnie looks me over carefully, a new curiosity about me, about the expression on my face. "That's attractive. You want to be with men?"

It was a fantasy I played with Melba. I'd never said it aloud before, but there it was. So it became a conceit to disguise my meetings with Winnie.

I would whisper to Melba, "You've been fucking someone, I can tell. Who is he?"

"Which one would you like him to be?"

"The dancer. Him I'd like to see." I knew then I could not turn back.

"Not the big guy who bought me a drink? Big hands, loose hips?"

"Too scary."

Melba laughs, "Well, next time, you choose."

It's Peter's voice, older, who leads the chorus. "Winnie talks to me all the time. Tells me all about you, everything, Chris. She lets me watch." These intimate conspiracies join us. "You know how she talks."

Of course I knew. How was I to stop myself from wanting them, all of them?

"Oh, babe, that bad boy whispered in my ear and I felt his tongue thick and warm punctuating his nasty talk, hips or lips, he kept at me, lips or hips and he bumped me, rubbing his crotch against me. He was so tall. I could feel his hardness pressed up against my breasts right through his pants. We danced around the floor. You saw him, how close we were, rubbing himself up and down my front."

I listen. She says this all a bit breathlessly, disheveled, with her shirt turned around, her panties dangling carelessly from her purse. The heat in her voice makes my throat swell, my tongue tight. I'm filled with feelings of contradiction, paradox. She sits quietly with no explanations, listening carefully, waiting for the rage to subside. And then she senses my desire in my aching breath, my trembling. She knew these were not questions. Simply my own heat. Tell me, oh tell me, just the lies if you please, how you do what you do when you do and do again, you say, you do again, I want to know, the angle, the posture, the organ, the pleasured senses, the whiling of the hours, the hapless surrender, the seduction, tell me, show me.

I spend the rest of the evening in helpless suspense, a slavish focus holds me through my dreaming, and the intensity I feel goes unrelieved. Melba had fallen asleep without letting me near her, so whetted, her lovers palpable in my insomnia.

"Chris, I see them, all that smooth flesh across rippling waves of muscle tissue. Look at them. They're like gods." Peter confesses deep into the night. "The safe endomorph, the cute dark trainer who lurks about the pool, tight curly hair cut close to his skull, wonderful bones in his face, and my eyes do follow when he stands profile to the mirror beside the sauna. I watch him pull his tank top over one shoulder, flexing his abdominals, one hip jutting out. Then he tightens his pectorals. Self-absorbed, exhibitionist, I love that in men."

Peter, in the dark, nodding, can hum that sweet refrain.

"Are you working hard? Are you getting big?" she demands even as she climbs on top of him, bolstering him with both fists working between her legs, arching back as his hands slide up her torso to crush her breasts. Her eyes are on me, and as she leans forward to press her chest into his hands, she smiles and winks at me.

I step from behind the door and see her straddling a pillow with him positioned behind her. "I tell you what's really nasty," he says with his chin on her shoulder, his mouth in her ear.

"God, I feel you right up through my spine."

"Tell him," now it's Peter's voice, urgent, urging, "say the words." They time their breathing, a sharp inhale as the other exhales in a wordless syllable, engaged.

Melba peers out from half-lowered eyelids, her tongue marking Twig's cadence, wordlessly staring at me in the doorway.

Yes, I watched you, watched you dance. All the little discoveries, the taste of your kiss, the faint aromas I imagine you bring, a little late, a little out of sorts. I can taste an ocean.

I looked up and saw Wick. He put his hands on my head, then covered my ears, and the only sound I could hear was my own breathing.

Melba was crying now, blotting the wet with her shirtsleeve, but watchful, staring at the child's sleeping form. "Twig told me he was shooting at the moon, you know. He wasn't trying to shoot anybody, just firing away at the giant turtle eating the moon," she snuffles. "Old story, a myth."

"Who are you talking about?"

He held us both together, whispering in our ears. I felt his hand on my shoulder, his lips in my ear.

"Twig was shooting at a turtle in the sky."

"What turtle?"

"It was something about the Lunar New Year from his childhood. Maybe he was trying to write a song, a fairy tale. I don't know. We went for a ride. He was hungry. We hadn't eaten all day." She stood carefully, tucking the child's legs under the bedspread.

"So you had the day together."

Idle hours, the day becomes evening.

"Yes. He had an idea for a song he wanted to write down. And he said I could help."

"In Oakland?"

She looked down. "Yes. It's the first whole day we've had to be together, without everyone watching." She staples her words into my chest. "Nobody was with us, all right? Nobody knows."

But they will. I lay spent between them, but alert. I felt her trembling against the two of us as he continued to massage and knead our damp skin.

"We slept together the first time the night after that fight at the café. Twig and Peter and maybe Wick were all arguing. We were talking and nobody was around. Peter said Twig had been stupid for fighting, especially because it was me. But he was treating it like a joke. Beat on a white man, that sort of thing. I saw Twig waiting outside Wick's door later and he was crying, Chris. He said he was going to have to leave. Then I came upstairs with him."

I need to leave now. I want to take myself away and leave her, leave them to each other.

"Twig could have killed that guy at the café as easily as not. He wasn't going to stop. He wanted to hurt himself, hurt something."

"He did."

And I was held there even as all my passions were sated, chilled.

"It was as if we were afraid to be alone together. That we would have to spend the night, wake together in the morning."

I felt his hands groping, reaching for our sex, felt his tense breath hot in our hair, in our faces. So I stayed.

"In his own mind, Twig told me he was already dead. He had already died a thousand times, in camp, on the streets, in jail. He's been in jail, you know. One more time would be easy."

"Yes. I understand." You wanted him. The hurt boy.

"We smoked a little. I told him to unwind, that it was all over. But he wasn't done yet, I could feel him, still angry, still unfinished, so deeply incomplete. Have you ever felt that way? I know you have."

"No. Yes. I don't know."

In that time, I learned to feel unfinished, done and undone.

"I wanted him to finish in me, kill me if he wanted. I don't mean literally, but in a way, yes."

"And I died."

Wrong song, again, the wrong movie.

"It's not you. It's not about you at all, poor Chris. It's what I felt in him. Even when we were making love, Chris."

I hold you in my arms for this other.

"That loneliness, that anger stays so deep I can feel it, touch it for a moment. I wanted him to give that to me. But I could only hold it for a moment, feel his spirit coming into me. I couldn't keep it. So I kept pushing. That's why I spent the day with him. I wanted to wake up next to him, draw him in, make him give me what he has in him, everything. I did it. But it let something else out. And now it's my fault."

"Maybe we should go home now?"

Slip over the garden wall, through the woods, and over the bridge.

"Not yet. Let me finish." She sees the child stirring and holds her breath.

"You can wake her. I want to make breakfast. We haven't eaten anything in a while."

"Listen to me, Chris. I'm not going to talk about this part anymore."

"Sure, I'm listening."

Please, I implore, quietly, only to myself—home, coffee, a shower. I can't leave her.

"We went for ride. I said something stupid when I was ordering food at the drive-in. And they said something back and then Twig wanted to leave. But I yelled at them. It was me. So it's white hippie bitch, this and that, with a monkey. Twig drives off. But I wanted to go back. I made him go back to fight them, to kill them." She speaks quickly, her ragged breath caught in her throat, whispering quickly.

"And he shot at them?"

She trembles and turns in my arms as our hands and mouths find her.

"No, no. He was talking about shooting at the turtle that was eating the moon," she sobs.

"Was he stoned or something?"

"Yes, we both were. But when we drove by, they saw the van coming and started waving and yelling at us. Twig put the gun out the window and fired in the air, but it was a little popping sound and they couldn't hear it. I knew they couldn't even see the gun. So I said I wanted to shoot it too."

"And you shot at them?"

"I pointed at the building. I wanted to break a window, something they could see and hear. What do I know about guns? I never shot one before. I pulled the trigger twice. And I broke a big window. It exploded all over the place. Twig told the police he did it."

"And they believe him?"

"Yes. I don't know."

"You're not going to tell them?"

She looks at me from the door that leads down the hallway to the bathroom. "How can I? I can't go to jail, Chris. I can't." The child stirs and sits up as Melba turns her face away and I hear the bathroom door closing, the hysteria in her voice echoing down the hall. "I'll only be a second, babe." Her voice trembling, "I want to wash up before we go home."

There had been a slight confusion when Twig went missing in jail. "They lost him?" I asked?

"His papers. It's all paper. They are all illegal here," Winnie repeated. "I've explained this to them. They will be deported if the authorities start looking into the businesses they've organized here. If an investigation occurs, they might wish to examine everyone's immigration papers more carefully. Then Twig will be very unhappy, as well as the real Huynh Ba Lan and family."

Peter poked about the garden. "That's the song I hear. Call it Uncle, call it Dixie."

Winnie nodded. "The Huynh family plays an active role in the anti-communist movement in Long Beach. Lincoln knows them very well. They have extensive connections. Twig will submit for the good of the families. When he is convicted, he goes to jail, he will be Huynh Ba Lan again. Besides, where could we send him?"

"There's no place they can send him or anyone anymore," Peter answered. "The war's over. They lost. We lost."

I hadn't been asked, but I felt I had to participate, show my concern or arouse suspicions. Nobody wanted to repeat the obvious, except me. Melba had two jealous guardians. And for my sake, they were going to send the other one to jail. "They're losing a son."

"What's the matter with you people?" Wick implored.

"You people?" Mary sat with Uncle as he napped in the shade. She stared at Wick. They rarely spoke to one another anymore.

"Mary, you know, the last time I looked, there's still no refuge west of the Mekong, but the camps in Olongapo might have a space for all of them."

Peter paced across the garden to the wall, where a raised bed of cilantro sat above a barrel of new basil. "These folks have a fistful of green thumbs. I'm going to make us some lunch right here."

Mary continued patiently, holding Uncle's hand in her lap, "When Twig speaks to the public defender, he must say he wishes to plead guilty. If he says nothing, apologizes, asks for the mercy of the court, they may be lenient."

"If he says nothing, the criminal laws that traditionally govern our exclusion stand without comment." Wick had been reviewing the history of immigration policy in his sermons, and for him, it was all of a piece, the larger conspiracy. "We have an opportunity here to do some good for everyone, a greater good."

Auntie shook her head and joined Peter at the wall. He handed her a small bouquet of herbs. She rubbed basil between her fingers, chewing thoughtfully on a sprig of lemon thyme. "We're not Communists."

Wick tried again. "Why don't I pack them all up and move them back to Oakland? We can hold a demonstration, testify on his behalf."

"Oh, this is very good lemon basil," Peter said, making bouquets for Mary. "That's perfect, Wick. They could wear something traditional, hawk their trinkets on the steps of the courthouse."

"No way, Jose." Winnie sounded like Uncle. "Have you taken a head count lately of all the cousins? There were only a few, not counting the girls, when you brought them here, in our name, to work for us. Now there's ten more for every one, and you know they want to know who the real Indians are. And then what? Where'd they all come from, anyway?"

"Originally from Laos, isn't that what Lincoln said?"

Uncle rouses himself as he hears Wick evoke him. He stretches one leg after the other, but remains seated on the plastic divan, waving Winnie's supporting hand away. "Thank you. Everybody sit down now. Just leave it the way it is." Uncle waves his hand in disgust.

Peter joins him. "Uncle's right. Let's keep it simple, a little media savvy. So he pleads guilty. Of course, he can't stand there mute."

"Twig should tell them something sad. But," Uncle cautions, "these things have a way of getting out of control."

Winnie sits beside him. "Lincoln's right."

"Not much. One small sad story."

Wick shakes his head sadly. "But we have an opportunity here."

"Enough," Auntie declares. "Everyone understands already. The cousins can stay here, but not so many. They have good businesses here. It's safer here." She begins gathering sprigs she finds cleverly planted in the folds and fissures about the wall. "Chris, would you find me something to hold these fresh herbs? I want to take some home with me." She touches my shoulder in passing, "It's lovely here, and they do such beautiful work. You know, Christopher, this is the first time I've seen the house in such good shape. Peter says we should have lunch right here outside in the garden."

Everyone knows the discussion is over. And no, Wick, you don't get it. No more quibbling, please. No more community, no Twig who will do his duty. It's the family, it's always been the family. And I still have Melba.

"They're right, Wick. Leave it be."

Wick shrugs and leaves without another word.

Peter rises. "Of course. Let's eat. Eat everything, let's eat it all before we're all dead and buried and then something comes along to eat the remains, and so on, ad infinitum. That's all there is, people. That's it, that's what we're here for."

I ignite the butane stove to heat the stock. Winnie unwraps fresh noodles, raw beef, scallions, and bean sprouts. The condiments lie waiting, the fresh-picked basil leaves in a heap, chili paste, and the industrial-sized bottle of hoisin sauce the cousins keep. They use it like catsup. Auntie dips soup as I arrange the bowls. "Isn't this nice? They've taught us to use lemon grass in the broth." The slightly acid sting in my nose blends seamlessly with the steaming citric broth that colors thin slices of flank steak. The rank grass deepens the sweetness of the meat, of the onions and sprouts.

Uncle eyes the pale sauvignon offered around. "You guys don't keep anything to drink around here? I always have a little Hennessy by the stove to cook with. Daisy always had a little tucked away for me."

"No brandy, Lincoln," Mary says, then Winnie repeats the phrase, word for word.

"Hell, she's right. Bad for my sex life, anyway. Gotta keep the home fires burning. Have you tried snake wine? Ran into a bottle of it in Canton City. Had a genuine snake floating in it, embalmed in the alcohol."

"It's a traditional aphrodisiac, Chris." Peter knows food and sex are the only safe topics at the table.

"Well, that's the reputation it has. You know, boys, I drank this stuff with a cousin in the village one time. Home brew. He claimed it was real fire water. Blow your pants off, if you'll excuse me. We never finished the bottle and I slept clear through dinner. Strong medicine."

Peter works the table. "Uncle, it sounds more like a contraceptive strategy to keep the population in check." He pours another glass of wine, drinks it, then refills his glass.

"Eat something, Lincoln," Auntie says mildly as she and Winnie clear the bowls into the house.

Peter sits. "I'm going to lead a tour of the fleshpots of Asia, Uncle. A roll in the hay of the villages. A jeepney through the rice paddies. Chris, you should go, you've never been. A pasha on the backside of a water buffalo. Watch a marriage arrangement from behind an Oriental screen, the lovely Ming Fa marries a rooster." Peter picks away at our scabs. We recognize each other by the faint smell of skunkweed, esters of cannabis that emanate from our pockets, buds wrapped in plastic, hash resins worked into the fabric of our clothing. We smile at one another, sniff, and smile.

Mary looks distractedly at Winnie and signals their exit.

Uncle empties his glass again and looks at us in disgust. "I'm going to drown before I can get drunk here." He lets his voice drop a decibel for the sake of the retreating women. "Anyway, sex in the village? With what? Dead barnyard animals? Half a pig? Be serious. You think anybody in China cares who's fucking who? They're all farmers, damn it. If something fucks something, doesn't matter if it's plant or animal, it better damn well reproduce and in quantity so that you save two, or divide one, and make more, right? You want bright city lights, TV, and, all right, a little of that snake wine. Anyhow, all you got there is a bunch of native girls with lipstick on their faces these days."

"That does take some of the romance away from the wooing. What about a cruise, then? The Pearl River Delta Queen. A steamy love boat up the Yangtze, visit your mother, your mother's other?" Peter looks to Uncle, but we can see his efforts are wasted.

"So what you have here," Uncle waves his arms to embrace the house, the garden, the trees, "what you have here, boys, is illusion, kind of like the movies, right?"

Peter can always talk back. "Twig's gone. Bugger the butler, three women, five pretty boys, nine eunuchs in row."

Is Lincoln even listening?

"Peter, I know Twig. I know his family. Winnie talked to them already. It's like this, boys. I don't care who's screwing who. But the dope train running through here is derailed and out of service right now. And we're that close to losing our money because of it." He looks at Peter now, a sorry stare. "We can't have Wick trying to save the world again while we're still living in it. Let's keep this all in the family. That's enough for me." He rises to stretch himself. "Great lunch, fellas, but you really oughta keep a little nip around. Now, me, I'm going to have a snooze inside."

I knew we should all run, run as fast and as far as we could. But I didn't know how to start. What should I take, and what could I leave behind, be done with, abandon? Or even where?

Peter slides up beside me. He's been smoking and drinking. "It's a conspiracy of witches and bitches, Christopher."

I feel his fingers at my neck, searching for a pulse. "Don't." I can't hide from him. "Please don't touch me."

"You've got knots and knots, Chris." He continues, working his fingers through my shoulders. "Lots of knots."

I sit here in the dark of the garden, our jungle, and feel a dampness, that wanton emptiness that needs filling. For once, I don't want him to tell me how I feel, what I think.

"Twig's going to hang himself, and you're going to let it happen. You want that."

Yes. I want him dead, out of my life, away from Melba. It's nothing personal, but it's all so personal. "I know it's my fault."

"Now stop that. You were doing so well. Play dead."

"I can't."

"You'd damn well better. For Winnie, too."

He lets the silence hang between us. I search in the darkest corners for some bit of angry fire to account for the heat I feel. I see it clearly. Winnie married Lincoln to be safe. And Melba chose Twig to be free.

Maybe I dreamed it. She comes back to the apartment late with her leftovers. The light from the fridge, then the bathroom. She showers, slides into bed, and I feel her coolness, her distance. You know I reach for her. I can't help myself. She's been with him.

Peter reminds me. "But you want this to happen. We can come together. You haven't forgotten, dear boy."

"I heard the two of you, but you know that too. It doesn't really matter that it's Twig she's been with."

"Who?"

"Dear Winnie. You don't mind? She told you. Twig wouldn't have me any other way."

But I think some other, not Winnie. I fuck her. She doesn't resist me. But I don't feel any response from her. I can't finish without her, but I can't stop myself. Her face is turned away and I'm looking for something, anything. Then I find her stupid pillow. Finally, she struggles against me. I want my hands at her throat.

"I know it feels—what—wrong, a mistake for now," Peter says. "But it was intense, wasn't it? All of us, all three of us together? I thought you'd understand. Isn't that what you want?"

"I want to kill her." I look down. "Melba, I mean."

Wick sweeps by in his robes. "I'm going to make a perfect fool of myself, I've decided, organize some futile demonstration and rage against the historical conspiracies that surround us." He waves at a cloud of gnats. "Why do I bother?"

"Nobody wants that, Wick. Eat something. Get high."

Wick sighs and stretches. "I feel so absolutely inspired by the absurdity of it all, because I want to inspire myself with the awe of others, walk naked in the streets, feel alive. Why else are we here, boys? We're ghosts, shades passing in the night. Can you feel yourself? You can't even get mad. Do you own yourself? Have you ever?"

"Save the race?" I knew that was illusion.

"What damn race? Half the population of the world?"

"Survivors, just the survivors, Christopher."

"By definition, we've been saved."

"That's the problem, Peter, that's exactly the problem. We need to save ourselves, again, survive the rescue."

I could never make myself understood, ever. "Wick, I have to tell you. I don't understand anything, nothing, and not you especially."

"Dear Christopher, I know."

Was it that he didn't want me to understand?

"You all are overwhelmed by gratitude and shortly to be annihilated by acceptance. It's what makes America great. You feed on the debris washed up on these shores, the hungry, hopeless, and hapless become the blueplate special for the all-you-can-eat steam table buffet. The only integrity you have left comes in a take-out carton Lincoln would poison the world with."

"Stop talking to him, Peter. You're nuts, Wick. It's over."

"To explain the infection I planted in all of you. That's the equation, isn't it, the meek or the mocking? We have to fight it in ourselves. That's what makes us all crazy. The measure of acceptance—but who's measuring, and who's creating the measure? What are we to the world, or to each other? Have we created enough necessities to test and expand our capabilities? If my eyesight's falling, is it because I want less to see? It's chicken-and-egg time. Fry them both, because we haven't the time anymore to figure out which came first."

I don't want to know anymore. I just want to hang on to it, to Melba, and the hell with everything else. If Twig goes to jail, so be it.

"Oh, Chris, Chris. How quickly you let him go. Let's make sure he goes for the right reason. Let him fry to save his father, his family, whomever. Any other way, the family loses face, Auntie and Peter are caught protecting you and yours, while Melba makes a quick exit. No one's at the other end of the string you're holding. Go on. Pull it. Loose end, right?"

I prefer, however, to divide myself and drive them all away from me.

I never sleep well. I spend the days trying to put the house in some order, avoiding the office, the telephone, and then I find myself in the car at dawn, driving with the new sun in my eyes as I aim for the city, towards Winnie. What remains undiscovered I will reveal to her. What I want is Winnie to say, to tell me what to do.

"That's not possible, Christopher."

251

What's not possible? She's wearing a ribbed cotton nightshirt under the white silk robe she gathers at her throat against the hour of my arrival.

"Wick's right," I tell her. "I want to save Twig from jail."

"And Melba? Is that what she wants?"

"I think so. Maybe."

"Maybe? Maybe we should start with a simpler question. What do you want?"

"I thought I never wanted anything more than you. But that couldn't be. Now there's Melba. And I have Twig standing outside her tent holding his candle, lighting the entrance, his flame, his sacrifice. How can I make him go away?"

"Out of sight, out of mind. In jail, the memory of his steadfast loyalty will soon seem absurd."

"Uncle has some influence here."

"Uncle knows it will be to everyone's advantage to keep Twig in jail for as long as possible. What does Melba want?"

"She still wants him, but she's gone away."

And Peter still looms over me. "Listen, we don't want Candlewick and his lunatic fringe, do we?"

"What does Wick have to do with any of this?"

"That's the other shoe, Chris." Peter smiles. "Twig and I, we'd been sleeping together. And Wick's outside the door."

"What are you talking about?"

"You and me. Don't you see, we're lost. We're divorced from our history, our fathers. We should never have been. I didn't see it until now. The fact that we can't keep our lovers should tell us. But I don't feel like committing suicide. I feel free, absolutely unencumbered, responsible only for myself, my own survival. We don't inspire great acts of loyalty, if you haven't noticed, Christopher. Maybe Uncle and Twig are the only real men. Why was Melba willing to start a war at the drive-in? For Twig, Baba Lan, a warrior, not for you, who would never think to war with Jack."

This drivel is Wick's curry, yogurt, and LSD regimen. Seek peace, seek annihilation. But Peter's right. He reminds me. It's like Lincoln's ma— a Ute in Denver at the end of the Trail of Tears, the diaspora of the remainders, the last of the tribe, orphans and widows. You refuse to breed with the conqueror, and choose instead a fellow survivor. At least by giving

Twig over to his own illusions of saving the family, there won't be the need for so many explanations or excuses. Leave the boasting, the history, behind. No one need explain the dour needs, the guilty pleasures we indulge.

Wick repeats his mantra: "Breathe, then work to stimulate the pubocoggygeus muscle—draw the muscles of the vagina and anus towards the navel. The Chinese practice this as part of the art of qi gong."

Twig's final sentencing came after an unusually long delay, nearly six months, during which he was held in various municipal and county jails. There had been disturbances in the first, a small riot that prevented the routine processing of prisoners awaiting their court appearances. In the second month, Wick had pressed Peter for bail to which Lincoln, against his better judgment, finally agreed. But when a cooperative bondsman had finally been located, the jail had lost Twig's records and could not locate him. Two Lans, a Wong Tui, a Ba Nguyen, no record of a Huynh, had been released from custody. The authorities had even given early release to an African-American being held on a similar charge. In that case the circumstances were nearly identical, only the name of the restaurant was different. He had been charged with firing a pistol inside a Denny's Restaurant up the block from the Jack in the Box in Twig's case.

Wick led a small group of students to court the day Twig was sentenced, promising a silent protest. All were in mufti, no backpacks, no blue jeans, no placards, except for Wick, who wore the white robes of mourning and his necromancer's hat, which the bailiff had him remove as they sat down. They stood when Twig entered the courtroom. They caused no disruption, but when Twig was ordered to stand before the court for sentencing, they stood in solidarity.

The judge asked Twig if he had anything to say before sentencing. Twig quietly repeated the story Peter and Winnie had cooked up. Even Wick approved. It was so politically correct, so expected, they felt sure he would receive a minimum sentence. His hopes for completing his rehabilitation from drugs, the mention of his concern for his parents, a family reunion, all seemed reasonable.

The judge took the unusual step of reading the probation review aloud before sentencing, taking note of the unusual presence of Wick and the well-dressed students.

First, the court noted the unusual amount of time Mr. Lan had been lost in jail, and went so far as to apologize to him and his public defender. There was no excuse, and the judge, though not personally responsible, wished to apologize as a representative of the American judicial system. He also took note of Mr. Baba's circumstances. But he added that criminal behavior may not be absolved, that personal responsibility for one's actions in a civilized society may not be waived. "If we are not responsible for behavior that is caused by the circumstances of our lives, some physical or mental impairment congenital to our natures, how can we hold ourselves responsible for anything we might do?" He looked directly at Wick and his group, as if he too were appealing for sympathy, understanding. He saw an orderly group of young Orientals, the boys in blazers and rep ties, the girls distinguishable in their businesslike outfits by the subtle shine of their hair, a brocaded collar here, a broach there, pearl earrings. At that moment, a precocious cutie from UC Berkeley gave him the finger.

Finally, on the point regarding Mr. Lan's desire to bring his parents together, the judge remarked that such ambitions were laudable in that they extended to a universal need for family, for children and parents to remain united, a practice long neglected in many impoverished communities in this country. But in these circumstances Huynh's personal ambitions had become a disaster for American society. "Dr. Candlewick," he said, directing his remarks at Wick and his group, "immigration to the United States often requires the utmost sacrifices, even to the abandonment of old cultural ties, traditional loyalties that, while appropriate elsewhere, have turned the rules governing entry into a Chinese fire drill."

Discussion: Judicial Council Rules 414, 421 & 423 (attached). Enhancements: (none) Case Evaluation: Appearing before the Court is a 20-year-old, single male who pled guilty to one felony count of Section 246 of the Penal Code (Shooting into an inhabited building). This represents his first contact with the criminal justice system.

Mr. Lan appeared to be truly remorseful and felt his state of inebriation influenced his behavior of violence. He also felt the victims initiated the crime by expressing racial slurs, but felt he could have handled it if sober. Although he believed that no bullets struck the building, two bullets were retained at body level from the building, slightly missing the glass directly in the path of the workers. It is fortunate that this incident did not result in tragedy. His actions endangered multiple victims, involving the threat of great bodily harm by the discharge of a loaded weapon in their direction. The victims were particularly vulnerable as they were performing their routine work duties unaware of any threat to their lives. The crime was obviously premeditated, as the defendant returned to exact revenge. The crime was performed in a reckless manner without regard for human lives.

The mitigating factors are the defendant's family, the fact that he carried out the crime while intoxicated, which is not his normal demeanor. He is willing to accept the consequences of his behavior.

It is recommended by this deputy that probation be denied for the seriousness of the crime and the threat to the community. It is recommended that the defendant be committed to the Department of Corrections for the midterm. Suggested term: Crime, Sec. 246 PC (Shooting into an inhabited building). MIT (yes.) AGG (yes.) Range: 3, 5, 7. Enhancement: None. Total Term: 5 years.

Probation denied. Five years. Sec. 246 PC (Shooting into an inhabited building).

Recommendation: (1) A restitution Fine of not more than $10,000.00 be imposed pursuant to Section 13967 of the Government Code. (2) Probation be denied. (3) The defendant be advised of a subsequent Five (5) years period of parole Supervision. Respectfully submitted, Velia de Lunes.

1 AUGUST 1983, *on the way to Mandalay.*
Ahoy, Christopher Columbus,
This flight is interminable, five hours in, six hours to go,
and reading an item from *Natural History:* "Human excrement is a central feature of paleoethnobotany because accidentally preserved feces, called coprolites, often contain traces of undigested food, particularly seeds." Here are the extruded details: ". . . when feces are charred, desiccated or waterlogged, they often contain numerous identifiable plant fragments which indicate the content of the human food in the tested culture. . . . "

By the sheerest coincidence, we had coprolites on a shingle for breakfast. That and a decaf coffee will make it very easy for some future paleoethnobotanists to discover the source of our remains should we be so unfortunate as to be found with this food in this condition. Yes, they'd mutter, people of the late twentieth century occasionally hurled themselves through the sky with feces in their stomachs. Authorities could not agree—was it shit before entering the stomach that caused them to commit suicide? Or was it the discovery that shit had been ingested that caused them to wish they were dead.

I sit next to an animal activist. These horsy-faced white demons, unfed, they reveal themselves, insidious and irritable *gwai*. One deals with these apparitions as one might with gangs, bandits, bullies, and beggars. Perishing far away from family. Sacrifices outside the household buy them off. Like the food police that come down on the Chinatown market-place. White meat? I give you veal. Farce? I give you foie gras. Culinary execution? The Dungeness crab. Think factory fishing boats, the cramping, numbing death their catch endures in the refrigerated holding tanks.

P.S. Hempstead Heath. Rule Britannia: I was stopped at customs and all the dried meats cured in honey were confiscated. When the dog began barking, they dumped my bag of dried grapefruit skin on the floor, looking for drugs. I left them autographed copies of my latest cookbook and all was forgiven save for Lassie, who kept lunging at me, strangling himself at the end of his leash in a paroxysm of revenge. Must have caught a whiff of something on my breath.

I leave Peter's letters at home. Mary can't see well enough to read them, and it's a side of Peter she knows too well, like Wick. Their absence is disguised in silence. Standing by the picture window that frames her bayfront view, Auntie Mary spends her final days watching the pelicans in the estuary. Huddled together, they form islands of old men's walking sticks, their heads and beaks the crook of *ah' bak's* third leg.

Auntie and I have lunch once a week. Winnie calls both of us to make sure. It's Winnie who stays close, steadfast. Winnie manages the bodies, but Mary knows where they're buried, which closets stay closed, who has been gone too long and requires a search party to recover the bones.

"No big deal, right?" She keeps dim sum frozen for company, but eats only her medicinal teas, noodles, and drinks boiled water. "No stinky guys, no dead cigars, all morning reading newspapers on the toilet." Her chair and footstool in the entry hall guard the front door and watch TV. The taro plant, the imitation Ming ossuary umbrella stand, a teak coatrack, a goldfish almost transparent in a pan of water and marbles are bathed in the flickering static of the television she never extinguishes, electric candle fire to light entry and exit.

Mary is so old now she's reverted to my childhood Cantonese. She likes to walk by the water, feed the ducks, the geese her gated village has encouraged by restoring the riparian flyway with its perspective of stacked airplanes waiting to turn the corkscrew for their landing at SFO. The hum of the freeway, the occasional explosion of jet engines burning fuel, the clammy smell of the Bay seep past the fencing. We wander towards the water, Auntie with a bag of bread crumbs and rice, armed with her latest slingshot, a stainless-steel wrist rocket strung with elastic surgical tubing to clobber the seagulls that bully her favorites.

"Keep a look out," she orders. The greenshirts discourage feeding and confiscate weapons. Look but don't feed. Stupid rule. Especially here where it's hard enough to distinguish the residents from their wild companions. I guard the path while she fumbles with a marble from her supply in the goldfish bowl. She lets fly at an old gull with one eye diving at the terns.

"Da nay wah! Mo yung, ah. Ah say kay!" Her language has become the vocabulary of irritable old men.

"They're scavengers, eat up the garbage, Auntie."

"Don't be stupid. Nobody eats garbage if they don't have to. They like rice, bread, and a little meat, like anybody. Thieves and beggars have the best taste, the greediest appetites, but no manners. I shoot at them to keep the pretty little babies near me."

"The little ones aren't babies, you know. Just little birds. Different species."

"You're so smart. Wha!" She shouts suddenly. "I almost got 'em. Frozen peas make good ammunition. Lethal, but fair. If I miss, they can eat it. But that guy I want to kill, make him dead. Too old, too smart now. Doesn't know how to find food for himself. And he won't eat garbage.

He hides near my house. I watched him eat a small baby. So he deserves it. Like the cats."

"Auntie, you wouldn't shoot a kitty?"

She stops herself and in tactful English replies, "Oh, no. Never the pet cats. But people leave cats they don't want right here and they go wild, eat birds, spread disease, that sort of thing. I told security about the situation when somebody saw me throwing rocks. But they can't do anything about the cats. And the rules protect seagulls. There's no shortage of seagulls, is there? Extinct seagulls? They're flying rats. Eat everything from the top to the bottom."

"No cats, Auntie. That's a felony in suburbia."

"No cats, no cats. I know. But I want to get that bird for my own satisfaction. I saw him do it. He made me mad. He eats everything and wants to live forever."

Auntie with a slingshot has surprising strength and an athletic coordination I never knew she had. In her eighties, she can draw out her stainless-steel catapult like a Mongol archer. Her lean torso twisting, she torques her upper body to brace against her right hip, left leg extended, knee bent as if she were on horseback. Locked and loaded, her left arm is a stiff line to her target. At full draw, her elbow cocked like a stiff battle pennant, a wing of death, she nestles her right fist in the silk scarf she wears like a headband holding her hair in place, disguising the bald patches she refuses to cover with a wig, both eyes wide and glaring. Her release when she lets fly is rock steady and her right hand remains locked to her skull. Her left hand, wrist rocket locked against her forearm and the spread of her gnarled grip, swings round to clear the catapult and its projectile in a natural arc of deadly accuracy.

And she drops that gray bird at ten yards as it swims past, an ugly, obvious dying, left floating with its one eye on an island of burnt rice, floating like a kombucha mushroom, a medicinal fungus growing in an herbal tea.

She has killed it dead. "Nice shot." I am, of course, horrified at her blasé, but I admire her skill.

"I practiced on pigeons in the park before they built the garage."

"In front of God and the police department?"

"Before God, Peter and Paul's at the park on California Street. Not Portsmouth." She still believes in David and Goliath.

"Which one would you rather be?"

"The winner."

I think Auntie always knew. I was only a naive participant whose small confessions she could encourage, but to no end; I was always her pet who could manage simple secrets, but not like Peter or Wick in his asylum. Or even Lincoln from the grave.

"Thank goodness for Winnie, right? Lincoln knew best." Auntie ignores my silence.

And then the greenshirts, the condominium police, were on us like white on rice.

Winnie borrowed advice from Auntie to prevent foreclosure and the forced evacuation of the remaining habitants, including Wick's charges, the tribal cousins he'd encouraged to spite us all. After Wick's breakdown, she renegotiated the leases in Santa Lucca's tiny business mall and retired what was left of the enterprises the authorities had been investigating all along. The café was rented to Ali Achmed's and a dance collective that transformed themselves into an organic vegetable market. The extra space was subleased to a bicycle mechanic who had been experimenting with multi-geared, ultra-lightweight frames and fat tires to maneuver on the mountain trails.

Twig's Ba Lan Huynh confession had its effect. In the few stories that made the news, it appeared as if he was right to search for a reason for being where he was, but he was wrong, so wrong, and so sorry to assume that he could make it his own.

Winnie discovered that what had begun as an offshoot of the weaving and jewelry-making business had blossomed into several dubious enterprises under Wick and Peter's benighted direction, none entirely illegal (the massage parlor and medicinal opium cultivation not withstanding), but in their effect a public nuisance. The tribal cousins were never charged, but were referred to a court-appointed social worker who would provide direction for their future enterprises. What Wick had said was true. There really wasn't any place to send them. To avoid malicious prosecution for the marijuana shading the Memorial Wall, Peter fled to Europe—first to Amsterdam, then to Rome—then to Israel as a consultant to develop kosher Chinese food, and on to teeming Asia. And in our way, Melba and I stayed, Melba by telephone for long enough to witness the final stages of Wick's demise, for which no one could be held responsible, not Auntie Mary who longed for it, and not Lincoln, who lingered quietly for another year. Not even Wick.

During Wick's trial, even the court agreed that ". . . there could be no willful participation on Dr. Candlewick's part because of his obvious mental impairment." And as long as the court found no direct link to Uncle Lincoln's estate, that Wick's name was everywhere listed as a charitable trust, and not that it was actually a small part of a larger holding under Uncle Lincoln's direction, and that Winnie, with power of attorney to manage the properties would and did present an operable plan that would quash the suit brought by the city's zoning commission even though "the properties in question presented a public nuisance," in violation of as many codes as the city manager could muster, the court would follow the recommendation of Wick's probation report and place him in the county halfway house for drug offenders until such time the probation office, with the advice and consent from his therapists, would release him to the court for his final disposition.

Winnie had simply let Wick burn himself out. His final decline began when the massage parlor was shut down. Winnie leased the offices to a group of chiropractors and homeopathologists that specialized in psychotherapeutic rolfing, an intensely painful but apparently effective therapy for recalling traumas embedded at birth in the interstices and junctures where muscle and bone first knit. My limited understanding of the technique has the massage therapist separating those attachments between tissues, muscle groups, and bones that were formed by traumatic events, to restore the natural elasticity bestowed at birth. Melba understood the therapy, having experimented with the treatment in New Mexico. She provided us with the literature suggesting that even the flexibility inherent in the skull maneuvering the birth canal may sometimes be restored in a practice that requires a thorough wrenching of the ears. Manipulating the various points with techniques that are sometimes quite painful—twisting techniques, a gouging practice with elbow, knuckle, knee, then blunted hardwood dowels as large as fence posts, as small as pencils—practitioners are required to exhibit a high tolerance for the suffering of their patient.

With Twig in jail, Wick's audiences dwindled to none, and his public confessions drove away the few remaining disciples. On the verge of complete collapse, he put himself in the hands of a therapist. I met her once, an attractive young woman from India, dark skin, and a lovely caste mark at the center of her forehead, but with bright red lipstick and a coincidentally unfortunate resemblance to Leslie Luis, our cousin's dental assistant, who would be responsible for the final coup de grâce. When Wick's therapy began, he admitted privately that he could only stand the pain by identifying it with the erotic passivity of his practitioner, she who stood beside him while he lay screaming, bathed in tears, as the agony of a particularly stressful event worked its tortured path through stretched ligament and wrenched muscle. His passion for her may well have been the cause of his final breakdown; after all, she gave witness to his birth, his toilet training, sexual climax, and, of course, quite nearly his death.

There was, of course, considerably less traffic in the former elementary school's parking lot. The stream of cars was gone. The cousins no longer lounged in the doorway to the massage parlor in bath towels. The occasional patient seen limping from therapy evoked a benign respect, even sympathy, from the neighbors who might hear an occasional bellow of pain to confirm the respectability of the establishment.

Even now, Wick still has trouble separating such events. "How can I not want to watch my own conception, her making me, giving birth to me, fucking me? Can you imagine fucking to create yourself while sucking at your mother's breast?" Dr. Delmore, his psychiatrist, believes that such confusion belongs to a larger syndrome closely related to the abuse of all the psychoactive drugs Wick ingested before his breakdown. By equating the ecstatic qualities these drugs induce with a genuine religious experience, literally seeing all things as one, he is seduced into his mania, unable to separate himself from the other. I tried to explain once that we were all after precisely that effect. But I didn't. It sounds so foolish in the retelling.

I once sat without speaking during one of Wick's group therapy sessions. "You see, it's important for us to be able to know that we're not the birds and the bees, not the rocks and stones, not one with the tree that we're hugging," the doctor patiently recited. "We need to keep— we need to restore our separate selves."

Meanwhile, before the assault that would lead to his incarceration, the rolfing actually made Wick seem more rationally persuasive. Although he could barely walk, he could sit comfortably on the floor in what resembled a full lotus, and from that position, a pillow in his lap for a desk, he could stay for hours, providing direction, advice, philosophizing on the oneness of the universe, and dealing finally with an audience of one, the single part-time building inspector looking into complaints from the neighbors. The two of them would sit together, Wick locked to his pillow, the young inspector dazzled by the innocent nudity the children and adults displayed, as Wick carefully explained how and why the commune existed, revisiting several medical traumas in his youth, actually dental traumas that his father allowed when they lived in Hong Kong. I suspect that they both were imbibing because the inspector often stayed for dinner—I stumbled across his sleeping form one morning on my way to the pool for laps.

Finally, the building inspector, persuaded by the head of the Board of Design and Review, a young woman with a recent degree in urban planning, who threatened his immediate discharge, recommended to the city council that no retroactive building permit be granted and that the wall be removed—there had been rumors that skate rats were eyeing the unusual topography for their own ramp. The cousins just shrugged. There weren't any skate rats in Cambodia. The wall was never dismantled, however, because soon afterwards Santa Lucca closed the building inspector's department for lack of funding.

Unfortunately, unknown to all of us, the cousins had continued the production and distribution of Vietnam War memorabilia they had begun in the camps. What we should have suspected from their reputation for cultivating opium poppies in the most unlikely climates actually disguised an entirely different clientele, the MIA market. The market in Thailand to tourists was nothing. But the market in the United States was vast, representing a myriad of interests, from veterans organizations to military surplus chain stores that supplied the various survivalist movements, as well as journalists who had served or wished they had served in Southeast Asia. Silk escape maps, the bone jewelry, and especially the ID bracelets—all of it came under suspicion.

The cousins' crafts industry had been manufacturing American military serviceman dog tags, the rolled edge, older tooth-notched models that rictus secures, complete with name, serial number, blood type, and religion. The names were copied from a public index and the tags sold in various guises—in authentic pairs, as they might have been issued; singly—representing all branches of the service, some with plastic inserts the ground troops employed to muffle their sound in the bush. In the complex world of army surplus and military memorabilia, the dog tags, claimed as misidentified graves registration surplus, found their way into the morbid market that included silk topographical maps of Vietnam, standard issue in the aviator's survival kit. The cousins were also distributing commemorative rings—or facsimiles—manufactured from the metal of downed American aircraft the North Vietnamese awarded their soldiers for valor. Their unique octagonal shapes stamped with the silhouette of the aircraft from which they were made were later fabricated in aluminum to emulate the lightness of the titanium skin of the B-52 or F-104.

The dog tags sold as icons for the MIA movement were quickly dismissed as bogus by the knowledgeable because they were anachronistically notched. Still, the tags were valuable to leftist resistors, who collected them to demonstrate the futility of the MIA search, to attach themselves to the victory of the National Liberation Front forces. America doesn't just love winners; we love everybody.

All these horrors were attached to the commune and considered as part of the review for building permits. At one city council hearing, a neighbor tried to introduce bone product carvings as the grisly remains of downed pilots. There were macabre rumors that our cousins had at their disposal the remains of human skeletal fragments. That they were not human bones was finally reported, but they were subsequently misidentified as dog bones, canine teeth, which of course set the Humane Society as well as antivivisectionists questioning our presence in the neighborhood.

A graduate student from Berkeley, a Chinese from Taiwan coincidentally named Wong, finally identified the teeth and bones as belonging to a Southeast Asian rodent, large rats the émigrés reported they had trapped in the refugee camps, a fact Peter had steadily maintained throughout the scandal that eventually moved beyond the *Santa Lucca Journal*'s "City Council" column and ran for nearly a week in both the *San Francisco Chronicle* and the *Oakland Tribune*. It didn't do Peter's reputation as a gourmand much good at the time, but he had already set himself adrift, in exile. Tastes change. Appetites require only variety, finally, the only constant.

In the midst of all of these public disclosures, Wick's therapeutic confessions resulted in his final collapse. His breakdown made the back page of the shopping weekly.

"I know this must be embarrassing for you." On the first day of her testimony, our dentist's Leslie is unaccountably wearing the identical oxford blouse with a short lavender tie around the collar, the same matching cummerbund and charcoal skirt the assistant district attorney has worn to court. "But I want you to tell us in your own words exactly what happened when you were attacked by the defendant."

"Objection, your honor. No attack has been established to contradict the defendant's contention that the incident in question was no more than a lover's tryst. In fact, Dr. Candlewick continues to maintain his innocence in this matter."

"Your honor," the prosecutor began.

"Sustained, sustained, Mr. Wong. Ms. Abrams." Cutting both attorneys short, the graying justice peers down from his high seat, rising slightly to close the distance between himself and poor Leslie. "Ms. Luis," he murmurs, "may I call you Leslie?"

"Sure, your honor."

"Leslie, then. Could you tell me, tell the court, something about yourself and how you happen to know the defendant? It says here you're a dental assistant. Dr. Candlewick is a patient of yours?"

Responding to a complaint by neighbors about loud music, the police had found Wick, unconscious, bloody, and beaten in Leslie's apartment bedroom. He was admitted to John Sloan Medical for treatment and the following day he told a police guard that he wasn't trying to hurt her, but that they were romantically involved and he had planned a night of kinky sex. He told the police that she misunderstood the recording which he took from Dr. Wong's office. He planned to tie her up and take photographs of her. He said that she had given him keys and a garage door opener, which he had lost during the struggle. The charge was attempted rape.

"No, your honor," Leslie smiles at the judge's innocent gaff. "Dr. Candlewick is Dr. Wong's patient. I'm his assistant. I'm working for my degree. I'm going to be a dental hygienist when I pass the boards, but I'm not done with school yet."

The prosecutor speaks. "Your honor."

"You may continue, Mary." The court room is peppered with gleeful snorts from the jury box. "Please excuse the court," he beams, nodding at the bailiffs at the door, who are staring at their shoes. "Ms. Luis, I beg your pardon. Please continue."

"Thank you, your honor. Ms. Luis," she begins, "Leslie."

The judge nods. Wick's lawyer slumps in his chair.

"Please tell us in your own words what transpired the evening of the first and early in the morning of the second of February."

"Like, it was what I always do. Well, not exactly. I was studying for my perio midterm, so I was up kind of late. But I was in bed before eleven. I usually watch the ten o'clock news, but I didn't because I needed to concentrate for the exam and I always do better if I get a good night's rest." She pauses and looks at the judge.

"Water?" he asks kindly.

"No, I'm fine." She bites her underlip for a brief second, then begins again. "So, suddenly, in the dark—it was about three in the morning—I wake up with somebody's hands around my neck, like, strangling me, and I'm hearing music all at the same time. I kind of recognize the music from Dr. Wong's office? Some oldie."

"Yes, go on." Ms. Abrams, the judge, Wick's lawyer, even Wick, all nod.

"Like a musical but from the movie? And I think I must be having a nightmare. I'm almost sure I'm at work, because I don't have any music like that and I only listen to soft rock, so I'm, like, sure I'm going to wake up any second. He pulls me by my neck and I'm on the floor. By the time I hit the floor, I can feel my own rug under me. I thought to myself, my God, this is, like, really happening in my own apartment?" Incredibly, little Leslie smiles at the memory of her realization.

"So I feel, like, his hand in my face? This guy's singing along to the music, like he knows the words. It was really weird."

Ms. Abrams interrupts. "Did he say anything to you during the struggle?"

"No. He was just singing, something about kisses and Shangri-la."

Wrong movie, it's the wrong movie again and never a musical.

"And then?"

"It's dark and I can't see anything, but I feel his fingers near my mouth."

Wick visibly stiffens at this point in her testimony. He winces as he rubs his fingers against his thumb, still heavily bandaged, the dressing stained with a bright yellow antiseptic. His face is heavily bruised, his lips swollen. There's tape holding more gauze along one ear, and the swelling under both eyes has relaxed to reveal the cuts healing alongside his broken nose.

"So I, like, bit him, real hard on the thumb."

"Your honor, would you please direct the defendant to raise his hand for the court."

"Objection, your honor, self-incrimination," Mr. Wong croaks.

"Never mind, Mary—rather, Ms. Abrams. Mr. Wong, sustained. It looks painful. Would the court reporter note Reverend—rather, Doctor—Candlewick's presence. Please continue, Leslie."

"Okay." She takes a breath. "So he let go when I bit him and I could, like, breathe again. He was yelling like crazy, like I really hurt him. He must have bumped into my nightstand, because my clock radio fell right next to me. I grab it. I can see him pretty good in the dark now. I mean I didn't know it was Dr. Candlewick right away, but I could see him coming at me? So I swung the radio and smashed it into his nose."

"You hit him with your radio?"

"Yep. Smashed him right in the face with it. A bunch of times, real hard, because I broke it. I mean, it still works, but I must have cracked it when I hit him."

"And you were able to escape to the apartment next door?"

"Not exactly. He was sitting on top of me still, but kind of dizzy? I hit him lots of times. But he wouldn't get off, or maybe he couldn't move because we were stuck between the bed and the wall. So I wrapped the radio cord around his neck and I choked him. He kind of slipped sideways off me when I jerked the cord. I guess I was, like, strangling him upside down, sort of?"

"Good, good, go on."

"I was, like, you know, behind his back then. And I had a good position, so I pulled the cord tight until he stopped moving. I mean, well, I could have killed him by accident, I was so scared. Like, I'm really glad I didn't hurt the old guy."

"Yes? Glad you didn't hurt the defendant?"

"I mean, he's sort of like a patient, you know. And when the police and the ambulance came, and I saw him, I saw what I'd done, I felt sorry."

"Sorry for your attacker?"

"Well, not that part. I felt sorry for Dr. Candlewick. I know him. And I know I hit him a couple of times right in the mouth. He's going to lose those front teeth from the gum damage. I mean, I know this kind of stuff, deep tissue trauma. That's real damage. He's gonna need a periodontist."

"You know, that is, you are acquainted with Dr. Candlewick?"

"Yes."

"And you've heard his lawyer, Mr. Wong, suggest that Reverend Candlewick—sorry, Doctor Candlewick—and you were having an affair. He will go on to suggest that you strangled him as part of some sexual practice that you and he indulge in?"

"Kinky sex. I know." Leslie blushes.

"And you deny that."

"Yes. None of that's true."

"Are you aware, were you ever aware, that Dr. Candlewick was anything more to you than a patient, in his mind if not in yours?

Leslie hesitates. "Well, yeah."

"Please elaborate."

"Well, he asked me out once. He said he was a licensed therapist as well as a minister and I was, like, talking about being nervous around exam time. Like, people do that? They ask me all the time and I haven't, like, even passed my boards yet."

"Do what?"

"You know, like, ask me advice about their teeth. They know I'm interested. How to brush, electric versus manual, fluoride treatment, whiteners."

"And?"

"I'm happy to tell them what I know."

"No, I meant what you said to him."

"I told him no. Like, this was months ago. And he's old enough to be my grandfather. I've seen his chart."

"Go on."

"So I told him I enjoyed talking to him. Just friendly, nothing more, just talk. I said that if he wanted more than that, he needed to find someone else."

"Anything else, any other contact in or out of your place of employment?"

"He asked for a photo of me. This is in the waiting room? He said he'd even take the picture if I let him."

"And did you give him any picture? Or did you allow him to take your photograph?"

"No. Never."

"Dr. Candlewick—I'm quoting from his police interrogation, exhibit one, your honor—says that you exchanged gifts. Have you ever given or received gifts from him?"

"No."

"He describes them as love potions."

"No way. I don't know what a love potion would be."

"Goldenseal, it says here."

"Oh, that stuff. It's Dr. Wong's idea. You know, toothbrush, floss, gum picks. Doctor gives goldenseal away. It's an herb to stop gum bleeding."

"But these were not personal gifts from you? Not love potions?"

"Nope."

"Thank you, Leslie."

"Oh, Leslie?" The judge has risen slightly, in deference to her obvious pluck.

"Yes, judge, I mean, your honor?"

"How did the exam go?"

"I got an A," she twinkled.

"A-plus, Ms. Leslie Luis, A-plus." He beams.

There is scattered applause around the court room.

"Order, order. Mr. Wong?"

There was the faint aroma of apple pie baking in the oven, coffee, fresh cream, and a wheel of cheddar by the stove in the cafeteria of the court house where Wick's lawyer and I met after the prosecution had rested its case.

"What are you going to do?" I asked him.

"Have some of that pie. Then I'm going to plead insanity. It's open and shut. He's a licensed clinical therapist who has flipped his wig. He's inside calling all the guards pigs, *sieg-heiling*, all that, so we need to remove him from the premises, if you know what I mean. Happens all the time. You know anything about his family, this commune thing he's got going? He wants me to find a translator for a character witness he says speaks Cambodian. Now what's that all about, right? He's so wired I can't get a word in edgewise. All I want is permission to do a blood test and testify as to his medical and mental condition. Obviously, he's not responsible. And you're his guardian?"

"Yes, he hasn't any family."

"Well, Mr. Wong, you're friend's nuts as far as I'm concerned. Fruit-cake, okay?"

"Yes, I know."

"I've talked to Mary, to Ms. Abrams, already in chambers. The district attorney's office, the judge—we all want him hospitalized, but so far, he's refusing to cooperate. I should tell you as his friend that we have an ace in the hole, that is Mary, ah, the district attorney."

"Yes?"

"Deniable QT, but Mary's got a friend in the DA's office, in San Francisco?"

"Yes."

"Well, everybody's aware of the circumstances surrounding Dr. Candlewick's resignation from his directorship at Shepherd's Haven. I should have remembered, but it came out when I indicated I would argue his public service record."

"What exactly are you referring to?" I already knew, of course.

"The charges of child molestation. The review board recommended his dismissal?"

"Yes, I know about that. What do you want me to do?"

"Talk to him. Nobody wants this to go any further."

"Yes."

"Great. Let's sign the papers and find a key, put him away for a while so he doesn't hurt himself," he says, eating his pie with a spoon. "By the way, you look kind of familiar. Do we know each other from some time, some place?"

"I don't think so."

"Would you believe I know Dr. Candlewick? Went to his church camp when I was eight years old."

"Really. Did he recognize you?"

"No, thank God. But you, weren't you something at Shepherd's Haven?"

"My brother, Peter Pan."

"Right, right, oh yeah." He paused. "But I remember you, too, Christopher Columbus, I remember you. Small world."

"Not anymore."

With all the public attention, the police department asked the state agricultural board along with the public health commission to inspect the property. Medicinal opium was discovered, poppies carefully cultivated in one sun-drenched corner of the wall, and that led to the order for seizure of the property and the threatened foreclosure.

With her usual foresight, which was considerable given the explosive real estate market at the time, Winnie had been able to leverage loans to the maximum value of the property before the bank could move. She put the money into a savings and loan investing in low-income housing, became an officer of the company, and sold her shares before HUD saw the tidal wave of bankruptcies in the industry. She, Peter, and Auntie formed a limited partnership, Keepsake Trust, investing in seized properties and land, and as one of their holdings now owned the Santa Lucca shopping mall outright. Of course, Winnie had her own brief troubles with immigration, but Uncle had married her, and the loopholes were closed.

With Wick out of our lives, Peter took a ten-year lease on a pied-à-terre in Amsterdam to expand his food business, and was discovered while catering shoots at Cinecittà in Rome. Melba dabbled with aromatherapy, and her marijuana garden, with Peter's advice, became a series of microgardens providing boutique vegetables to the restaurant industry, which she sold when she finally moved to Italy.

After we buried Lincoln, Winnie invited me several times for dinner in the city. She had returned to the penthouse on the Embarcadero with a wonderful post-earthquake view of the Bay. I finally saw no reason to resist. But I live alone. I do most of my work in Santa Lucca and take the bus into the city whenever I must. I'm seldom in Chinatown where there's never any parking unless you pay rent for the underground garages. And all of the attendants remind me of Twig and the cousins. Besides, I love walking alone along the trails on the mountain where I am the only one of me in sight.

8

Sudden summer storm, a little rain, fog sinking down the slopes of the coast hills. The mottled sky, gray, opaque, foreshortens the landscape. The hills, large trees, streets, houses on the hillside are brought up in sharp relief. The neighborhood seems smaller, toy-sized, bound all at once by the humidity, the fetor of skunks and dead opossum, of gardens, earth, wet wood, the stink of sour chimneys leeching old winter fires, the street dappled with old blossoms and young fruit.

On the telephone, Wick whines. He calls whenever he feels the compulsion. He's been in and out, living at the Praxis Connection, the county's halfway house for drug offenders, where they practice the art of living in the world. When he's up and running, he can stay with Mary. But I get the dark side. I am his big brother at therapy group, eavesdropping on others, his other, mine own. I listen, inhale his schizoid gas (although I've been warned not to inhale too deeply). I've had to learn to disconnect him, hang up when he turns on me. There's some perverse pleasure in that, some sanctioned, but unhealthy, revenge, for the benefit of Mr. Kite.

He's having a bad week. "Hasn't anyone noticed I'm better? Is Mary afraid of me? Where's Peter?"

"Peter's in Rome being an actor. Remember?" Ah, Giulietta.

At times, the only reassurance that I'm not a part of his lunacy is the second click after he hangs up, the guardians who monitor his outgoing calls. I always say good-bye a second time. Once in a while, Wick announces he is calling from the world outside (I hear the sounds of street traffic in the background), casually impatient now that he's connected to me, and a more sinister suggestion that the conversation can be more wide-ranging and serious in content when no one is eavesdropping. So he's waiting for me, waiting for a chance.

"Of course, I remember. That was a test. You know I'm bipolar, schiz-ophrenic," Wick concedes. "I only call you when I want to feel excite-

271

ment. I use you shamelessly." He's hungry for sensation, any sensation. He narrates his treatments to stall me, keep me on the phone.

"It's real brain damage they're looking for these days. I've had neurological testing." His patter is didactic. "They think the right hemisphere of the old squash was damaged. The ether in the DMT, they say. I'm undergoing bilateral therapy. They whisper in my ear, they make me write in red ink with one rose-colored lens so my left eye doesn't see what I'm writing. We scramble on the floor on all fours like babies." He says he thinks it's working because he can catch a Frisbee for the first time since his collapse and sit for hours on the floor without discomfort. "They may even sign me up for volleyball because I show evidence of binocular development. You know, I can see in 3-D again. I never liked to use that side of my brain before. But what I see has a great deal more interest for me now. I can see colors better. Are you listening?"

Weather's changing by the coast. The warm dry air from the inland plains meets the ocean's prevailing weather, swirling fog filling the treetops of the inland canyons, creating an ocean of white noise, a soundless void. Young trees lean against the older trees; they commence to bend, to sway and stretch, a cracking at the barre.

"I'm listening."

"It's just that when I have to solve problems, you know, control my excitement, things like that, it doesn't feel good. I don't want to do it. And when that happens, I call you for a quick feel."

"Cut it out," I warn him.

"I do apologize, Christopher. That slipped out. A kick in the ass."

"Good-bye."

"Wait. Did I tell you I have a mother and a father now? I know I mentioned my mother to you before, but I have to have a father. Everyone does. Imagine that."

At the track, it's a jogger's corps de ballet. I run the coastal forest trail instead. Against a changing sea, evenings, birds shriek, surf hisses in the sand as it reaches up the beach. Here, the warm gale inhales, then exhales endlessly, a spark ignites tinder, summer lightening. I hear fire, brush burning, manzanita exploding, a cracking eucalyptus. Walking, to a slow jog, then to a run. The air smells used. Pollen tickles my nose and eyes. I wait to break sweat, wait to feel my adrenaline desensitize the itch. Men and women of middle age run, cranky, down the path.

I won't play.

"Dr. Delmore's my mother's boyfriend, did I tell you? They're not really married, but they do live together. Everyone's so honest here. We know about everyone's private lives. So egalitarian. Mother says she can't be mother unless I accept Del as daddy. Then today I heard she's left him. Isn't that pathetic? And they think we're crazy."

"Call again, Wick. Good-bye."

"I do have to hang up now," he concedes. "But listen. Everybody knows. You always looked exactly like him. You have Lincoln's eyes. You even have Lincoln's lies. You could even have his wife. Again. You love her so. Hmmm? Auntie Winnie, all yours to build that next little love nest? Or would it be for three? Think, Chris, the possibilities are positively repetitive. But we've done that before, haven't we?"

"Good-bye, Wick. You've reached the asshole stage." He knows me. I can't hang up. He makes me feel again.

"Please. I forgot. I called to wish you happy anniversary. It's your second. Tell Melba. The honeymoon's not over."

"Sorry, sorry. I'm not responsible. I'm just impossible," he hums to himself.

I let him have the final word, listening for the house extension's click. Only then do I whisper, "Good night."

In the summer heat, grass fires ignite the hillsides and threaten those who built on the highest ridges, in the winding cul-de-sacs, on the edge of public sanctuaries, those whose dreams reached beyond the safety net the county's fire district can afford to provide. Boraide bombers flatten the ominous orange edge of flames on the horizon, but gray smoke rises relentlessly as steam, turning white as it drifts across the sky. Late in the afternoon, more planes as the smoke turns black, the burn igniting structures. The hot air shimmers above the marching flames and the smell of greasy smoke is everywhere. The sound of the planes drones listlessly against the hissing envelope of wind. The burning makes the wind sound like an asthma in the trees.

It's the third of July. More fires for the Fourth. On the radio: In the Straits of Hormuz, an American battleship SAMS an airbus on a twenty-five minute hop to Dubai, killing 290 guest workers and the crew. Electronic detection mistakenly identifies it as an enemy fighter with an Exocet preparing to launch at range, nine miles and closing at mach 2.

To relieve my own anxieties, Melba's looping indecisions as she waits for Twig, or our serial infidelities, my own deceits, our mutual fantasies, I have taken up jogging in the early morning along the dirt path that travels the circumference of the watershed. Or I go to the gym, squeezing sets to disco when aroma of sweat is still faint from the evening before, more mindful now of the body fading. I buy a bicycle.

I feel strangely exultant after Wick's calls, free, alone, independent, but alone. There is a rush of birdsong, a nonsensical blast of heraldic chirping as a stray cloud covers the face of the sun and drops the air temperature a few degrees; momentarily the thick summer foliage turns dark, pendulous, a somber moment as the cloud wipes away the apparent light before the world brightens, its passing shadow on the west hillside leaving dark footprints, something prehistoric passing over the land. It's the sound of them, the birds, ludicrous echoes of their avatars, the territorial chirping, scattered and holding their place like an orchestra tuning up. There is that fear at the symphony when the pre-performance cacophony seems endless, a madness uncontrollably lunatic until the violin finds one note and then the rest of the orchestral voices find that note. The baton taps the edge of the podium. All is order, symmetry. I pour coffee over a heaping tablespoon of raw sugar to carry to the computer and add a rice cracker to the clutter. The phone rings. It's Wick, to wish us happy anniversary.

After Melba moved to Oakland, to Cuzco, to Rome, my nights were filled with falling dreams, dreams of being trapped. I'm in an imaginary labyrinth beneath the Golden Gate Bridge. It is an enormous tubular cavern and I race about on scaffolding, testing doors shaped like the hatches on a submarine. Each door opens to reveal a long fall to the water. Suddenly, the gravitational oddity 45 degrees to reality, the right-angled illusion overwhelms me and I begin to fall. I wake up smiling, relieved at the logic of my dreaming. Suspended in midair, I will fall.

Ivy curling around the window of the basement where I make my bed these days reminds me of Melba's new hairdo, a little shorter now, red with a henna rinse, crimson ringlets, the final image from dreaming to wakefulness, a silent riot of twisting curls, my absent wife.

Wick has jinxed me. He promised me that my love would last. Wick, the divine, the therapist, the felon, assails me. I want him to tell me why

Melba left and how I'm supposed to feel, but his fantasies come like waves overwhelming all that I ever was, and I am lost in the confusion of our mutual obsessions. What happens when your confessor is a lunatic?

Peter also has his bad patches. "Christ, listen to me. I couldn't help myself. American jazz in Rome, foreign movie time. It was the music, that black singer with the voice like sex floating through the room, warm with sunlight."

I should let Peter and Wick confess to one another.

"I've been handsomely propositioned by a wanna-be, a German skinhead who loves his Cong girlfriend and wants to understand the culture."

In Honolulu? Amsterdam? Rome? Where does he find them?

"Very sexy, Chris. He tells me he's really gay, his daddy still impressed between his tight cheeks. It's always these overprotective fathers who bang the kids. Who would have guessed?"

"Peter, where are you calling from?" I want him to talk to me about who we were, who we are now. Even business, but he doesn't care, never wants to listen.

"Outside Rome. I've got this marvelous little trattoria that's closed for the summer. The kitchen and dining room are mine for a month. Santa something or another, little stone houses, all peach and crumbling plaster, fields of sunflowers, TV antennas."

I listen. I've heard it all before.

We lunch on the terrace overlooking the Bay, the ferry terminal, Melba's favorite spot to say good-bye.

"I was watching Ramdas make tea, and it was then I knew that I would give myself to him, that I would make love with him, freely, without hesitation, without guilt, without contraception. You don't understand the polyandrogeny in me; in fact, I hardly understand it myself, which makes the mystery all very lovely, makes me want to reach out and touch where I'm not supposed to touch, to stare back when stared at, to peer forward as if I were slightly nearsighted. I can hardly believe that he can be so bold, that I am not nearly so bold." She tilts her head to look past me at the ferry heading towards the dock.

"Conjuring intimacy with a stranger, yes, I like that."

She was seated on the terrace drinking a latte, the sun lighting her head and shoulders, the glare from the gymnasium's bay window falling across the plastic table, her reflection in the dark glass, the stink of motor traffic, roasting coffee, now and then the sweet aroma of new hay, smoke rising from the tiny meerschaums seasoned potheads favor welling up on great columns of warm midday air. She likes to be watched, and here, where she could watch people, people could watch her.

She reminds me, "I love that, being watched. First, not acknowledging that I know. To pretend that I am blind to a surreptitious glance, a gaze that evaluates sexual opportunities my physical features offer. That I'm not aware a man is staring at my breasts, my nipples hardening in the chill breeze, imagining me naked, wondering if I might be wanton; I love that, wantonness."

"And why this one? This Ramdas? Tall, dark?"

"You'll laugh. At least I hope you're slightly amused by all this. I am."

"His intellect."

"Yes. Well-spoken conceits and innuendo make me crazy, every time. You and I had that."

"Really?"

"Yes, yes, I think so. Wasn't it with you?" she teases.

She's radiant. I want her, love her still.

She wants some dark, attractive hunk—or in this case, a young stud who listens carefully to her words, who hangs on her every syllable, a man who watches the way she phrases a notion, an idea, who laughs with her. And big hands, a man who likes to touch, touch her, of course, physically comfortable. A man who watches her, who she knows has his eyes on her, who she can embarrass occasionally when she knows he's watching and nobody else is, and she does something that makes him see her.

"Sometimes when I know I have someone looking at me, say in a store, a café, and I feel his eyes on me, I'll touch myself, finger a nipple, make it hard, then turn as if I'm looking over my shoulders at something— not him—so he can see my nipple hard against my shirt.

"He'd been watching me for a while, touching myself, first one breast, then the other, until I had them both hard, you know, I spent all of ten minutes touching myself here and there, and this wonderful lusting kid, he was so excited. I couldn't help myself. I pretended to stir my latte with my middle finger then I sucked off the chocolate, staring at his crotch. Wanton and lewd. I surprised myself."

I promised Melba we'd meet to give Twig a ride home. His final three months were spent in a minimum-security facility outside Fresno, and he didn't want the Huynh family's social worker to make the drive. So he called Melba, who had recently returned from Peru to farm boutique vegetables under the freeway. I drove.

She was wearing muddy denims and work boots, a Columbus Travel and Tour aloha shirt, baseball cap worn bill-side back. She gave me the raised-bed mini-horticulture tour, six-by-twelve beds sitting on sawhorses, a tub of new planting soil she folds, working air into the bedding to make it light and fluffy. She spread five hundred seeds per three square feet, long rows with heavy lettuce at one end and the lighter lettuces at the near end where the filled tubs were stacked underneath the freeway where she parked her new van. The sunny space, shared with Caltrans, included a tool shed, as well as hookups for electricity and water the helpful on-site foreman made convenient. "He's a real charmer, but a baby. Calls me Ms. Wong. He lets me use the telephone and hide from the rain whenever he's around."

She wants to sit between his knees, barebutt on his shoes, rub her cheek against his sex, feeling all drippy and wet and feel his toes tickling her bottom.

The heavy whine of traffic above us is deafening. I point to the car. "You don't mind driving?"

The I-5 corridor is a flat, monotonous highway, a dry plain broken by occasional glimpses of the concrete aqueduct that carries a clear mountain stream from the Sierra Nevada mountains to the deserts of Southern California. In our way, we have learned to leap through space, over obstacles our natures invent, bridges our words barely describe.

"I got a postcard from Milo—remember Milo? He's living in Santiago, married, this time, with more kids. I asked him to send me a picture, but he hasn't. Didn't mention Asia. Bastard."

"I'm sorry."

"Got a long letter from Peter. He's still in Rome, so wonderful. He sent seeds for me to try. He said you might be going to China for him?"

"I'm thinking about it. Winnie thinks we should sell the travel business, put more into the food market."

"But you hate to fly. Poor Christopher Columbus, going east, going west."

We pick up Twig at the bus station in town. We shake hands, then there is a longer, thoughtful embrace between them. He is voluble, easy with us. He looks the same—younger in fact. He's been away at school, summer camp, a long holiday. Young, bright eyes, quick, disarming smile, asking after Peter, Auntie, Winnie.

The flat, dry Central Valley highway, a stretch of undeviating tedium he follows with excited comments after each of the gas station-motel-restaurant plazas that appear every thirty or forty miles. He even makes jokes about the Jack in the Box drive-throughs we invariably pass during our four-hour ride. He scans the horizon for the next sign of commercial habitation, chattering over the details to fill the void between us.

Does she want him still?

"I've haven't been waiting, Chris. But I'm loyal to my friends."

When Melba smiles, the lines around her eyes forming as she wrinkles her nose, my wide-eyed gamin seems older.

"I picked up a trade: dry cleaning," Twig chirps like a *cholo*. "The hustle was doing *bonnereaus,* prison French for starched shirt, pants, jacket, something neat and clean. Guys put their pants between their mat and the steel frame. But if you want it done right, you have to pay to be creased down and sharp, you pay to be *bonnereau* down.

"I made Catholic chapel janitor before the dry cleaners. Then I got the Protestants, then the Jews. So I worked it as an all-day job. I used to bust my ass once a week. Strip the floors, wash everything. The rest of the time, an hour or two, get up late, leisurely shower, get ready for lunch. Do an hour, dusting. Had it made. But it was interim. I wanted dry cleaners because it was a voc, a trade. Looks good to the parole board. I made money with it too, doing *bonnereaus.*"

In bed, later, Melba weeps. I remember her slightly arched, with a pillow under her back exaggerating her small breasts, her nipples pink and relaxed, anxious, anticipatory, welcoming, warm hands, small with slender fingers, wrists, fine pale skin and a vegetarian diet that makes her pubic hair, underarms, smell like oatmeal and fresh herbs.

Twig tells her, "I got your postcards, you in Peru, on the Inca Trail. Man, that's so cool. That place was on TV and I had pictures of it hanging on the wall. Machu Picchu. The *vatos* thought you were an Indian. I told them you were my sister and they all wanted to be friends."

"Please don't cry."
She looks down. "He learned a trade. He went to jail for me."

"So, like I said, the freeman quits. They put us on a trustee basis. Then, shit, I'd walk out of the shop with twenty orders a day. I had guys who wanted their T-shirts pressed. I even had guys who wanted their drawers pressed. I mean, goddamn."

"He never wrote, not a card or letter."
I didn't know.

"My hustle got so good I told the cousins to stop sending money for the canteen."

Too much time has passed.

"So, yeah, I do two-thirds of five years for good behavior, minus six in the county, makes two years, eleven months, and a day."

At Altamont Pass, the angled windmill farms silence him. We drop him off in Oakland, and he leaves us, steps from the car without saying another word.

We make love on a cot in the tool shed under the freeway. She seems relieved. "The space is virtually free until they want it back. The soil's portable. The harvest is seventy-five dollars a tub, delivered. And I've got a deal for squash blossoms."

"The ones you used to batter and pan-fry?"
"Yes, you remember those?"

"Of course."

"You want me to explain, don't you?"

Not any more. "You want me to invest?"

"It's the scale, well within my personal universe, all mine. I mix salads, different types of lettuce, from rocket to romaine, oak leaf, escarole, butter. The restaurants call and tell me what they want. This week they want spinach, radicchio, endive, or a tub of mixed. See?" She lifts a handful of salad to reveal the flowers in the mix. "Nasturtiums, marguerites, squash blossoms, pansies. I toss them into the tubs to make the salad pretty. I make sure everything's rinsed clean. No pesticides. Sometimes the chef gives me the leftover lunch. Peter says I should write a cookbook for gleaners."

"Don't forget Ewell Gibbons poisoned himself." We can still do this, Melba. We can.

She laughs. "I don't mean collect road kill. I'm going to keep it local; it's more a tour of the public parks."

We listen closely these days. Worry over the details, the little things. That's what we need now, to live, for ourselves, alone.

We marry. There is first the explosive flash, then the sound of a kitchen match scratching the side of its box. In the darkness that follows only the bright halo of flame from the match is clearly discernible against the muslin scrim, but shapeless silhouettes slowly begin to take the form the sounds passing through the cloth screen suggest. The chimney glass rattles impatiently against metal as the match flame touches the mantle of a kerosene lamp. Soft light diffuses across the entire scrim. The table upon which the lamp rests is a shadowy etching, but a hunched figure, a man sitting in a ladder-back chair with his back to the audience is clear, the left shoulder fixed, the right shoulder rolling back and forth, driving an invisible arm, making a rubbing sound not immediately recognizable. The figure reaches across the table for a bowl from which liquid pours. Ink, the friction of an ink stick rubbing against a stone, the tell-tale aroma that fills the calligrapher's nose as he begins his practice, working the stick into an inky slip, passing a dark tincture across the mulling smells of the dampening garden, old incense, charcoal fire, sandalwood, musk, and patchouli oils, wafts over our redolent family, the smell of ink. The man stands, casting a grotesque shadow across the screen. He moves about a room that quickly takes shape as he fires candles and smaller oil lamps strategically illuminating various figures, mostly animals in human postures, a boat with rigged sails, a ragged landscape in miniature depicting trees, mountains and a satellite of sorts suspended from a stick. The calligrapher flourishes a writing brush as he takes his seat again, this time perching on the chair's edge, one leg folded under, the other heel parked on the chair, an elbow locked against his knee to steady his hand, the boot's toe tapping a hesitant tattoo.

Once upon a time there was an old fisherman and his wife who lived at the river's end where it flowed into the sea. They had a rich life. As the tides turned twice a day, the fisherman's nets were always filled with something delicious that had swum downstream to the ocean or something from the bottom of the sea, the ambitious or the simply curious that had tried to work its way past the fisherman's traps. Behind them lay fields and forests, and as the seasons turned, his wife's vegetable gardens, their small orchard, duck pond, and two-pig sty provisioned them.

At the end of their day, when the weather permitted, they sat on benches overlooking the sea and cooked the fisherman's catch-of-the-day in a rich vegetable stock from his wife's garden, turning a bit of roasted meat on a spit, sipping warm wine, nibbling smoked eel, watching the sun slip below the horizon as the white line of breakers formed on distant reefs where the sky met the sea and rolled toward the land, ending in a soft curl and a hiss, the surf's feathery edge lifting like a dried brush from the warm sand.

The calligrapher elaborately dips his brush, drawing ink. Two small figures, a man and a woman bent with age, pass across the muslin screen, one drawing a net, the other squatting to dig with a trowel.

The fisherman and his wife ate taro and duck wrapped in lotus leaves, an earthy mélange of dark mushrooms, bracken, and tree fungi, pigeons stuffed with candied fruit peel and sweet rice, steamed puddings made from quail eggs and honey, then tasted seasonal fruits, pear-apples, grapes and oranges, summer melons, lichees, durians, mangoes, various seeds, and coconuts until they fell back over their perches, swollen senseless each evening, stunned by such largesse. And as they lay there, their faces reddened by the heat of the fire, breathing with some difficulty, they would complain how empty their lives were without children to keep them company.

Oh, no. Such a pity.

How empty.

Sshhhhh!

"Think how a son might relieve the tedium of our days," the fisherman would begin.

"Someone to look after us as we grow older," his wife would say.

To partake of their prosperity, to help them mend nets, fences, the roof's thatching, to marvel at the bounty they gathered in all seasons, to mind their wishes, to reward them with respect and loyalty—the advantages of a son were endless, and they would list as many as they could remember having imagined the night before or invent new ones until they finally fell into a deep and abiding slumber, a dreamless void that left them utterly refreshed and enthusiastic the following morning.

One day the fisherman discovered an enormous two-headed fish struggling mightily in his traps. He leaped into the water with his club, quickly dispatching it before it did further damage to his nets. As he wrestled it to the river bank, squeezing it in his arms, he saw the fish was gravid, a long string of translucent eggs trailing in the shallow water. Safely ashore, he sliced the belly of the fish carefully from tail to gills to scoop the roe, when, to his surprise, a human figure slipped to the sand, folded, wrinkled, but undamaged.

It was a young man, naked and whole, whose features and frame, gently rinsed in the river, seemed well proportioned and fit. Lying on the warm sand in a delirium, he struggled to catch his breath as he unfolded from the awkward coil he had formed inside the fish, his teeth chattering, his skin the mottled blue of the fish's belly.

The fisherman lit a fire and made tea, allowing the youth small sips as he struggled to wake himself. As he later explained his regaining consciousness to the fisherman and his wife, "I could not distinguish between dreaming and wakefulness." His first coherent words were of thanks and gratitude to his rescuer, but he could not explain himself further. He had no idea how he came to be inside a fish, no idea from where he'd come, who his parents might be, his age, his past. Twice he reached for what he imagined to be his purse, declaring his intention to reward the fisherman, but discovered nothing. "I owe you my life," he said. Finally, he politely averred his willingness to do whatever the fisherman wished in exchange for having released him from the belly of the fish.

The fisherman was overwhelmed by the look and comportment of this young man, quite handsome, well spoken, so gracious in his manner, the son he had always wished for. As they sat by the fire, the fisherman described the rich life he and his wife led at the mouth of the river, concluding, "Thus, we have everything we require and more than the two of us can ever hope to use. If you would remain with us, share our life, become a part of our family. . . . " The fisherman stumbled with his words, daubing at the tears welling from the loneliness he felt.

The young man reaches out and touches the arm of the fisherman. They embrace.

Music. A flourish created by the sound of a stick running across bamboo fencing, punctuated by the clap of two slabs of wood brought sharply together.

We leave the fisherman and his newly begotten son walking slowly homewards and observe his wife, who has discovered a thick cardboard box lashed with duct tape beneath a tree where she was wont to gather mushrooms. She hears a low, self-absorbing chuckle emanating from within. The box trembles slightly as she first observes it, and a rich smell of warm yeast and toasted rice invites her careful examination. Nestled in a bed of ailanthus leaves and polystyrene pellets she finds a baby girl, wrapped in layers of swaddling. As the forest light touches her face, her tiny mouth, the shape of a rosebud, smiles delicately and her eyes snap open to reveal bright black seed pearls. As she presses the infant gently to her breast, the infant's sweet warm breath awakens such tender feelings in the fisherman's wife that milk immediately dampens her blouse as drops form at her nipples.

Murmurs of polite envy wash over the audience.

The calligrapher daubs water on the scrim as the fisherman's wife brushes past with the suckling infant in her arms. The fisherman and his son face the sea as the calligrapher pours the liquid from his cup over the bushes. And now a pretty show of lanterns painted with suns and moons, passing clouds, running horses, plants growing from tender shoots to flower, then fruit, families at work and at play. Lacquer petals hung from the lantern frames spin slowly in the heat of the candle fire.

The seasons passed quickly. The infant girl, pampered and chubby, flourished. She ran before she could walk, strong, willful, a quick tongue, in every way an adorable child whose doting parents watched in awe as she grew more beautiful each day, each month, each season.

And as the shadow of one child after another crosses the scrim, each one taller than the other, I see a darker silhouette, the child's mask tangled in the curtain.

But their isolation suggests the unspeakable.

Here the illusions collapse. Here on the mountain that once divided the clear from the impure, here on what we once imagined could be the Mountain of Flowers and Fruit, I rest. I have no desire to seek the secret of immortality from the Buddha, the immortals or the sages who stand all about me seeking some escape from the Wheel of Reincarnation.

Twig had slipped LSD into the punch. The fragile chain of protein lysergic acid thrived and recombined with fructose and mango pulp, banana, blackberries, and a slurry of shaved ice and vodka in a silver loving cup the adults shared discreetly, secure from the children and pets. The moiré of fading sunlight through the bamboo screens began to twinkle and shine with darts of neon hues. I moved slowly down the driveway past the shiny four-door Lincoln Leviathan mating with a Daihatsu Charade, thunder lizard humping an ancient armadillo, windshield glass staring at me, waves of nausea, the smart smell of spilt gasoline. Gravel sticking to my kneecaps, I embraced the trunk of the buckeye oak, nuzzled my face against the bark, imagining my chin sprouting pubic hair. Words began to disintegrate, soap bubbles: I, ego, life, death, nothing. The elastic band of consciousness stretched to its darkest limits began to contract, and the familiar nausea, then words, then fear, then shame came rushing back, flew past me, an irresistible tidal wind that stood me on end, my arms wrapped around a tree, weeping for the would-be dead, old cars, and the drug I reminded myself I'd ingested an hour ago by my watch and the ballpoint tattoo that marked the time I noted in the palm of my hand.

Where am I?

Isn't it Mary I see in a wheelchair with an IV hanging from an armature attached to a post, muttering pleasantly at the doctors who walk like priests through the hospital corridors, past the ranks of nurses who are allowed to genuflect, the orderlies and attendants who huddle in corners? Here is the prison of life and death, here the mumbled apothecary that are prayers, the regimen of blood and bowel movements measured.

No, it's Peter shuffling down a hospital corridor in his unfastened hospital gown in Amsterdam.

But no, it's me. I've had an allergic reaction to blood transfused, too many histamines, allergic to vintage blood, I feel as if a cat is sitting on my face. Childhood asthmas blossom hives in the folds of my ears, between my fingers, circle my wrists like bracelets of rosebuds, make my eyes burn with grit and ashes, ashes.

Have I died yet? This is just the beginning. Once the shunt to the world is established, a little Novocain under the skin, a quick stick, tape, then a saline drip to keep the vein from congealing the blood around the intrusion.

"Save the vein," the nurse barks across my chest.

Four hundred cc of Benadryl, of all things, the drug of my asthmatic youth, taken intravenously, has the kick of amphetamines. As the blood drips into my veins, I can feel the cat entering the room, rubbing up against the nylon calves of med techs, then climb the wall and cross the ceiling, dropping softly on my face, hot waves of oat fields, hay prickling my nose, my chest constricting, hives growing from the tips of my ears, my cheeks, blooming across my face, my lips swelling, the allergies of a lifetime in transfused blood. Then Benadryl in a drip, in solution through the IV—pharmaceutical nirvana—all the antihistamines I have ever ingested come rushing forth to manifest the avatar of antihistamines, bliss. Am I dead? This is only the beginning.

Flocks of bicyclists glide past the garden wall, neon flamingos in Day-Glo tights and spinning chrome, knees angled like cranking pistons, heads turned, chatting casually as they converge at the corner, drawn by the music.

The garden paradise blooms hives.

"Mr. Wong? Christopher Columbus? Do you know where you are?"

I'm blinded by lights swirling in a room with green walls and a red door. "Call me Chris. God, I hope you're not my dentist."

"County General Hospital, it's Monday morning, Chris." A nurse in green scrubs loosely knotted at her neck takes my pulse. "I'm going to remove your IV. The tape will sting when I pull, okay?"

"Yes, I'm awake."

She smiles, "Am I the last one to congratulate you? I understand you just got married. Quite a party."

"What happened to me?"

"We're not sure. Something in the punch?" she giggles.

"Must have been."

"I can't imagine where you might go on your honeymoon. Some trip, huh? Bummer."

Melba's shadow, a bit unsteady in platform shoes, looms across the scrim, caught by the flickering candle fire. So tall—as she turns, her wavering stick figure stretches beyond the top of the illumined curtain. Arm in arm, two children kneel, bowing low, touching their foreheads to the ground before the seated figures of father and mother. The candles are extinguished one after another. The family is complete. But there is no place for them to go. They are here forever, the illusion frozen at the moment when the last open flame steadies as the soft breeze in the garden dies and becomes a tableau, a paper-cut embroidered on white muslin.

While waiting for the ferry on Hong Kong Island, I catch the aroma of the leis Melba and I wore on our wedding day, jasmine blossoms Peter had brought from Honolulu, heady perfume to defend against the rank odor rising from the harbor that precedes a monsoon.

It was a silly season. We were married after the Tree of Heaven's entire entourage returned from Las Vegas. Twig dumped his last opportunity to play the "Hawaiian Wedding Song" for themed nuptials forever. They were booked for a week-long wedding celebration Winnie had arranged for a friend of Uncle's, Mr. Wong, a Chinese millionaire based in Jakarta who managed lumber exports for the Indonesian government. The youngest son was now secured by a small franchise of high-end shops retailing gourmet cookies in malls throughout Southern California. Mine was the last wedding Twig would ever play.

It was a time. Melba took Winnie and Mary shopping at secondhand stores for wedding costumes, although Winnie would have preferred a run through Paraphernalia, Yves Saint Laurent, or the new Vanity Fair factory outlets. Instead, they combed through the racks of vintage clothing and cast-offs. Melba, in her element, warned them to look for coffee stains, cigarette burns, insects, and unwashable underarm stains. Winnie was able to slip into satin bell-bottoms and a blouse with a beaded neckline sized to fit a child. Melba chose for herself an ecru satin slip, really an undergarment. In her hair she wore cornrows of puka shells and one of the flower tiaras Auntie had woven for all of them, with tiny wood-flower pods, the kind that Wick brewed to make a mild hallucinatory tea. Of course, Auntie wore a tux.

Among our wedding souvenirs I keep a shadow box that displays Mr. Wong's wedding invitation (no relation), a red garter and bow tie, plane tickets, a hotel key to room 999, and a gambling chip with an embalmed bridal bouquet whose flowers all have faded to that same necrotic hue captured in Winnie's video of the qi gong master's scrotum. Despite Melba's best efforts, Winnie had managed to find and transport several cartons of "Keepsake" freeze-dried floral bouquets for our ceremony. Although we all laughed about it, Winnie had the idea to merchandise the product, reassured that I was always wrong.

"You see," she kissed me in all our company, "you can freeze salad." It was Winnie who took title to the word "Keepsake" for their investment company.

A card arrives from Winnie announcing a visit to the cemetery in spring. Uncle Lincoln, the husband of a cousin to an auntie's sister, a Daisy I can never recall. I try, but I can never let the question go. Auntie Mary? And Winnie, my father's wife? Didn't Mary counsel adoption? Families are a confusing, seductive preoccupation.

So it is in the end as it was in the beginning, as it will be for all time. Peter and I are Lincoln's and Auntie's bastards, somehow, the amputated members of no distant clan, sterile, utterly mutable, stamped by our common experience, our brief history, writ in a single generation. Observe that fine yellow line that erosion marks beside that steep slide to the Pacific Ocean. See that ochre ring, that indelible whorl across the face of a redwood burl, read them for us, our signal calligraphy etched in the matter that we eat, that is consumed and digested, the albumen capturing the salty detritus in the oily broth coating the sides of Lincoln's stockpot, the kitchen spill.

Until she died, Auntie still bothered to put everything that's left over into little white boxes she stored in her refrigerator. She bagged them for me and, I suppose, for Wick too. Like Lincoln, Auntie, Peter, and Winnie always wanted everything eaten so nothing would be thrown away. The years have passed. We have done our work, lived our lives. Lincoln gone,

Mary gone. Peter and I, Winnie, Wick, Melba and the company she keeps are what remain as family. Now I remember.

Enveloped in a warm summer evening in Rome, we're perched together at an outdoor table propped between a wall and the a curbside parade of parked cars and motorscooters. Berto's been delayed. Lazio, Melba's latest lover, avoids our little anniversary. But Hanif, our accountant solicitor, has joined us. Lit by candles in shallow dishes on the cobbled pavement, flickering against a dull mix of ancient disco and the bossa nova, our waiter, Paolo, hums not unpleasantly as Peter and Wick study and complain over the familiar bill of fare. Melba has Paolo's devoted attention as she questions the preparation of each dish, the choice of pasta, the fish, *"A vapore?"* She lets the final syllable linger as he describes the complexities of the meal's preparation, his fingers dancing across his chest, his torso curved in a seductive embrace. She catches his hands and shakes her head laughing. "I'm going to let Paolo choose for me," she announces. "Surprise me, *caro.*"

Wick reads from the newspapers and magazines he's collected on the train, inventing translations as he scans the headlines. "Now here's a surprise, Peter. Look at this headline: *'Dove ti porta il cinese?'* We're notorious in Rome."

"Paulo's the owner's nephew," Melba informs us. "He's only here occasionally, when he's not studying engineering or computers or something. But isn't he just? So sweet." She splashes mineral water in her wine. "I told him to bring you the veal, Chris. It's harmless. This *vino,* Peter, must be last month's vintage. But waste not." Our glasses meet. She whispers a stagy private toast for all to hear. "Free at last?"

"The Chinaman, *il cinese,* is a much beloved labor leader of the left wing. They call him that because he has small eyes," Hanif explains, dismissing any responsibility for the opinion with a shrug and offering his empty hands. "It's a term of affection, at least in this instance. The Italians think so." Hanif is nephew and namesake of an uncle who was a business agent for Lincoln.

"A Roma, non ci sono sorprése," Peter offers the table, studying the menu. "A Chinese godfather."

All of us had spent the entire afternoon with Hanif who, with his secretary as witness, had us signing contracts certifying our legal positions in Winnie's carefully crafted trust, allowing, among a blizzard of other entanglements, our marital divorce, but maintaining our financial responsibilities in the family corporation, Keepsake, Inc., by finalizing Melba's adoption, which Mary arranged before she died. The timing of the adoption and divorce was a technicality our change of venue somehow resolved, Hanif reassured us. No surprises, then—legal custody to ensure a fair division of our family responsibilities—and that we would always be together, always a family. That was the dream Auntie Mary held closest to her heart, and Winnie's Keepsake, Inc., had become its corporate realization. Mary had even married Wick for good measure, even though they had lived apart for the rest of her life. He needed her medical insurance. He had a role to play. He would guard the door.

"But it's all in the family now," Hanif assures us, "and this is my first of many glasses of wine I will drink to all of you and your family—especially, *la signora* Winnie, who I only know by her voice on the telephone, and the respect I have for her knowledge. She does not have the bound feet." He looks around anxiously.

"To big feet," we toast.

"I think now that freedom is overrated. Let my fetters and chains be. You know I only rattle them when I want to be fed." Peter slips his slight frame between the chairs, shaking the table, but gracefully, aging but still agile, dexterously pinning the wine glasses that threaten to spill with his fingers. *"Perfetto."* He caresses the nape of Melba's neck, strokes her hair curling around his fingers. "Lovely to see you, my dear, under any and all circumstances."

Peter had napped most of the afternoon in Hanif's office as Wick watched over him. "It's his heart. Arteriosclerosis and high cholesterol. He's had the problem for years. I'm twenty years older and have six times the energy."

"But he's very careful. Red wine, fresh vegetables, very little meat," Hanif recites, *"il cinese,* Peter Pan."

"Unfortunately, he inherited the problem from both sides. He's lived longer than he might have. Haven't we all?" Wick adds, cranky, stiff from too much watching. He needs to retire, to resign, but Mary picked him all those years ago, chose him over Lincoln when we needed a crossing guard, someone to emulate, to shape our speech, to disguise our assimilation, our family. Like Wick or Hanif and his uncle, once Iranian and twice Persian in America, his generation understood the needs of the diaspora. That's why Mary chose him.

Melba laughs as Peter eyes the passing Paolo. "Me, me, Peter. Tell me about Twig. He's doing well?"

"Twig won't be traveling much. He's been in the hospital." Our eyes shift quickly to attention; a look of sympathy, of concern, crosses Hanif's furry brows. We have crossed an enormous divide into new territory, and we are all wary. "A bad flu season, a very bad winter."

"But excellent for business." Hanif knows. Twig manufactures hemp fabrics for the counterculture, for the green movement, taking advantage of extremely low labor and material costs in Asia as well as excellent connections with old friends. "Bad luck. And you. Chris?" He lets the question slip to wring every ounce of reassurance from our company, perhaps mindful of the actuarial tables governing our delicate balance. "You're in good health. You eat Italian for your heart, like your brother?"

"Absolutely, Hanif. I love Italian food, all of it, especially pasta. Unfortunately, I eat everything," I snap a breadstick to share, "but, fortunately, I didn't inherit Peter's cholesterol levels. I was adopted."

"No!"

"*Sì.*"

"But so was I," he says with recognition and warmth, with solicitous gratitude. "*Vero*, my mother was from Spain with no family left when she died in childbirth, and my father left me with cousins when he went home. Then he was killed in an earthquake. His cousins kept me, fed me, sent me to school. I grew up outside Rome, but they kept my father's name for me. It was not unusual, not in Italy, not at the time. We are a big family, still all together. We even have family in San Francisco who did business with Peter's father, I believe. We all come from places and times that share the need to keep the family connection. Even orphans like us, Christopher. We're the chosen. We need a special eye."

Wick nods. "You can never trust the state. Never. Loyalty requires blood, given or taken, fictively speaking, that blind metaphor. The family is always first."

Hanif loves debate and like a good lawyer raises an objection. "But I am the state, I represent the state."

"Laws merely codify practice. There are so many circumstances where social code is unwritten, unobserved, unequally applied, Hanif, you know; I know you know." Wick rose from his place at the table with some effort. "Please."

Paolo arrives with platters of glistening pasta covered with clams, mussels, periwinkles, flakes of dry chili and black pepper.

Wick refuses to be discouraged. "I was never charged with criminal liability for my acts. The statutes of limitation recognize the timely order of forgiveness and repentance. But my church, my corporate body, was financially liable to the day of my death. Only in America."

"Wick's been spending too much time in the Farnese *palazzi*. All those cherubs peeping at the bulging Hercules in labor as they sing for the Madonna and St. Stephen's piercings."

"Peter, please." Wick is lost, forlorn, unable to recognize that he is safe now, with us, with his family. "I'm trying to make a point here. Perhaps Hanif should understand what happened in the past is past." We are what remains, what's left over, a family.

"And just look at what they say about us in this magazine: '*Ma poi, dove condurra i suoi occasionali compagni da strada il cinese? Sarà il cinese esercitazióne in caso d'incendio.*'"

Melba seems bored. "Eat, Wick."

"There's a larger situation than you see here in the magazine," Hanif explains patiently. "The immigrants—the Chinese in any case—move too fast. They rented apartments to use for storage. This was discovered when some old buildings collapsed from old age, and the city council began their investigation. Rome doesn't want a Chinatown, you know. I represented your family at a meeting where the Chinese business association signed an agreement not to cluster too many Chinese businesses in one neighborhood. It's better—or at least it's what they want. You all know there are so many *cinese*—from Croatia, old East Germany, the old Soviet bloc, Albania. They go to New York, to San Francisco. Winnie said you have a cousin Mai who wishes to immigrate?" He shrugs. I'm the only one to return his smile. His hands are empty.

I read old letters I once wrote to those who watched over me, letters that remind me of who I was, what I am, what I might be.

16 JUNE, *Shenzhen*

Dear Peter,

You never told me the ancestral homecoming would be down forty miles of bad road following a wagonload of chickens hitched to what's called an iron buffalo, a two-stroke steamroller smoking diesel. Walking through the neighborhood, I got caught up in a line that led through a long, dark communal kitchen, then into a courtyard as large as a stadium, where there was a food bazaar that featured a new product for international trade: boiled elephant skin. Our competitors are trying to sell Lipton's chicken noodle soup to the Chinese market. No TV here. Who stars in the revolution?

16 JUNE, *Hong Kong*

Dear Winnie,

The sea is brown and littered for about a mile out, but now a restless green, a blue, a red—here is the color metaphor for jade, for glaze, for all the enamel work and embroidery. China's art emulates waters, streams, rivers, all to the sea, all shades of the sea, and finally I understand something about the relationship between art and nature. I felt the need for some sort of religious experience, to help organize the chaos, the constant tension between the vertical and the horizontal, the yin, the yang. Where's the beef? The tourists are gone. Too much smoke rising from the middle kingdom. I ate in a restaurant alone, a Muslim all-beef menu. A large restaurant, with waitresses, hostesses, and busboys hovering while I sat alone with my potstickers, seafood soup, peanuts, onion cakes, a mélange of kimchi, and a beer and tea, alone without even a book to read. They watched me delicately devour everything, slowly, I alone, in the middle of an institution, a restaurant, the center of Chinese social life, a table for twelve, all by myself. I was like some aesthete, some hermit, a mad monk, the glutton.

22 JUNE, *Canton City*

Dear Peter,

I'm eating everything, I figure if I get sick, United would have me in an American hospital in ten hours, less if I put myself in the hands of my homies in Honolulu. I graze on the street: onion cakes and congee, jellied trotters, the paws from some endangered species, grass soup, three-bites-in-a-box I found at the end of a queue I didn't even know I was in, turtle flesh, living crustaceans, snails, shrimp, all manner of bugs, rice rats marinated and roasted on a stick, and the sautéed thighs of frogs at a small lunch stand overlooking a flooded field where I watched them being gathered, heard their cries, their mournful calls echoing from the kitchen to their kin in the rice paddies. Watched Australian TV video. Keeping my head down.

23 JUNE, *Hong Kong again!*
Beef and beer for a change. Spotted dick. Lovely. The English love to play with their food with words, teasing, loving, they handle it like a toddler handles fecal matter. Whereas the Chinese see their food in mythic proportions. The phoenix dawn, dragon's eyes, the edible fauna and flora mythic. The lion head, a Chinese meatloaf steamed in a cabbage wrap, becomes stuffed cabbage to the Hungarians, rice and pasta, east meets west. Chicken, the ubiquitous pig, and shrimp, macerated and mixed with black mushrooms and all the water-logged greens that are fresh in the market. Cilantro, pepper, sesame, soy—all the world's a farce for the table, multiple meats, the gleaning from the tree, from the earth, from the sea.

25 JUNE, *Bak Fa Village.*
I can see for a hundred klicks from the gun tower in the village. Old men with good eyesight but too crippled to work effectively in the paddies become crop watchers, issuing early warnings when they see the dust of bandits rising on the horizon. That's why you want a thick door. Remember Mary's niece? Wouldn't the doors, the slop buckets, the stools make great artifacts as the PRC turns to plastic knock-offs?

"Not-for-pets" Street, where all manner of reptile, mammal, bird, and fish wait to be slaughtered fresh for the table in front of these restaurants that lined this alley. Saw a puppy flayed and twitching as it was gutted in a pan of warm water. Saw a cage full of silent puppies further down the street. All manner of snakes, several Komodo dragon lizards, turtles, frogs, pigeons, chickens, and opossums. I also saw a pangolin shivering at the bottom of a stack of cages holding all of the above. Hunan people are very close to the Cantonese in their love of a culinary challenge. Turned to meet the weight of a stare trained on my neck and found myself staring into the eyes of an owl. I made Cantonese sounds in tones, gestured to people who were staring at us as I took pictures. People laughed and pointed and named the arrivals I feigned my pleasure and appetite at. I was horrified, yes, but the dog, once butchered, looked like spring veal, anemic, tender.

I had a walk out into the fish ponds and fields that feed the markets of Changsha. The rain has stopped, though the clouds remain threatening. The fish ponds are large, square-acre lakes no more than three feet deep enclosed by concrete curbs that channel the effluent waters draining from every cornice, tiled catchment, gutter, and toilet in the city. The rains' effects are everywhere. The Xiang River is very high. On the road to the airport, anxious crowds gathered at the banks to watch the waters flow. I did not hear any talk of flooding, so I think that the people simply gathered to watch what the river parades past the city, an interesting assortment of garbage like the flotsam of fresh Changsha melon I photographed in the fish ponds, maybe an interesting alignment of boats, or the corpse of an animal, or worse. People who are not organized into specific work units seem to have a lot of time on their hands, time to watch traffic jams, time to watch the river pass.

There was an excellent chicken that tasted like chicken, fresh tomatoes, bitter melon, french fries, and liver—potatoes are big in Changsha—water fungus, fresh fried tofu, steaming rice, and melons, ubiquitous and complete with Sprite and a few knocks of white lightening.

Lovely afternoon punctuated by a kamikaze ride through the afternoon traffic jam on the way to the airport. The driver stopped at the main gate to pick up his girlfriend, who stuffed into the back seat with the explanation that she would only ride a little way. His next stop was at a tire shop to load a wheel he was having fixed.

2 JULY, *Macao*
Crossing the Pearl River Delta by hydrofoil from Hong Kong to Shekou, cocooned in the hovercraft, sealed behind the crackled glass, I see in the infinite fissures a kind of Chinese calligraphy, a subtext only I can read. The sun refracts through the crystalline fissures, hot sun pouring past rain clouds dispersing in the wash of the jet foil. The window is as detailed in its fractures as a translucent glaze, here done in polymers, plastic etched by the salt spray of the South China Sea, and its message: the history of Kwantung. I fly at midnight to restore the Han.

4 JULY, *Beijing*
Watch as I slowly turn my back on all of this, Peter. I went to a trade show in Beijing and followed a silk trader, a Russian woman dragging a plastic cargo bag through the silk market. Sweat on her breasts, and brow, she's short and tough. I could see the dirt ground in her eyebrows when she caught me staring. Then I got swindled in an exchange of RMB.

Beijing again. Getting over the highs and lows of the capital city and its sybaritic comforts. Western toilet, instant hot water, fast food. Downside, ripped off again very smoothly in a hundred-dollar try at exchange. I never learn. I bought lovely flour dough figurines, a scholar and a fisherman, turned to mold in the morning, ephemeral as the week.

Inauspicious day of petty bickering that began with a fight

over getting congee for breakfast and winding up at the Beijing hotel and burning myself on a cup of hot orange juice. China needs us. Had a brainstorm. I call this series "Water Creating Wood with Elephant Skin." It's just pasta. But the spicing features medicinal herbs, the metaphorical as well as the actual I can package freeze-dried. Elephant skin is actually the skim of tofu, but the fungus is a snap.

To avoid the furnace of a Beijing summer, I walk the city well before dawn. I leave the *hutong's* compound and follow the geometry of the boulevards, watch the horse-drawn drays clopping through the streets, pulling a parade of comestibles down Wanfujing. The teamsters ride contraptions invented to take advantage of the detritus spilling past the edges of the industrial millennium, the truckwork and suspensions stripped from automobiles, with flayed tires rolling beneath a carriage assembled with iron scaffolding and scrap lumber. Arks of teetering cages rumble past. The major traffic intersections stockpile and distribute summer melons, vast, fragrant pyramids iridescent in the light cast by the carbon arc lamps frying clouds of insects. Before dawn, the smoke from charcoal-fired braziers baking bread, the smell of onion cake and egg omelet perfume the marketplace, mingling with the odor of offal, of fresh blood spill, of river ice.

When the sky begins to lighten, I backtrack, keeping to the alleys as the rumble of the first buses, the taxi brigades, begin their static loops, diesel exhaust burning my sinuses. The smog disguises the sunrise. The ochre light seems to emanate from the city itself, as if the night was simply the respiring effluvia of a city asleep, and the light, its absence. There is a freshness to the morning. The slaughter of carcasses disappears and the city water trucks wash the markets with high-pressure hoses, quickly. Trucks and hand-pushed carts piled with fresh produce wait impatiently. Merchants sweep the water into the gutters and work furiously to cover their allotted space with potatoes, eggs, greens, noodles, bean curds, peppers. The morning lights up "charcoal alley," where the briquettes are pressed and stacked.

I watch as a peddler separates clusters of garlic bulbs, creating a mound as tall as he can manage. He sweeps the chaff into a pile with a twig broom, then sets fire to the light parchment skin, which rises like a phoenix in a cloud of flame. Fragile ash chases smoke and dissipates into the ether of the hot summer dawn.